RADICAL PHILOSOPHY

2.07
Series 2 / Spring 2020

Protests, lockdowns – and then?
Radical Philosophy Collective 3

From one Arab Spring to another
Gilbert Achcar 5

Chilean revolts and the crisis of neoliberal governance
Sergio Villalobos-Ruminott 9

Nationalisms by, against and beyond the Indian state
Rahul Rao 17

Critique without ontology
Daniele Lorenzini and Martina Tazzioli 27

Masses, class and the power of suggestion
Andrea Cavalletti 41

Hegel's natural assumption
Hammam Aldouri 53

The philosophical disability of reason
Keti Chukhrov 67

The social life of black things
David Lloyd 79

A motley crew for our times?
An interview with Marcus Rediker 93

Reviews 101

  Andrea Long Chu, *Females*
  Nora Fulton 101

  Lucas Richert, *Break on Through: Radical Psychiatry and the American Counterculture*
  Steffan Blayney 104

  Brenna Bhandar, *Colonial Lives of Property*
  Alyosha Goldstein 108

  Amit S. Rai, *Jugaad Time*
  Chris Moffat 112

  Ratna Kapur, *Gender, Alterity and Human Rights*
  Emily Jones 115

  Michel Henry, *Marx: An Introduction*
  Ekin Erkan 119

  Dan Kidner & Alex Sainsbury, *Nightcleaners and '36 to '77*
  Nicolas Helm-Grovas 122

Black-Palestinian Solidarity conference
Gary Foley and Suzannah Henty 126

Editorial collective
Claudia Aradau
Brenna Bhandar
Victoria Browne
David Cunningham
Peter Hallward
Stewart Martin
Lucie Mercier
Daniel Nemenyi
Hannah Proctor
Rahul Rao
Martina Tazzioli
Chris Wilbert

Engineers
Daniel Nemenyi
Alex Sassmannshausen

Creative Commons BY-NC-ND
Radical Philosophy, Spring 2020

ISSN 0300-211X
ISBN 978-1-9999793-6-2

Protests, lockdowns – and then?
Radical Philosophy Collective

When future historians try to make sense of the epochal transformation that began in 2020, one of the things they will need to consider is the relation between the mass protests that marked the beginning of this year (along with so much of the previous one) and the drastic measures taken in February and March to contain the spread of Covid-19. Like any complex process operating on something approaching a world-wide scale, the nature of both protests and the subsequent containment measures have varied according to place and context. The immediate framework, in each case, has so far remained national or regional, rather than global. All the same, what is perhaps most striking about the protests, the pandemic, and the relation between the two is the degree to which they all demand to be understood as properly 'world historical' phenomena, marked by unprecedented forms of convergence, synchronisation and overlap, if not yet by direct coordination. Routine use of the word 'unprecedented', these days, is itself without precedent.

In one sense, of course, the pandemic has offered embattled national governments all over the world a perfectly timed excuse to stifle all significant forms of dissent. Some of these governments may have been saved from imminent collapse. Although it may sometimes seem that they already belong to another era, it's essential to remember just how widespread, how radical and how determined mass protests had become over the course of 2019. In the final weeks of the year, the press was still full of reports stressing the scope and stamina of popular revolt, in one place after another. Reviewing a 'year of street protest' in the *Financial Times* on 23 December, for instance, Gideon Rachman was struck by its 'sheer geographical spread ... Protests large enough to disrupt daily life and cause panic in government have broken out in Hong Kong, India, Chile, Bolivia, Ecuador, Colombia, Spain, France, the Czech Republic, Russia, Malta, Algeria, Iraq, Iran, Lebanon and Sudan – and that list is not comprehensive.' While Hong Kong's students and the French *gilets jaunes* may have dominated European headlines, governments were overthrown in Sudan and Algeria, and in the autumn the prime ministers of both Lebanon and Iraq were forced to resign. Although it received scant attention in Europe or the US, massive and sustained protest once again brought Haiti to the brink of collapse, if not revolution. Profoundly reactionary and polarising regimes further inflamed tensions, everywhere from Bolsonaro in Brazil and Modi in India to Orbán in Hungary. Yemen, Palestine and Kashmir faced newly profound threats to their political survival. Along frontiers too ramified and too numerous to mention, workers, migrants and people of colour have been treated with a brutality that exposes the real priorities that shape the world for all to see.

The broad context for the 2019 mobilisations is all too familiar, and testifies to the essentially structural quality of these priorities and their immediate corollaries: the increasingly intolerable consequences of neoliberal economic policies; the social costs of austerity, mass unemployment, grotesque inequality and outright destitution; the scapegoating tendencies of authoritarian and fascist regimes; the unrelenting experience of precarity and growing despair about the future – all compounded by climate change, environmental degradation, war-mongering chauvinism, the legacies of slavery and racism. Even the most forceful measures taken to contain the spread of Covid-19 will do nothing to address these structural problems, of course, and in many ways and in many places they have already intensified them. Whether it's a matter of accessing healthcare or of finding a way to make ends meet, there is obviously nothing 'equal' about the impact of an epidemic in societies shaped by class, race and disparities of wealth and privilege.

On the other hand, it's easy to see that some of the steps taken by governments and corporations, officially in response to Covid-19, may also greatly strengthen their hand in any future confrontations with their own populations. Although grounded in long-running campaigns against migrants and 'extremists', and although framed by our unending wars against drugs and terror, the rapid adoption of newly invasive forms of surveillance and policing may already indicate a point of no return. If for the time being such steps may be most easily taken in places like Israel, China or Singapore, many other governments (including Italy, the UK and the US), with the help of big tech companies, have already seized on opportunities to ramp up their digital surveillance and other security measures, with no clear end in sight.

That's one side of the story. But it's complicated by at least two factors. One is the way in which many governments have now been obliged, by public pressure and often in flagrant contradiction of their most basic principles and ideological reflexes, to reaffirm the need to address public problems by public means. No doubt big pharma, private medicine and the corporate sector in general will do everything possible to profit from the pandemic, and the way that most wealthy countries have so far responded to the economic disruption of 2020 (repeating the pattern set by the banking bailouts of 2008) gives a clear indication of their underlying priorities. Nevertheless, in a place like the UK, explicit veneration of the National Health Service, precisely as a universal public service, has quickly imposed itself across the political spectrum, and even in a country like the US support for a comparable public service may grow significantly in the coming months. Further public pressure may demand the conversion of short-term forms of welfare and income support into something more durable. As feminist movements have long stressed, the politics of care and social reproduction may also play an increasingly central role in future struggles.

The other factor returns us to one of the more striking aspects of the 2019 protests: the fact that so many of them made similar demands in similar terms and at similar times, and proposed similar solutions to similar problems. In Lebanon and Iraq as much as in Chile or Sudan, huge numbers of people mobilised to reject the existing order of things in its entirety. Mass refusal of Lebanon's sectarian political system is exemplary here, as is the rejection of Chile's whole governing class. *¡Que se vayan todos!* remains a pertinent slogan, with an ever wider comprehension of *todos*. It's the world system as a whole, as a system, that has become the chief target of protest in so many places that, in the past, both internally and externally, have been kept in check by reliable means of divide and rule. Recourse to these ancient forms of domination may prove harder to justify in a world that is starting to realise the full extent of its unity and interdependence. We exploit or are exploited in keeping with one and the same set of basic laws. We work, produce and consume according to the rules prescribed by a single economic logic. We share a single planet, and live in the shadow of shared forms of catastrophe.

So many of the perils we face are the same for everyone. The way we address them, in the coming months and years, may well reinforce the differences that already structure our world in dominance and inequality. Or not. Perhaps more than ever before, this stark alternative can now be formulated as an actual political choice.

7 April 2020

From one Arab Spring to another
Gilbert Achcar

The crisis of the neoliberal stage of capitalism has been unfolding spectacularly under our eyes in recent months, provoking ever greater social upheavals in an ever greater number of places.[1] Events in the Arab region fit into this general global crisis, to be sure, but there is also something specific about the region. There, the neoliberal reforms have been carried out in a context dominated by a specific type of capitalism: one determined by the specific nature of a regional state system characterised by a combination in various proportions of rentierism and patrimonialism, or neopatrimonialism. What is most specific to the region is the high concentration of fully patrimonial states, a concentration unequalled in any other part of the world. Patrimonialism means that ruling families literally own the state, i.e. its apparatuses and resources, whether they own it by law under explicitly absolutist conditions or just in practice, as a matter of fact. Such ruling families regard the public sector as their private property and treat the armed forces – especially the elite armed apparatuses – as their private guard. These features explain why neoliberal reforms achieved their worst economic results in the Arab region, of all parts of the world. Neoliberal-inspired changes implemented in the region resulted in the slowest rates of economic growth of any part of the developing world and, consequently, the highest rates of unemployment – specifically youth unemployment.

The main reason for this is that neoliberal dogma is based on the primacy of the private sector, the idea that the private sector should be the driving force of development, while the state's own social and economic functions must be curtailed. 'Introduce austerity measures, trim the state down, cut social expenditure, privatise state enterprises and leave the door wide open to private enterprise and free trade, and miracles will happen', says the dogma. However, in a context lacking the prerequisites of ideal-typical capitalism, starting with the rule of law and predictability (without which long-term developmental private investment cannot happen), most private money tends to go into quick profit and speculation, especially in real estate along with construction, rather than into manufacturing or agriculture, the key productive sectors.

This created a structural blockage of development. Thus, in the Arab region, the general crisis of the global neoliberal order goes beyond a crisis of neoliberalism into a structural crisis of the specific type of capitalism that is prevailing regionally. There is therefore no way out of the crisis in that region by a mere change of economic policies within the continued framework of the existing kind of states. A radical mutation of the whole social and political structure is indispensable, short of which there will be no end to the acute social-economic crisis and destabilisation that affects the whole region.

That is why such an impressive revolutionary shockwave as the Arab Spring rocked this whole region in 2011. This was much more than a series of loosely connected mass protests. The prospect was truly insurrectionary, with people chanting 'The people want to overthrow the regime!' – a slogan that has become ubiquitous in the Arab region since 2011.[2] The first revolutionary shockwave of that year forcefully shook the regional system of states, revealing that it had entered a terminal crisis. Almost every single Arabic-speaking country saw a massive rise in social protest during the 2011 Arab Spring. Six of the region's countries – that is, more than a quarter of them – witnessed massive uprisings. And yet, the 'lesson' according to the IMF, the World Bank, those guardians of the neoliberal order, is that all this happened because their neoliberal recipes had not been implemented thoroughly enough. The crisis, they claimed, was due to an insufficient dismantling of the remnants of yesterday's state-capitalist economies. The solution, they said, was to end all forms of social subsidies, in even more radical fashion than had already occurred.

However, governments of the region did not do *more* of what the international financial institutions have been advocating because they were worried about the political consequences. They had good reason to worry. Unlike Eastern Europe after the fall of the Berlin Wall, when people swallowed the bitter pill of massive neoliberal changes in the hope that it would bring them capitalist prosperity, people in the Arab region are under no illusion that their countries will become similar to Western European countries. In order to impose further neoliberal measures on the people, brutal force is therefore required in most of the region's countries.

The full implementation of neoliberalism does not go hand in hand with liberal democracy as Fukuyama's 'end of history' fantasy claimed thirty years ago. The first such radical implementation was in Chile, of course, under the rule of General Augusto Pinochet. In Egypt, it is currently taking place under the post-2013 restorationist dictatorship led by Field Marshal Sisi – the most brutally repressive regime that the Egyptians have endured in decades. The Sisi regime has gone the furthest in implementing the full range of neoliberal measures advocated by the IMF, at a huge cost to the population, with a steep rise in the cost of living, food prices, transport prices, etc. People have been completely devastated. The main reason why their anger did not explode once again on the streets of Cairo on a massive scale is that they are now deterred by state terror. But the full implementation of the IMF's neoliberal recipes has produced no economic miracle, and it won't produce one in the future. Tensions are building up and, sooner or later, the country will erupt again.

Unfortunately, both the left and the workers' movement in Egypt are in bad shape. They have suffered a painful defeat – not only due to the brutal return of the repressive state, but also because of their own contradictions and illusions. The major part of the Egyptian left has pursued a politically erratic trajectory, switching from one misconceived alliance to another: from the Muslim Brotherhood to the military. In 2013, most of the left and the independent workers' movement supported Sisi's coup very short-sightedly, subscribing to the illusion that the army would put the democratic process back on track. They thought that the overthrow of Morsi and the Muslim Brotherhood, after their year in power, would reopen the way to furthering the revolutionary process, even though the overthrow was brought about by the military.

This terrible blunder discredited the left as well as the independent workers' movement. As a result, the left-wing opposition is much weakened and marginalised in today's Egypt. This is another crucial reason why people have not mobilised massively against the new neoliberal onslaught. When there seems to be no credible alternative, people tend to accept the regime's discourse that says: 'It's us or chaos, us or a Syria-like tragedy. You must accept our iron heel. It will be tough, but at the end of the day you will find prosperity.' Most Egyptians do not really buy the last promise – prosperity – but they are still paralysed by the fear of falling into a situation much worse still than what they are enduring.

Linked to all this is another specificity of the regional revolutionary process, of which Syria is the most tragic illustration. The Arab world has experienced the development over several decades of an Islamic fundamentalist reactionary current, long promoted by the US alongside its oldest ally in the region, the Saudi kingdom. Islamic fundamentalism was sponsored by Washington as an antidote to communism and left-wing nationalism in the Muslim world during the Cold War. During the 1970s, Islamic fundamentalists were green-lighted by almost all Arab governments as a counterweight to left-wing youth radicalisation. With the subsequent ebb of the left-wing wave, they became the most prominent opposition forces tolerated in some countries, such as Egypt or Jordan, and severely repressed in others, like Syria or Tunisia. They were, however, present everywhere.

When the 2011 uprisings started, Muslim Brotherhood branches jumped on the revolutionary bandwagon and tried to hijack it to serve their own political purposes. They were much stronger than whatever left-wing forces remained in the region, very much weakened by the collapse of the USSR, while the fundamentalists enjoyed financial and media backing from Gulf oil monarchies. As a result, what evolved in the region was not the classical binary opposition of revolution and counter-revolution. It was a triangular situation in which there was, on the one hand, a progressive pole – those groups, parties and networks who initiated the uprisings and represented their dominant aspirations. This pole was organisationally weak, except for Tunisia where a powerful workers' movement compensated for the weakness of the political left and allowed the uprising in this country to score the first victory in bringing down a president, thus setting off the regional shockwave. On the other hand, there were two counter-revolutionary, deeply reactionary poles: the old regimes, classically representing the main counter-revolutionary force, but also Islamic fundamentalist forces competing with these old regimes and striving to seize power. In this triangular contest, the progressive pole, the revolutionary current, was soon marginalised – not or not only due to organisational and material weakness, but also and primarily because of political weakness, of the lack of strategic vision.

Nevertheless, a new generation has entered the struggle on a mass scale in the region in recent years, one that came of age through and after the 2011 Arab Spring. The bulk of this new generation aspires to a radical progressive transformation. They aspire to better social conditions, freedom, democracy, social justice, equality, including gender emancipation. They reject neoliberal policies and dream of a society in sharp contrast with the programmatic views of the Islamic fundamentalist forces that hijacked or tried to hijack the uprisings to direct them towards their own goals.

This huge progressive potential came back to the fore in the second revolutionary shockwave that started in December 2018 with the Sudanese uprising, followed since February 2019 by the Algerian uprising, and since last October by massive social and political protests in Iraq and in Lebanon. Sudan, Algeria, Iraq and Lebanon have been boiling since then, while all other countries of the region are on the brink of explosion. The Covid-19 pandemic will undoubtedly suspend the revolutionary process for a while – it has already ended the weekly mass demonstrations in Algeria and the various forms of protests in Iraq and Lebanon – but it will only worsen the conditions that led to its ignition in the first place.

Protracted revolutionary processes, such as the one that is unfolding in the Arab region since 2011, are cumulative in terms of experience and know-how. They are learning curves. The peoples learn, the mass movements learn, the revolutionaries learn, and the reactionaries learn as well, to be sure; everybody learns. A long-term revolutionary process is a succession of waves of upsurges and counter-revolutionary backlashes – but these waves are not mere repetitions of identical patterns. The process is not circular, it must move forward or else it degenerates. People grasp the lessons of previous experiences and do their best not to repeat the same errors or fall into the same traps. This is very clear in the case of Sudan, but also for Algeria, Iraq and Lebanon.

Sudan and Algeria, along with Egypt, are the three countries in the region where the armed forces constitute the central institution of political rule. Of course, armed apparatuses are the backbones of states in general, but it is direct military control of political power that is peculiar to these three countries in the Arab region. Their regimes are not patrimonial. No family owns the state to the point of making of it whatever its members wish. The state is instead dominated collegially by the military high command. They are 'neopatrimonial' regimes: this means that they are characterised by nepotism, cronyism and corruption, but no single family is in full control of the state, which remains institutionally separate from the persons of the rulers. This explains why, in these three countries, the military ended up getting rid of the president and his entourage in order to safeguard the regime. That's what happened in Egypt in 2011 with the dismissal of Mubarak, and last year in Algeria with the termination of Bouteflika's presidency, followed by the overthrow of Bashir in Sudan, all three carried out by the military. However, when this happened in Egypt, there were huge illusions about the military among the population, which were renewed in 2013 when the army deposed the Muslim Brother president Morsi. These illusions were not reiterated in Sudan or Algeria in 2019. On the contrary, the popular movement in the two countries has been acutely aware that the military constitute the central pillar of the regime that they wish to get rid of.

But there is more than just that difference at work in Sudan. There is a leadership that embodies the awareness of the lessons drawn from all previous regional experiences. This is mainly due to the role of the Sudanese Professionals Association (SPA), which started in 2016 with teachers, journalists, doctors and other professionals organising an underground network. As the uprising that started in December 2018 unfolded, the association developed into a much larger network involving workers' unions of all key sectors of the working class. It has been playing the central role in the events on the side of the popular movement. The SPA was also instrumental in the constitution of a broad political coalition involving several parties and groups. These forces are presently engaged in a political tug of war with the military. They agreed temporarily on a compromise that instituted what can be described as a situation of dual power, somewhat reminiscent of the situation in Russia after February 1917. The country is ruled by a council in which the leadership of the people's movement is represented alongside the military command. This is an uneasy transitional period that can't last very long. Sooner or later, one of the two powers will have to prevail over the other, which will inevitably entail splitting the other.

The real spearhead of the Sudanese revolution is constituted, however, by a network of 'resistance committees' that involves several thousands of mostly young and politically unorganised people in big cities' neighbourhoods and small towns across the country. These committees are defiant towards the existing political parties and refuse to centralise their activities and statements, insisting on the preservation of their local autonomy. They are as radically opposed to military rule as they are to Islamic fundamentalism, especially since both were represented in power under Omar al-Bashir. They decided to authorise the SPA to speak for them, but they keep it under vigilant scrutiny as well as they exert a critical pressure on the whole political process.

The popular movement in Algeria is remarkable for having staged huge mass demonstrations every week for over a year. Its stamina is truly exceptional. But it has no recognised and legitimate leadership. Nobody can claim to speak in its name. This is an obvious weakness, in stark contrast with Sudan. Forms of leadership naturally change over time, but we haven't entered some postmodern age of 'leaderless revolutions' as some want to believe. The lack of leadership is a real and far-reaching impediment: a recognised leadership is crucial in order to channel the strength of the mass movement towards a political goal. This exists in Sudan, with all its contradictions, but not in Algeria, nor in Iraq or Lebanon.

The role of women in the second wave of the revolutionary process in the Arab region is another very important feature, and a further indication of the higher degree of maturity achieved by the popular movements. In Sudan, Algeria and Lebanon, women have participated massively and very visibly in the demonstrations and mass rallies as well as in heading them. In the three countries, feminists have been a crucial component of the groups involved in the uprisings. Even in Iraq, where women were hardly visible in the initial stage of the protests, they got increasingly involved, especially since the students joined the mobilisation.

The big question in Algeria, Iraq and Lebanon is clearly this: in a situation shaped both by the endurance of mass mobilisation and by the new opportunities for oppressive state interventions provided by the menace of Covid-19, will the popular movement succeed in finding ways to organise, like their Sudanese brothers and sisters did, in order to amplify their struggles' impact and achieve major steps towards the fulfilment of their goals, or will the ruling classes manage to quell each of these three uprisings and defuse them? The fate of the Sudanese revolution will very much impact the regional revolutionary process in its entirety. There is ground for hope, albeit not for optimism given the difficulty of the challenges lying ahead.

Gilbert Achcar is Professor of Development Studies and International Relations at SOAS, London. His recent books include Marxism, Orientalism, Cosmopolitanism (2013), The People Want: A Radical Exploration of the Arab Uprising *(2013) and* Morbid Symptoms: Relapse in the Arab Uprising *(2016).*

Notes

1. Some material here is adapted from an interview in *Marxist Left Review* 19 (Summer 2020). It is rewritten and updated.
2. For a full account, see Gilbert Achcar, *The People Want: A Radical Exploration of the Arab Uprising* (London: Saqi Books, 2013).

Chilean revolts and the crisis of neoliberal governance

Sergio Villalobos-Ruminott

On Friday 18 October 2019, a long series of mass demonstrations began in Chile against the right-wing government led by president Sebastián Piñera.[1] Despite brutal and continuous police repression, these demonstrations persisted, day after day, with remarkable stamina and inventiveness, right through to 13 March 2020, when the risks posed by Covid-19 led Piñera to ban public gatherings of more than 500 people. It's easy to see why his government and its security apparatus might have welcomed the timing of such 'protective measures' as fortunate. For more than five months, many hundreds of thousands of people had taken to the streets, with a determination that shook the government to its foundations; the government's response, meanwhile, has shed a revealing light on the darker sides of the so-called Chilean miracle.

The decision that triggered the first protests was an increase in subway fares, which led high-school students (already stretched beyond their capacity to make ends meet) to plan systematic fare evasions throughout that October morning. The government, unable to understand the students' outrage, responded to these evasions by deploying the armed forces and announcing a state of exception – a measure that, although the constitution provides for it, is usually reserved for absolutely extreme situations. With the adoption of such an excessive policy the government's real intention became evident, namely, to impose this rise in the cost of public transport as part of an ongoing series of policies designed to intensify its long-standing neoliberal agenda.

The state of exception proclaimed by the government in the autumn triggered something else: in a society that still mourns those who disappeared during Pinochet's dictatorship (1973-1989), the army's presence on the streets precipitates the re-emergence of a traumatic memory related to repression, torture and the abuse of power that characterised the long years of military rule. This is a situation that the army and the political sector defending Pinochet's legacy have not been willing to recognise, let alone redress. Nonetheless, far from returning to their houses in fear, the Chilean people at large, in support of the student demonstrations, took to the streets and confronted military personnel face-to-face, occupying public spaces and cities, in a series of massive meetings (more than two million people on Friday 25 October, for example), that challenged not only the erratic behaviour of the government but its neoliberal strategy *in toto*.

The *real state of emergency*, in this sense, is not the one abruptly dictated by the government, but the one decided by the people's occupation of their streets, which is sustained only by their own tireless perseverance. Huge demonstrations subsequently took place almost every Friday, right through to mid-March 2020, despite the government's strategy of blunt criminalisation. Meanwhile, the main media outlets (newspapers and public television stations), owned by the same small clique that also controls most of the country's economic activity,[2] have been instrumental in disseminating images of horror, riots and looting of supermarkets, showing hooded protesters (*encapuchados*) setting fire to buildings, subway stations and bank offices. Consequently, the official narrative, reinforced by the media, adopts a well-known pattern: the protests are illegitimate and criminal insofar as they do not remain within the official channels of participation – the same channels which have repeatedly proven to be useless over the last thirty years.

It is not entirely clear how far the government itself has been involved in the creation of this climate of crime and social unrest (since many phone-videos show members of the police force igniting fires in subways stations and supermarkets), but there is no doubt about the government's decision to criminalise the protests and to subordinate the legitimate claims of the Chilean people to questions of institutional order and security. In fact, security has become the decisive marker of the government's discourse, leading to a constant increase in police personnel, expanding the budget dedicated to surveillance and technologies, of repression and a series of new laws rapidly signed off in congress that grant more powers to the police while at the same time reducing basic checks and balances that might guard against impunity and the excessive use of force.

The government made things worse with its deployment of the army the very night after the protests began (19 October 2019) and by the characterisation of the current situation as a war against a 'dangerous enemy' – i.e. students and unarmed hooded protesters. The situation was further aggravated when the government decided, a few days later, to remove the army from the streets and hand over the control of the protests to the *Carabineros*, the police institution disgraced by its historic participation in the crimes of the dictatorship and that is currently under investigation for one of the biggest fraud cases in the country's history. *Carabineros*, without any consideration for their own standard operating procedures and with a total lack of common sense, soon began using rubber-coated steel bullets to repress the demonstrations, causing ocular amputation to more than 400 hundred people; they have also been blamed for multiple cases of torture, illegal detentions, sexual abuse and several cases of rape. To this series of crimes and abuses, one should add the bombastic accusation, by President Piñera and other members of his government, incriminating Cuba and Venezuela for orchestrating an international plot against Chile.[3] A further 'intelligence' report from the Ministry of Interior went so far as to accuse, in December, Korean pop music groups (K-POP) of having a large influence on the social instability in the country.

In order to understand the logic that has enabled this tragicomic series of mistakes, it's essential to remember that Chile has usually been represented both as a neoliberal 'economic miracle' and as the exemplary case of a successful 'transition to democracy'. This narrative has certainly been challenged often enough by social protests, many of them led by high school and university students, during the last decades (2007, 2011, 2018, etc.).[4] However, the October thirty peso increase in the subway fare is consistent with a long-running series of government initiatives that have impoverished the population in favour of the richest people in the country, beginning with a tax reform that exempts the most prominent economic groups operating in Chile (groups to which the President himself belongs), while heavily taxing general consumer goods and basic services, most of which were privatised long ago. Thus, the thirty pesos came to represent thirty years of post-dictatorial governments, framing the historicity of these protests in a different way: it has become evident that people are not only protesting a rise of the subway fare, they are protesting *everything* that has happened during the last three decades. They are protesting this whole period routinely labelled our transition-to-democracy, that is to say, our transition to the post-dictatorial and limited democracy that began in 1990, after Pinochet left office and Patricio Aylwin took over.

The institutional mechanism that lends a strong degree of unity to this transitional period is the duopolic political system that allows control of the government to alternate between two political blocks, without challenging either the underlying economic path or the limits it imposes on democracy. This system continues to operate under the same constitutional constraints inherited from the Pinochet regime. Pinochet's dictatorship has been regularly and rightly characterised as a violent regime in which neoliberalism was first implemented in a Latin American country;[5] the subsequent transitional period, under the alternative administration of Chile's centre-left and then centre-right blocks,[6] should properly be considered as its institutional *continuation*.

By the same token, we should remember how the slogan that mobilised people at the inception of this transitional process, and which led to the massive voting against Pinochet in the plebiscite of 1988, was a promise of democracy as happiness for all ('*la alegría ya viene*', literally, 'happiness is coming'). This future democracy was supposed to bring justice and punishment to the perpetrators who committed crimes against humanity, along with transparent and effective democratic processes, social justice, and a new constitutional framework able to respond to the social, economic and political demands issued by people exhausted by years of persecution and repression. That is what this promise of democracy meant to us, at the time. The revolts have reminded everyone that the promise of happiness for all was never fulfilled. Genuine democracy, understood as mass empowerment, never arrived. Instead of gaining a new degree of control over their lives and futures, Chile's people have been subjected to ever more suffocating versions of the old neoliberal project.

The secret of the so-called Chilean miracle is plain to see: the dictatorship handed the country over to a new and recently educated neoliberal elite that was able to design both an economic system based on the principles of neoliberal economy, and the juridical framework (constitution, electoral system, configuration of political parties, etc.) necessary to protect the economic order, neutralise political dissidence and contain social unrest.

The neoliberal reaction was, of course, first and foremost a *reaction*. The series of civil wars and dictatorships that have devastated Latin America since the mid-1960s, despite their anti-communist rhetoric and well-known Cold War orientation, are to be understood also, and especially, as a systematic response to the democratisation processes that opened up from the mid 1950s to early 1960s, processes that were themselves partly enabled by successive waves of industrialisation and ensuing migration from the countryside to the cities. This systematic reaction led to a new concentration of power, wealth and land in the hands of an emerging elite educated in the principles of neoliberalism. Chile was the first country in which openly dictatorial military power established a strategic alliance with the so-called Chicago boys. The main result of that alliance was a change in the composition of the dominant class during Pinochet's dictatorship, since the new policies implemented in that period favoured the financial sector over more traditional industrial ones. In this sense, the Chilean dictatorship was a modernising regime oriented to the dynamics and demands of the global financial sector, at the expense of the classical national-developmentalist project.

Instead of its own version of a democratic-bourgeois revolution, during the 1970s and 80s Latin America was subjected to a revolution led by capital itself. After the Cuban Revolution and the intensification of the containment strategies that precipitated the 1973 coup in Chile, it became apparent that the socio-political and economic transformation of the region would no longer depend on a sequence linking urbanisation, industrialisation, proletarianisation and democratisation. Instead the new path towards 'modernisation' would be opened up by deregulated financial markets and new forms of speculative investment. The new business sector, which does not understand its performance in national or territorial terms, does not respect traditional legal constraints either. This is why Chile's contemporary configuration also permits the proliferation of notorious cases of corruption, cases that have been systematically disclosed over the last decade, involving prominent economic groups and indeed the whole political 'class'.[7] The so-called ethical imperatives of the traditional entrepreneur that Weber theorised as a key factor for capitalism's inception no longer play any significant role in a deterritorialised capitalism whose main imperatives are dictated by the flexible process of accumulation for accumulation's sake, without regard for the ever deepening precarity suffered by vast sectors of the population.

Chile certainly deserves its unenviable reputation as the exemplary case of an early implementation of neoliberal policies enabled by an authoritarian government. Once an effective opposition, both internal and external, had been mobilised to stifle Allende's moderate but progressive government, by 1973 Chile seemed to offer the perfect scenario in which to activate, in a sort of controlled social experiment, a whole series of measures whose principal goal was the total deregulation of the economy, i.e. the removal of production, wealth creation and wealth distribution from anything resembling popular interference or control. The recipe has since become familiar all over the world, and includes: privatisation of state-owned factories, of the health insurance system and of retirement plans, downsizing of the state apparatus, decentralisation of state administrative capacities, reduction of taxes on profits, wealth and imports, deregulation of international exchange, sharp reductions in public spending, loosening of the credit system, etc. Once it was safe to do so, the package also included a move away from overtly dictatorial repression, with the eventual elaboration (in 1980) of a constitution and a legal framework that secured, limited and supervised the national exercise of democracy. This framework was designed above all to prevent the political system from falling back into the hands of a government responsive, as Allende's government had been, to the demands of the people themselves – hence the relentless demonisation of this government both as totalitarian or undemocratic, and as responsible for fiscal disorder and economic chaos.

Through the 1990s, when most Latin American governments were implementing similar policies amid social unrest, Chile's governing class could point to steady economic growth and development, in keeping with procedures and criteria recommended by the World Bank and IMF. Some sectors of Chilean society duly celebrated the transitional period by placing all hopes on such growth and the trickle-down policies associated with it. The truth however was more complicated, and the situation more fragile. Much of the prosperity enjoyed by some sectors of Chile's economy depended on a growing global demand for copper, driven in large part by China's manufacturing boom; the resulting rise in commodity prices made it easier for our transitional governments to postpone genuine economic reforms, while simultaneously deflecting attention via a human rights rhetoric that depoliticised each and every socio-economic claim in favour of a generic conception of abstract 'justice'.

It was during these transitional years that neoliberalism was intensified and perfected, with the final privatisation of water systems, the highway system, the public transport system, the total subsumption of higher education to the private sector, and the increasing dominance of the financial sector. Chile, a dependent and weakly diversified economy geared to the extraction of copper and other raw materials, remained a paradise for international capital. Its natural resources and labour market were exposed to predation by a deregulated legal system that offered little or no protection to the most impoverished and most vulnerable members of the population. Chile, in short, seemed to have done everything necessary to secure its 'modernisation' and socio-economic development.

At the same time, the so-called Chilean miracle has to be understood in its relation to a pervasive understanding of the country's exceptional history, one that links this apparent economic success to a political one: the success of a country that had gone through a paradigmatic and peaceful transition to democracy, after the bloody but necessary defeat of communism. Hypotheses about the Chilean republican tradition, about the incorruptible character of its leaders, about the growing prosperity of its economy, and about the infinite set of natural and human resources it enjoys are part of Chile's foundational fiction, one that has shaped the country's self-representation since its modern inception.

It would be quite easy, of course, to unveil this exceptionalist myth for what it is, by referring to the brutal history of inequality inflicted on the country's popular sectors, the number of military interventions throughout its history and the security policies deployed again and again against the civilian population, not to mention the 'anti-terrorist' and pro-corporate policies implemented during these same years against the Mapuche people in the southern part of the country. The extremely unequal distribution of income, the concentration of wealth and property in the hands of the few, and the blatant nepotism of the dominant classes (constituting a sort of 'caste' that has been in power since the beginning of the nineteenth century),[8] all testify to the real conditions that have led to the series of social demonstrations and revolts of the last five months. Nevertheless, what really explains the situation of the country over the past thirty years is not only the class division inherited from the nineteenth century, nor the legacies from the dictatorial regime, but the determination of the governing sectors to preserve the juridical framework that defines and limits its democracy. This constitutional framework, first instituted by the Pinochet regime and then confirmed during the ensuing transitional administrations, dramatically defines the limits of democracy by confiscating political agency from civil society and granting it instead to the duopolic formation that allows for superficial changes in the composition of government while ensuring continuity at the level of basic policy. A durable agreement seems to have been reached about how to lead the country, on both sides of an apparent 'political divide', while allowing members of either side to take turns implementing the measures required.

The constitution of 1980, carefully articulated and put in place by Jaime Guzmán (an extreme right-wing ideologist, a reader of Carl Schmitt and Juan Donoso Cortés, with clear links to the Opus Dei, and the final architect of Pinochet's institutional order),[9] was partly a reaction to the more democratic constitution of 1925, but principally it was designed to safeguard the sacred right to private property, a right that had been directly challenged by Allende's Agrarian Reform plans. But Guzmán was not only interested in preventing attacks on private property by state-oriented expropriation policies: he was equally interested in shaping a political system of equilibriums that would prevent the poor majority from advancing radical redistributive reforms. While some overtly repressive measures were scaled back after Pinochet left office, Guzmán's carefully designed electoral system (a variation of the D'Hondt system) has been preserved. This is a system that secures a non-proportional representation of the two blocks that dominate Chile's congress, while requiring, at the same time, two-thirds of the votes in the congress to pass any legislative initiative.

The veneration of this electoral system is the key to understanding neoliberal governmental strategy in Chile, which is anything but democratic.[10] This system not only regulates but also defines the political composition of congress and, more importantly, defines the general rules of engagement in Chile, from municipal and local elections to the presidency. It is not an exaggeration to say that the electoral system operates as a control mechanism that neutralises direct elections and any expression of the popular will, under the guise of proportionality and institutional equilibrium. Thanks to it, the whole system of political parties is articulated around the two dominant groupings, in a way that not only prevents other non-affiliated parties from truly participating in the electoral process but that also neutralises civil society and social movements in general, depriving them of all political legitimacy.

The preservation of Chile's properly 'juristocratic' limitations is one of the things that distinguishes it from some other Latin American countries, those that by the late 1990s began to embark on the reformist agenda that came to be known as the *Pink Tide* – an agenda characterised by new distributive policies, new constituent processes, official recognition of originary peoples and cultures, and a strong anti-neoliberal rhetoric. While Venezuela, Brazil, Bolivia, and several other countries were doing their best to bid farewell to neoliberalism (a farewell that unfortunately turned out to be only transitory), Chile was ruled by a centre-left administration that did not hesitate to embrace the most radical neoliberal policies.

Considering all this, it should not be surprising that on Friday 15 November 2019, Chile woke up to news announcing a 'Great National Agreement for Social Peace and a New Constitution' ('*Gran acuerdo nacional para la paz social y una nueva constitución*'). After almost a month of sustained civil unrest, when the government's weakness was evident, the full congress had met during the night and reached an agreement that both promised a new constitution and called on the people to end the protests. This agreement preserved the usual duopolic consensus, along with the distance separating this consensus from popular demands. Instead of trying to respond directly to these demands, and to the very concrete proposals made by a vast array of grassroots organisations,[11] the political parties in control of congress once again opted to preserve the existing balance of power. The real message sent by the Agreement was perfectly clear: in Chile, politics should and must only be exercised through institutional channels, by professional politicians. Politics must always respect the familiar balance among established political parties, and it must always proceed in accordance with the interests of those few economic groups that finance the campaigns and salaries that sustain these parties.

Today, in late March, after more than five months of protests, people are showing signs of exhaustion and despair. The indecisive management of the Covid-19 situation by the government has so far proven to be both criminally negligent and politically motivated, given its clear determination to quash the protests. In mid-March people were obliged to suspend their protests, but this was as a result of Covid-19 rather than in response to any concessions extracted from the government. The government has once again deployed the army on the streets, invoking the new state of emergency posed by the pandemic. The President currently enjoys approval ratings of less than 7%.

The woeful response of the government stands in stark contrast, meanwhile, to the impressive creativity shown by different grassroots groups during this time, from student boycotts and feminist mobilisations (with the performance piece *Un violador en tu camino*, 'A Rapist in your Path', quickly gaining a global audience),[12] to the unexpected solidarity of fans from different football teams, combining to form a solid and coherent movement against the government. In the current situation it seems that anything could happen, from a dramatic *coup d'état* on the pretext of a 'national emergency' to an eventual renewal and intensification of the protests.

Despite the recent suspension of protest, what remains clear after so many days of protest is that most people do want another constitution, a genuinely new one. The majority of the population demands a constituent assembly, a mechanism that should include gender proportionality and the recognition of indigenous peoples. The new constitution envisioned by most of the Chilean people is indeed properly *impossible* within the narrow confines of the nation as it stands; the simple incorporation of women, immigrants, Mapuche people and other minorities already demolishes the fictive ethnicity (Europe-oriented, heteronormative, patriarchal and Christian) that has fed the identity and image of the country.

The government and the political parties have likewise been clear in their positions about a new constitution. The centre-left block may be open to a constitutional commission, made up of members of congress along with some representatives chosen from the civil society, selected by the same electoral system that favours the established parties. The government, supported by the right, is adamantly opposed to any kind of constituent assembly, a measure which they associate with the reformist governments of Venezuela and Bolivia – places that for them represent nothing but chaos, anarchy, socialism and the past. Instead they propose a plebiscite to decide whether a new constitution is indeed necessary or not (as if nothing had happened in the last months), and in case the answer is 'yes' they are adamant that it must be undertaken within congress, i.e. within the same representational mechanisms that have neutralised politics in Chile for the last thirty years.

Although many leftist intellectuals still insist on reading the protests according to the hegemonic logic of articulation (via political parties) and representation, I think they are best understood as something else, as genuine revolts that go beyond the heavily-occupied political space of the nation-state and the ongoing subsumption of life by capital. The protests that began in October have dramatically and irreversibly undermined the legitimacy of Chile's neoliberal administration. They have exposed the Chilean myth for what it is, and restored the people's own capacity for self-organisation. For many of us who have been following the protests day in and day out, they exemplify the logic that Jacques Rancière derives from the famous mass secession of the Roman plebs – the moment when the plebs are said to have undertaken a kind of general strike, the moment when by leaving the city and their well-defined place in it for the relative freedom of the Aventine hill, they privileged their own potential and their own capacities, in violation not only of patrician commands but of the whole established institutional order.[13]

In Chile we need to take full stock of the radicality and singularity of this unprecedented series of disruptions. They are revolts defined less by a class identity than by an existential condition. The people on the streets do not respond to a party strategy, nor to a programme; they are there, protesting, since this seems to be the very last thing they can still do. The left consistently fails them, and the right consistently oppresses them. There is no apparent exit.

Referring to another set of revolts that were animated by a mixture of mass enthusiasm and despair (the 1979 uprising in Iran), Foucault evoked that 'play of sacrifice and hope for which each person, and a people collectively, is responsible', and which enables ' a people to confront an army, a police', and to disrupt the course of history.[14] Undertaken under severe pressure, as a sacrifice made for the sake of life and survival itself, such revolt should be understood first and foremost as a direct reaction to an existential threat. Furio Jesi makes a similar suggestion, reflecting on the Spartacist uprising:

> Every revolt is a battle, but a battle in which one has deliberately chosen to participate. The instant of the revolt determines one's sudden self-realisation and self-objectification as part of a collectivity. The battle between good and evil, between survival and death, between success and failure, in which everyone is individually involved each and every day, is identified with the battle of the whole collectivity – everyone has the same weapons, everyone faces the same obstacles, the same enemy.[15]

Jesi makes this point in order to distinguish the normative aspects of the modern notion of revolution from the more spontaneous and more elusive 'logic' of revolt. In the lived experience of such revolt what matters is less party principles or class identities than an almost visceral reaction to oppression, as the people involved come to realise that nothing could be worse than waiting any longer, waiting passively for an inexorable end, within the confines of the situation as it is.[16]

This is what has characterised the Chilean revolts, animated by a deep desire to end the oppressive and exploiting order that has been imposed upon the people under the cover of a progressive and globalising rhetoric. As many of their participants have recognised, what animates such revolt resonates to some extent with a version of what Giorgio Agamben calls 'destituent power',[17] a power of refusal that delegitimates the dominant order altogether and all at once. Such power acquires in these revolts an immediate material connotation, one that opens directly onto a demand for another kind of political practice and for another relationship to the political. Such destituent power is not concerned with institutional renovation or with the creation of a new order, it is instead motivated first and foremost by a logic of rejection and an end to 'business as usual'. And although invocation of such destituent power might appear to be in tension with people's desire for a constituent assembly and a new constitution, the truth is that Chile has never produced a democratic constitution – this still remains unthinkable, and perhaps not only in Chile, since the old liberal model of the social contract is clearly a fiction designed to confine political participation within clear institutional boundaries. The call for a new constitution in the context of our protests is precisely the expression of an impossibility. It's a demand to expose the flagrant illegitimacy of the actually-existing social contract in Chile, as forcefully as possible.

Although Piñera's government clearly seeks to exploit the repressive opportunities offered by the pandemic, it's still too early to say whether the consequences of Covid-19 will reinforce or dilute the recent mass challenge to Chile's neoliberal project. But what's already clear is that things can no longer continue as they did before. What has been most immediately at stake in the revolts in Chile, as in some other places, is not merely the victory of a class, or the continuation of a policy; what is at stake is the very survival of humankind. It's no longer enough to frame the alternative in terms of 'socialism or barbarism'. The immediate choice is rather one of 'revolt or devastation'. We will see which of these two prevails, soon enough.

Ypsilanti, March 2020

Sergio Villalobos-Ruminott is Professor of Latin American Studies at the University of Michigan, Ann Arbor. His most recent publications include the books Asedios al fascismo. Del gobierno neoliberal a la revuelta popular *(Santiago 2020), and* La desarticulación. Epocalidad, hegemonía e historicidad *(Santiago 2019).*

The photographs in this article were taken by, and are reproduced with the kind permission of, the photographer Orizon Severino Villalobos, orizonseverino@gmail.com. His Instagram feed can be found at Orizon_severino.

Notes

1. I am grateful to my dear friend Erna Von Der Walde for encouraging me to write on these events.
2. See María Olivia Mönckeberg, *El saqueo de los grupos económicos al Estado de Chile* (Santiago: Ediciones B, 2001), and *Los Magnates de la Prensa: Concentración de los medios de Comunicación en Chile* (Madrid: Penguin Random House, 2011).
3. We should remember, by contrast, how Piñera's government has been proactive in supporting the repeated coup attempts in Venezuela and the recent coup d'état in Bolivia.
4. On an earlier series of revolts in the country, see Sergio Villalobos-Ruminott, 'The Chilean Winter', *Radical Philosophy* 171 (January 2012), https://www.radicalphilosophy.com/commentary/the-chilean-winter.
5. See for instance David Harvey, *A Brief History of Neoliberalism* (Oxford: Oxford University Press, 2005) and Naomi Klein, *The Shock Doctrine: The Rise of Disaster Capitalism* (New York: Picador, 2007).
6. The centre-left block was first called *Concertación de partidos por la democracia* and now *Nueva mayoría*, while the right-wing was first called *Alianza por Chile* and now *Chile vamos*.
7. For nuanced analysis of the widespread fraud and corruption that is endemic to neoliberal Chile, see the volumes by María Olivia Mönckeberg, mentioned above.
8. See Mönckeberg, *El saqueo de los grupos económicos al Estado de Chile*; Ernesto Carmona Ulloa, *Los dueños de Chile* (Santiago: La Huella, 2002); Daniel Matamala, *Poderoso caballero. El peso del dinero en la política chilena* (Catalonia: Santiago, 2015).
9. See Renato Cristi, *El pensamiento político de Jaime Guzmán* (Santiago: LOM Ediciones, 2014).
10. This is what I have elsewhere called 'juristocracy', an immunitarian series of practices and mechanisms that drastically curtails democracy by putting a cultural and juridical framework in place to prevent contamination of the political system by demands coming from the socio-economic world.
11. These proposals have included a fair minimum wage, a fair retirement system, universal access to basic public health services, recognition of minority rights, relief of student debts, and so on.
12. It's essential to stress the crucial role played by feminist movements since 2017 in particular, movements that not only demand politics of recognition, but by doing so, shatter the whole patriarchal nature of neoliberal governability. See for example Alejandra Castillo, *Asamblea de los cuerpos* (Santiago: Sangría, 2019).
13. Jacques Rancière, *Disagreement* (Minneapolis: Minnesota University Press, 2005).
14. Michel Foucault and Farès Sassine, 'There Can't Be Societies without Uprisings', trans. Alex J. Feldman, *Foucault Studies* 25 (Oct 2018), 334.
15. Furio Jesi, *Spartakus: The Symbology of the Revolt* (Pennsylvania: Seagull Books, 2014).
16. It is worth noting, in passing, that this is exactly how Mariano Azuela's crucial 1915 novel *The Underdogs* begins. This text, better and earlier than any other novel on the same topic, presents the inception of the Mexican Revolution by focusing on the experience of Demetrio Macías, a peasant who rises up against the local *cacique* and the federal police. Demetrio's visceral insurrection was not planned nor was it articulated by the 'revolutionary agenda'. It sprang from an existential threat, from the unsustainable condition of a bare life that nevertheless tries to survive, and to persevere in its being. See Azuela, *The Underdogs: A Novel of the Mexican Revolution* (New York: Penguin Press, 2008).
17. Giorgio Agamben, 'For a Theory of Destituent Power' (Athens, 16 November 2013), http://criticallegalthinking.com/2014/02/05/theory-destituent-power/.

Nationalisms by, against and beyond the Indian state

Rahul Rao

On 26 January 2020, thousands of people cheered as four women hoisted the Indian flag in Shaheen Bagh, a predominantly Muslim locality in New Delhi, which had become the epicentre of protests against the highly controversial Citizenship (Amendment) Act (CAA) that was passed in December 2019. Three of the women referred to as the dadis (grandmothers) of Shaheen Bagh – Bilkis (82), Asma Khatoon (90) and Sarvari (75) – were leading figures in the sit-in protest in this locality that began soon after the law was passed and that has inspired scores of similar protests in other cities. The fourth, Radhika Vemula, is the mother of Rohith Vemula, a Dalit student whose suicide in January 2016 triggered widespread protests against caste discrimination. The flag hoisting, accompanied by the singing of the national anthem and other patriotic songs, marked India's 71st Republic Day, which commemorates the coming into force of the Indian Constitution.[1] It offered a popular counterpoint to the annual state-orchestrated military parade in the centre of New Delhi that is typically the focus of public attention. On the same day in the southern state of Kerala, seven million people formed a 620 kilometre-long human chain stretching from one end of the state to the other and took a mass oath to defend the Constitution against what they saw as the CAA's 'attempts to subvert and destroy it'.[2]

The demonstrations in Shaheen Bagh and Kerala were two of thousands that rocked India for nearly three months since mid-December 2019, when the CAA was passed. The Act offers a fast track to citizenship for non-Muslims fleeing religious persecution in predominantly Muslim Pakistan, Afghanistan and Bangladesh. Its opponents argue that in introducing a religious qualification for Indian citizenship for the first time, it strikes at the root of the Constitution's commitment to secularism. The Act follows on the heels of an effort to compile a National Register of Citizens (NRC) in the northeastern state of Assam, responding to long-running protests by the state's majority ethnic Assamese population against immigration from neighbouring Indian states as well as from Bangladesh.[3] This registration exercise, justly described as 'one of the largest purges of citizenship in history', required all people in the state to demonstrate proof of their citizenship.[4] While the Assamese agitation has historically been directed at all non-Assamese immigrants regardless of religion, India's ruling Hindu supremacist Bharatiya Janata Party (BJP) has championed the demand for the NRC (and has promised to conduct it on a countrywide basis) on the assumption that the exercise would disenfranchise mostly Muslims. It did not bargain for the possibility that many of the 1.9 million people (in a state with a population of 33 million) who failed to meet the onerous documentary requirements of the Assam NRC would be Hindus. The CAA is widely believed to be an attempt to offer a safety net for non-Muslims who fail to demonstrate proof of citizenship in the NRC exercise, putting in place a legal regime that will target primarily Muslims for detention and deportation.[5]

Numbers cannot adequately convey the scale or ferocity of the agitation against the NRC/CAA, which has drawn people from all communities and which commentators have described as the most significant upheaval since the Emergency of 1975–77. Within three weeks of the passage of the CAA, protests had taken place in 94 of India's 732 districts across 14 of its 29 states. Thousands of people were arrested. 31 were killed in an initial

wave of police repression mostly in BJP-ruled states.[6] Events took a darker turn in February 2020. The sit-in at Shaheen Bagh had inspired scores of similar protests in other cities. When one of these sprang up in Jaffrabad in northeast Delhi, local BJP leader Kapil Mishra invited his followers to clear the protesters off the streets if the Delhi police did not do so within three days.[7] His ultimatum was widely seen as a call to violence to which Hindu mobs responded with a brutality not seen in the city since the anti-Sikh riots of 1984.[8] 53 people, mostly Muslims, were killed, and Muslim-owned properties and mosques vandalised, while the police looked on and by some accounts even participated in the violence.[9]

Throughout this period protests against the CAA continued, drawing thousands of people onto the streets in marches and sit-ins and into conversations on social media where protest memes offered a running commentary on the intricacies of the law as well as the state's response to the movement that it had brought into being. The protests were remarkable as much for their peacefulness as for their earnest deployment of a repertoire saturated with symbols of national identity, which is the subject of my inquiry in what follows. Protesters wrapped themselves, quite literally, in the national flag. Images of leaders in the struggle for independence from British rule such as Gandhi, Bhagat Singh and especially B. R. Ambedkar – the foremost Dalit leader and chairperson of the Drafting Committee of the Indian Constitution – became talismans of the movement. Mirroring the leading role that Muslim and subordinate caste women have played in the anti-CAA protests, the pavement library that sprang up at Shaheen Bagh was named after Fatima Sheikh and Savitribai Phule, both pioneering nineteenth-century social reformers and educationists from these communities.[10] Protesters sang the national anthem and embraced the Constitution of India on a scale and with an affective intensity that is unprecedented, engaging in mass readings of its Preamble and lingering over its promise to constitute India into a 'sovereign socialist secular democratic republic'. Much of this came as a surprise even to seasoned analysts of Indian politics. Until recently it was thought that India did not have a tradition of constitutional patriotism akin to the United States.[11] In contrast to the aural ubiquity of the pledge of allegiance and the visual omnipresence of the stars and stripes, until 2002 the Flag Code of India prohibited the use of the flag by private citizens except on national holidays and until 2005 the flag could not be displayed on clothes. Commentators have remarked on the alacrity with which pious Muslims have adopted secular nationalist symbols to affirm their belonging alongside visible markers of religious identification.[12] In this article, I want to try to make sense of the reasons for the widespread adoption of a nationalist repertoire of protest in the current moment, before turning to a critical evaluation of its potentials and limits.

Nationalism by the state

The frisson inherent in the protesters' take-up of nationalist symbols derives in part from a recognition that they were being seized back from a Hindu Right which has deployed them as a stick with which to beat its opponents. The coercive imposition of a state-authorised nationalism has been central to the BJP's wider political and cultural agenda since its return to power at the federal level in 2014. The Shaheen Bagh sit-in was initiated by women who were outraged by the police brutality unleashed on students protesting on the campuses of the historically Muslim Jamia Millia Islamia and Aligarh Muslim University in mid-December 2019, immediately after the CAA had been passed. In early January 2020, masked members of the Akhil Bharatiya Vidyarthi Parishad (ABVP), the student wing of the BJP, physically attacked students and faculty at Jawaharlal Nehru University (JNU) in retaliation for their protests against the CAA, while the police looked on. Long considered the intellectual bastion of the left, JNU has over time become a microcosm of national politics with the rise of the ABVP on its campus mirroring that of the BJP on the national stage.[13] The ABVP attacks were reminiscent of similar provocations in 2016, which triggered widespread student resistance. On that occasion, ABVP harassment in collusion with authorities at the University of Hyderabad drove Dalit activist Rohith Vemula to take his life. Around the same time, ABVP activists accused communist student leader Kanhaiya Kumar, then president of the JNU students' union, of sedition in connection with a Kashmir solidarity event that he had helped to organise, and instigated the Delhi police to file charges against him. The state has made enthusiastic use of the draconian sedition law to crack down on dissidents of all stripes.

In addition to invoking the full wrath of the law, the state also responded to the 2016 protests on university campuses in an emphatically symbolic register. At a meeting with the Minister of Human Resources Development, whose portfolio includes the governance of universities, the Vice-Chancellors of 42 central (federal) universities agreed to fly the national flag from 207-foot high masts to counter what they perceived as a rising tide of anti-nationalism sweeping across their campuses.[14] (So there was a poignant irony in Radhika Vemula hoisting a flag of her own four years later.) In 2017, the Vice-Chancellor of JNU – widely perceived to be sympathetic to the Hindu Right and to have facilitated the latest round of ABVP violence – requested the government install a battle tank on the JNU campus as a way of inculcating in students a spirit of patriotism and an appreciation for the sacrifices made by soldiers.[15] Between 2016 and 2018, as a result of a Supreme Court ruling that was subsequently reversed, the playing of the national anthem was made compulsory in every cinema before a film was screened. It was not uncommon during this period to read news stories reporting vigilante attacks against people who were unable or unwilling to stand for the anthem.[16]

In her account of the visual politics of Indian nationalism, Srirupa Roy argues that 'the reproduction of the nation-state rests not on the existence of individuals who identify with the nation but rather on their ability to identify the state as the nation's authoritative representative.'[17] She suggests that this ability is acquired through repeatedly encountering rather than necessarily believing in the official imagination of nationhood. As she explains, 'the sights and sounds of the nation-state clutter public space, and it is their familiarity or pervasiveness rather than their persuasiveness that engenders public recognition.'[18] Recognition of the state as the authoritative representative of the nation is a complex affective transaction shot through with fear of state violence, gratitude for its benevolence, enchantment at its spectacle and boredom with its familiarity. Importantly, Roy's account of the institution of nation-statist ideology in India focuses not on its most recent iteration under the Hindu Right but on the early postcolonial decades of what is typically referred to as the 'Nehruvian' state. This begs the question of what might have changed given the intensification of the deployment of this ideology as a disciplinary apparatus under the current ruling dispensation. How are the emotional valences of symbols transformed in a context in which the state seeks to saturate public space with them in an attempt to repair what it sees as a deficit in public recognition of its ability to represent the nation? What happens to the affective and political capital of symbols when the state cares more about their pervasiveness than their persuasiveness?

One answer is suggested by Lisa Wedeen's landmark study of the cult of Hafez al-Assad in Syria, which, she argues, engendered a politics of public dissimulation in which subjects behaved as if they revered the leader even if they patently did not.[19] Importantly, Wedeen argues that the spectacles that constitute the authority of the cult anchor politically significant ideas that ground political thinking and frame the way people see themselves as citizens, even if their claims are not taken literally, providing a visual and aural language for *both* complying with and contesting the regime.[20] Separately, Lacanian psychoanalysts have developed the notion of overidentification to describe how people living under authoritarian regimes might attack the norms by which they are governed not with a direct and straightforward critique but rather through a rabid and obscenely exaggerated adoption of them.[21] As Slavoj Žižek argues, by taking the norms of the system more seriously than the system itself does, overidentification lays bare the hollowness of regnant ideologies and their claims to obedience.[22]

Neither of these scenarios for living under authoritarianism fully describes what is unfolding in India. Anti-CAA protesters appear deeply invested in the very symbolic apparatus that has been used to discipline them. At one level this can be explained quite straightforwardly: the protesters wrap themselves in national symbols to obviate the state's all-too predictable charge of anti-nationalism. Yet the deployment of these symbols is far from simply instrumental and defensive. The exuberant profusion of their creative reconfiguration, the evident sincerity with which they are invoked, the febrile pitch of contemporary public discourse and the sheer scale on which all of this is unfolding suggest that the protesters retain a faith in the power of these symbols to shield them from the violence of the state even when they patently do not. (A widely circulated video from the Delhi riots shows policemen beating a group of protesters, one of whom subsequently died, and taunting them by forcing them to sing the national anthem.[23]) This begs the question of how national symbols have managed to retain a degree of subversive critical potential despite their deployment as a disciplinary apparatus by the state.

Nationalism against the state

I suggest that the protests against the CAA are better understood as an instance of what David Lloyd has called 'nationalisms against the state'.[24] Lloyd reminds us that even as they seek to saturate the field of subject formation, anticolonial nationalisms are articulated in a variety of ways with social movements organised around other logics such as class and gender. When nationalism becomes annexed to the territorial state, the processes of articulation that maintain nationalism as an element of broader, more complex and internally antagonistic social fields are brought to an end. Yet these other movements are never fully absorbed into state-oriented nationalisms, persisting as a potentially disruptive excess over the nation and its state. As Lloyd explains, 'the possibility of nationalism against the state lies in the recognition of the excess of the people over the nation and in the understanding that that is, beyond itself, the very logic of nationalism as a political phenomenon.'[25] This 'excess' grows in those historical conjunctures in which the state becomes increasingly unmoored from the nation or at least from key constituents of it, as is evident in the BJP's unwillingness to consider Muslims a part of the nation and in its determination to subordinate and/or expel them from a reimagined Hindu nation-state.[26] In such moments, nationalisms against the state marshal the symbolic repertoire of nationalism to shame the state for its betrayal of the nation, with a view to repairing the disconnect between state and nation.[27]

This seems precisely to be the import of, for example, Varun Grover's defiant poem that in the few short weeks since it was composed at the start of the protests went viral, mutating into song and graffiti.[28] One stanza reads:

Hum samvidhan ko bachaenge,
Hum kagaz nahin dikhaenge,

Hum jan gan man bhi gaenge,
Hum kagaz nahin dikhaenge.

We will save the Constitution,
We will not show [NRC] papers,
We will sing Jan Gan Man [the national anthem]
We will not show papers.

Participants in the leaderless movement against the NRC/CAA have taken on the pedagogical task of reminding both the people and the state of the nation's founding ideology. Musicians have resurrected the less well known verses of the longer poem by Rabindranath Tagore from which the national anthem is extracted, poignantly drawing attention to lines that affirm the national belonging of Hindus, Buddhists, Sikhs, Jains, Parsis, Muslims and Christians – as if to underscore the betrayal inherent in the CAA in singling out one community for removal from the nation that the anthem sings into being.[29] It is an enduring irony that the man who wrote the anthem (as well as the song that became the national anthem of Bangladesh) was, for much of his life, a fierce critic of nationalism. In his 1917 lectures on nationalism, Tagore describes the idea of the nation as 'one of the most powerful anaesthetics that man has invented' under the influence of which 'the whole people can carry out its systematic programme of the most virulent self-seeking without being in the least aware of its moral perversion – in fact feeling dangerously resentful if it is pointed out.'[30]

The trope of 'saving the constitution', literalised in the names of political action groups such as the Samvidhan Suraksha Samiti and the Dastoor Bachao Committee that have sprung up recently, likewise represents the Constitution as endangered by the state and therefore requiring the protection of the nation. In his book *A People's Constitution*, the legal historian Rohit De attempts to unsettle the conventional view of the Indian Constitution as the discursive preserve of state and civil society elites. He opens the book with an image of the Constituent Assembly being 'flooded with telegrams, postcards, and petitions from schoolboys to housewives to postmasters, staking claims, making demands, and offering suggestions' while it went about its work of drafting the Constitution.[31] The story he tells about the Constitution in its first decades of existence is one of a document produced through elite consensus but enlivened by the use made of it by ordinary litigants, many from unpopular minorities whose rights were not always assured by the majoritarian institutions of the state. But it is still a story about litigants invoking the Constitution before a court that they hope will rule in their favour. The CAA's critics, in contrast, do not sound like they are waiting for a court ruling, convinced as they are of the incompatibility of the CAA with the Constitution and indeed of its potential to undermine it. It is as if the people have sought a direct relationship with the text of the Constitution, insisting on their right to interpret it unmediated by the authority of a secular clergy whose recent judgments have not always inspired confidence.

The Supreme Court is, at the time of writing, considering over 140 petitions challenging the constitutionality of the CAA. While it would be imprudent to anticipate its conclusions, it is sobering to recall that the Court has often chosen not to restrain the executive's majoritarian excesses, notably in three recent cases that implicate central elements of the Hindu Right's vendetta against Muslims. First, in November 2019, the Court brought to a conclusion the long running dispute over the Babri Mosque that had been demolished in 1992 by Hindu mobs claiming that the sixteenth-century mosque had been built on the ruins of a temple that marked the birthplace of the Hindu god Ram. After decades of litigation, the Court awarded the disputed site in its entirety to the Hindu parties despite acknowledging that the demolition of the mosque was illegal.[32] Second, in August 2019, the Modi government drastically altered the position of India's only Muslim-majority province, the disputed state of Jammu and Kashmir, by revoking the autonomy guaranteed to it by article 370 of the Constitution and downgrading its status to that of a territory ruled directly by the federal government in New Delhi. The move was accompanied by draconian measures including curfews, the incarceration of virtually the entire political class and the longest Internet shutdown ever imposed in a democracy. In January 2020, the Court ruled that the indefinite suspension of the Internet violated fundamental rights but inexplicably declined to pass any specific orders mandating relief.[33] Third, the NRC exercise in Assam – the results of which, recall, provided the impetus for the CAA – was conducted after much stonewalling by politicians as a result of the zealous oversight of a Supreme Court bench headed by the then Chief Justice Ranjan Gogoi who is himself Assamese. Indifferent to the obvious conflicts of interest at play, Gogoi's political views as an Assamese nationalist heavily shaped decisions about the constitutionality and conduct of the NRC.[34]

Faced with a fascist executive that commands a supermajority in the legislature and is unrestrained by a supine judiciary, the anti-CAA movement's nationalism against the state seeks to reiterate and protect an endangered vision of the moral values of the nation and ultimately to persuade or force state institutions to uphold those values. Unreliable as it has been as a guardian of minority rights, the Supreme Court has shown itself to be attentive to public opinion – for better and worse. For example, the outcry that greeted the Court's 2013 judgment upholding India's colonial-era anti-sodomy law may have played some role in persuading it to change its mind five years later.[35] In quite a different vein, upholding the death sentence awarded to Afzal Guru, a Kashmiri convicted for his alleged involvement in an attack on the Indian Parliament in December 2001, the Court justified its decision on the ground that 'the collective conscience of the society will only be satisfied if capital punishment is awarded to the offender'.[36]

Beyond nationalism against the state

Nationalism against the state aspires to strengthen the hyphen between nation and state to make the state representative of the nation from which it has become unmoored. This is the source of both its power and limits. Because it looks forward to a re-hyphenated nation-state, it cannot in good faith be accused of anti-nationalism or even anti-statism, even if it throws the full weight of its anger at the current incumbents of the state apparatus. Yet the presumption of 'good faith' in the debate over the CAA itself betrays a naïve Habermasian faith in the possibility of consensus on the rules of communicative reason. Nothing in the nationalism of the anti-CAA protesters protected them from the viciousness of the bad faith accusations of anti-nationalism that were hurled at them by the state and its acolytes. The most popular slogan of the Hindu mobs rampaging through northeast Delhi was 'desh ke gaddaron ko, goli maro salon ko' (shoot the traitors). In the face of such murderous disingenuousness, the imperative of solidarity with the victims and survivors of this pogrom and with their demands for justice is clear. What follows is offered less in the register of critique of the normative imaginary of a movement that could not *not* have appealed to a certain kind of nationalism in its struggle against the state, and more in the spirit of a search for what lies beyond this imaginary, circumscribed as it is by the telos of the idealised nation-state. If the very possibility of nationalism against the state lies in the recognition of the excess of the people over the officially constituted nation, then the performance of this nationalism generates excesses of its own. In this section, I offer some illustrations of such 'excesses' whose claims are difficult to advance even within the more capacious imaginaries enabled by nationalisms against the state.

First, the question of Kashmir brings the limits of this discourse into stark relief. While the struggle for self-determination in Kashmir has been ongoing for decades – since the late 1980s in some reckonings and the inception of independent India in others – it has taken on a particular urgency since August 2019 in the wake of the repeal of article 370, the abrogation of which fulfils the BJP's cherished ambition of integrating this Muslim-majority state more firmly into the Indian Union. In this regard, calls to defend the Constitution can be construed as a demand to restore the constitutional status quo ante vis-à-vis article 370. Yet to demand this is not to demand very much at all: by the time the provision had been formally abrogated, it had become a shell of its former self, hollowed out by successive Congress and BJP governments in New Delhi. There is something disingenuous in the sudden resurgence of left-liberal interest in Kashmir, newly rediscovered as a weapon with which to attack the BJP, given the historically bipartisan insistence on its status as an 'integral part of India'. Many Kashmiris resent how Kashmir has been drawn into the anti-CAA protests (if it is remembered at all) as one issue among many with which to criticise the government, bristling at the manner in which their demand for azadi (freedom) has been appropriated and resignified to express a plurality of other demands in the slogans of the current movement.[37] The tension arises from the fact that the desires of those protesting their forced inclusion in the nation (in places like Kashmir) are fundamentally different from those protesting their forced exclusion from it (in places like Assam), even if both processes are manifestations of the BJP's coercive nation-building. Calls to protect the Constitution cannot mean much to those who do not wish to be governed by it – unless the Constitution can contemplate a process by which it will no longer be applicable to unwilling subjects. But this is typically where law ends and politics begins.

Second, not enough attention has been paid to how adivasis (indigenous peoples), who constitute 8.6% of the Indian population, are likely to be disproportionately and differentially impacted by the NRC-CAA. While the politics of indigeneity – specifically the 'fear' of powerful ethnic groups of being reduced to minorities in their homelands – has underwritten the NRC, the demand for documentary proof of citizenship that it has entailed will be especially difficult for adivasis to meet given the greater likelihood of their being poor, rural, landless and nomadic and/or displaced.[38] The CAA is unlikely to function as a safety net for adivasis given that many do not identify as belonging to the major religious groups to which it promises citizenship. Indeed the combined effect of these exercises in governmentality might be to incentivise adivasis to become Hindus, a process that the Hindu Right already encourages through campaigns of coercive inducement that it calls 'ghar wapsi' (return home). Some of the most powerful moments in the protests against the CAA have arisen from gestures of everyday fraternity between religious groups – as when Hindus have formed protective cordons around Muslim protesters offering prayers, or when Sikhs have set up langars (community kitchens serving free meals typically at gurudwaras). Moving as they have been, the very ontology of these gestures – in which communities divided by something that can be identified as 'religion' nonetheless make common 'political' cause – can feel analytically incommensurate with what Alpa Shah calls the 'sacral polities' of adivasi lifeworlds in which distinctions between religion, politics and economics have never been very meaningful.[39] In such lifeworlds, the constitutionalism of the current nationalism against the state can seem presumptuous. In recent years, a movement known as Pathalgadi has spread particularly through adivasi villages in the state of Jharkhand. Responding to the threat of dispossession posed by land acquisition legislation, the movement has made itself visible through the erection of gigantic stone plaques quoting extracts from the Constitution that protect adivasi rights at the entrances to villages. Yet Pathalgadi evinces a paradoxical constitutionalism, asserting the exclusive sovereignty of gram sabhas (village assemblies) while in the same breath denying the sovereignty of other levels of government.[40] As some participants in the movement explained to journalists: 'We have all descended from nature and we worship it. We don't believe in the Indian Constitution, nor do we recognise government officials.'[41]

Third, the reference to nature invites us to think beyond the humanist discourses of liberal constitutionalism to consider how relationships between people and the environment have produced the current conjuncture. In the preparation of the Assam NRC, a xenophobic and arbitrary adjudication process has conspired with the paucity of record-keeping by people who are poor, illiterate, and have often had to move frequently as a result of war, partitions and environmental displacement, to deprive nearly two million people of citizenship.[42] As Arundhati Roy writes, the very impermanence of the nearly 2500 shifting, silty 'char' islands in the river Brahmaputra on which many of the most marginal farmers live has meant an absence of land deeds and other documentation that might establish their connection to the land as demanded by the NRC.[43] Whatever fences and border regimes are put in place, if current projections of climate-induced displacement in the region are correct, we must expect migration only to grow. It is estimated that by 2050, one in seven people in Bangladesh will be displaced by climate change, with up to 18 million people having to move because of a rise in sea level.[44] This will offer grist to the mill of the Hindu Right, which for decades has used the spectre of 'illegal migration' from Bangladesh to whip up anti-Muslim hysteria in India.

Nowhere in the world are the forms of international cooperation necessary for better management of land and water resources or indeed the mitigation of the global climate crisis adequate to the scale of the task that they face. But these processes are particularly deficient in South Asia which remains one of the least integrated regions in the world thanks to the bitter legacies of Partition, war, contested borders, a lack of complementarity between economies, and the mistrust that comes from the sheer disparity in size between India and its neighbours.[45] There has been little consideration, even within the anti-CAA movement, of the international effects of an Indian law that presumptively declares the country's Muslim-majority neighbours to be persecuting states while setting itself up as a refuge for the non-Muslim victims of such persecution. In February 2020, a 20-year-old woman named Amulya Leona took to the stage at an anti-CAA rally in Bengaluru and attempted to lead the crowd in a chant that began with the words 'Pakistan Zindabad!' ('Long live Pakistan!'). It was unclear where she was going with this because she was violently taken off the stage by event organisers and police before she could finish; we hear her repeat the Pakistan slogan several times interspersed with cries of 'Hindustan Zindabad!' ('Long live India!').[46] A Facebook post by her from several days earlier suggests that she was trying to articulate a position of pan-South Asian fraternity.[47] Such views cannot easily be accommodated even within the discursive and affective realm of nationalism against the state. The Hyderabad MP Asaduddin Owaisi, who was on the stage at the time and has been the leading Muslim political voice in the anti-CAA protests, immediately distanced himself from Leona, undoubtedly mindful of the portrayal of Indian Muslims in Hindu rightwing propaganda as fifth columnists sympathetic to Pakistan. The police filed charges of sedition against Leona, Hindu vigilantes offered a bounty for her murder, and even her own father was publicly critical of her actions.[48] And yet, in the fraught international context produced by the NRC-CAA, the politically naïve slogans of a young woman with a terrible sense of timing may be the thing we most need to hear.

Nationalism in the time of COVID-19

What threats, litigation and even the Delhi pogrom could not do, COVID-19 has accomplished. A hundred days and nights after it first began, the sit-in at Shaheen Bagh and other anti-CAA protest encampments in New Delhi and elsewhere were cleared by police as part of the lockdown imposed by the government in the wake of the spread of the coronavirus. As Raghu Karnad put it, political togetherness had yielded to the inexorable logic of social distancing.[49] Popular responses to the pandemic have sometimes been troubling, featuring racist anti-Chinese tropes and caste supremacist claims about the putative superiority of the traditional Namaste as a form of greeting that does not involve touching. The state's initial response has tilted heavily in the direction of securitisation (curfews and lockdowns) with rather less consideration given to the welfare of people disadvantaged by these measures.[50]

Leading these responses has been the figure of the Prime Minister himself, whose own discourse has been heavy on symbolism and citizen duty rather than state responsibility.[51] In what seems to have been a trial-run for a subsequently ordered 21-day lockdown, Narendra Modi asked people to observe a 14-hour curfew on 22 March 2020, as part of which he urged them to beat on pots and pans to demonstrate their gratitude for the efforts of medical and emergency workers. Many appear to have ignored, forgotten or misunderstood the instructions on physical distancing, congregating on balconies and in streets to participate in the moment with enthusiasm. Whatever superficial resemblance the gesture might have borne to spontaneous demonstrations in Italy, Spain and elsewhere, many who witnessed the moment first hand described it as evoking the soundscapes of Hindu ritual especially as people also took to blowing the horn-like conches commonly used in temple worship. The Leader had ordered and the People had obeyed. The last Indian able to stage such impressive shows of symbolic conformity might have been Gandhi.

Rahul Rao is Senior Lecturer in Politics at SOAS University of London and author of Out of Time: The Queer Politics of Postcoloniality *(2020). Photo credits: Chris Moffat.*

Notes

1. 'In Photos: Republic Day at Shaheen Bagh', *The Wire*, 27 January 2020, thewire.in/rights/in-photos-republic-day-at-shaheen-bagh.
2. Siddharth Premkumar, 'Kerala Forms 620 Km Human Chain Against CAA, NRC on Republic Day', *Outlook*, 26 January 2020, https://www.outlookindia.com/website/story/india-news-kerala-forms-620-km-long-human-chain-against-caa-nrc-on-republic-day/346282.
3. For an account of how the politics of Assam has shaped successive amendments to Indian citizenship law, see Anupama Roy, *Mapping Citizenship in India* (New Delhi: Oxford University Press, 2010), chapter 2.
4. Rohini Mohan, 'Inside India's Sham Trials That Could Strip Millions of Citizenship', *Vice News*, 29 July 2019, news.vice.com/en_us/article/3k33qy/worse-than-a-death-sentence-inside-indias-sham-trials-that-could-strip-millions-of-citizenship.
5. Arundhati Roy, 'India: Intimations of an Ending', *The Nation*, 22 November 2019, thenation.com/article/archive/arundhati-roy-assam-modi.
6. Sumant Sen and Naresh Singaravelu, 'Data: How many people died during anti-CAA protests?', *The Hindu*, 6 January 2020, thehindu.com/data/data-how-many-people-died-during-anti-caa-protests/article30494183.ece.
7. Sukirti Dwivedi, '"We'll Be Peaceful Till Trump Leaves," BJP Leader Kapil Mishra Warns Delhi Police', *NDTV*, 24 February 2020, ndtv.com/delhi-news/bjp-leader-kapil-mishras-3-day-ultimatum-to-delhi-police-to-clear-anti-caa-protest-jaffrabad-2184627.
8. Hannah Ellis-Petersen, 'Delhi protests: death toll climbs amid worst religious violence for decades', *The Guardian*, 26 February 2020, theguardian.com/world/2020/feb/26/delhi-protests-death-toll-climbs-amid-worst-religious-violence-for-decades.
9. Jeffrey Gettleman, Sameer Yasir, Suhasini Raj and Hari Kumar, 'How Delhi's Police Turned Against Muslims', *The New York Times*, 12 March 2020, nytimes.com/2020/03/12/world/asia/india-police-muslims.html.
10. Sneha Bhura, 'The story behind the library at Shaheen Bagh', *The Week*, 18 February 2020, theweek.in/news/india/2020/02/17/the-story-behind-the-library-at-shaheen-bagh.html.
11. Srirupa Roy, *Beyond Belief: India and the Politics of Postcolonial Nationalism* (Durham: Duke University Press, 2007), 6.
12. Rajeev Bhargava, 'The return of the secular', *The Hindu*, 26 December 2019, https://www.thehindu.com/opinion/op-ed/the-return-of-the-secular/article30397647.ece; Rahul Rao, 'Test of Faith', *The Caravan*, 29 January 2020, https://caravanmagazine.in/politics/caa-protests-shake-old-bounds-indian-secular-morality.
13. Ankita Pandey, 'Keeping India's Universities for the Rich', *Jacobin*, 27 January 2020, https://jacobinmag.com/2020/01/jawaharlal-nehru-university-india-fee-hike; Samanth Subramanian, 'How Hindu supremacists are tearing India apart', *The Guardian*, 20 February 2020, theguardian.com/world/2020/feb/20/hindu-supremacists-nationalism-tearing-india-apart-modi-bjp-rss-jnu-attacks.
14. Anuradha Raman, 'National flag to fly at all Central Universities', *The Hindu*, 18 February 2016, thehindu.com/news/national/hoisting-of-tricolour-to-be-made-mandatory-in-all-central-universities/article14086309.ece.
15. Staff Reporter, 'JNU VC asks govt. to install a battle tank on campus', *The Hindu*, 24 July 2017, thehindu.com/news/cities/Delhi/jnu-vc-ask-govt-to-install-a-battle-tank-on-campus/article19341486.ece.
16. BBC News, 'India national anthem no longer compulsory in cinemas', 9 January 2018, bbc.co.uk/news/world-asia-india-42618830.
17. Roy, *Beyond Belief*, 14.
18. Roy, *Beyond Belief*, 18.
19. Lisa Wedeen, *Ambiguities of Domination: Politics, Rhetoric, and Symbols in Contemporary Syria* (Chicago: University of Chicago Press, 1999), 6.
20. Wedeen, *Ambiguities of Domination*, 19–24.
21. Stevphen Shukaitis, 'Overidentification and/or bust?', *Variant* 37 (Spring/Summer 2010), 26, nictoglobe.com/new/articles/V37overident.pdf.
22. Slavoj Žižek, 'What the hell is Laibach all about?', last modified 11 March 2009, youtube.com/watch?v=1BZl8ScVYvA.

23. Anumeha Yadav, 'Ground Report: Delhi Police Actions Caused Death of Man In Infamous National Anthem Video', *Huffpost*, 1 March 2020, https://www.huffingtonpost.in/entry/delhi-riots-police-national-anthem-video-faizan_in_5e5bb8e1c5b6010221126276.

24. David Lloyd, 'Nationalisms Against the State', in *The Politics of Culture in the Shadow of Capital*, eds. Lisa Lowe and David Lloyd (Durham: Duke University Press, 1997), 173–97.

25. Lloyd, 'Nationalisms Against the State', 192.

26. The most authoritative exposition of this ideological worldview remains V. D. Savarkar, *Hindutva: who is a Hindu?* (New Delhi: Bharti Sahitya Sadan, 1989), originally published in 1923.

27. See Pheng Cheah, *Inhuman Conditions: On Cosmopolitanism and Human Rights* (Cambridge: Harvard University Press, 2006), 38–40, for an argument along similar lines.

28. The full text of the poem can be found at https://lyricsraag.com/hum-kagaz-nahi-dikhayenge-varun-grover/.

29. Moushumi Bhowmik, 'The Art of Resistance: Unsung verses of India's national anthem shine a light on the idea of India', *Scroll*, 7 January 2020, https://scroll.in/article/948836/the-art-of-resistance-unsung-verses-of-indias-national-anthem-shine-a-light-on-the-idea-of-india.

30. Rabindranath Tagore, *Nationalism* (London: Macmillan, 1917), 42.

31. Rohit De, *A People's Constitution: The Everyday Life of Law in the Indian Republic* (Princeton: Princeton University Press, 2018), 2.

32. *M. Siddiq (D) Thr Lrs v. Mahant Suresh Das and others*, Civil Appeal Nos. 10866–10867 of 2010, sci.gov.in/pdf/JUD_2.pdf.

33. 'Status quo SC likely to continue in Kashmir; SC avoided primary responsibility of judicial review', *Firstpost*, 10 January 2020, firstpost.com/india/article-370-jammu-and-kashmir-supreme-court-verdict-on-restrictions-petitions-updates-latest-news-today-foreign-envoys-visit-7885211.html.

34. Arshu John, 'Sealed and Delivered: Ranjan Gogoi's Gifts to the Government', *The Caravan*, February 2020, 26–55.

35. Compare *Suresh Kumar Koushal v. Naz Foundation*, (2014) 1 SCC 1, and *Navtej Singh Johar v. Union of India*, WP (Crl) No. 76 of 2016.

36. *State (NCT of Delhi) v. Navjot Sandhu @ Afsan Guru*, Appeal (crl.) 373–375 of 2004, https://indiankanoon.org/doc/1769219/.

37. Listen especially to Mehroosh Tak, 'Hindutva and the University', Teach-in at Queen Mary University of London, 22 January 2020, thepolisproject.com/hindutva-and-the-university.

38. Ananya Singh, 'How Will CAA and NRC Affect India's Tribal Population?', *The Citizen*, 31 December 2019, thecitizen.in/index.php/en/NewsDetail/index/9/18101/How-Will-CAA-and-NRC-Affect-Indias-Tribal-Population; Jawar Bheel, 'Citizenship Amendment Act (CAA), and the Tribal Community (Adivasi)', *Round Table India*, 18 Dec.2019, roundtableindia.co.in/index.php?option=com_content&view=article&id=9773.

39. Alpa Shah, 'Religion and the Secular Left: Subaltern Studies, Birsa Munda and Maoists', *Anthropology Of This Century* 9 (2014), http://aotcpress.com/articles/religion-secular-left-subaltern-studies-birsa-munda-maoists/.

40. Nandini Sundar, 'Pathalgadi is Nothing But Constitutional Messianism So Why is the BJP Afraid Of It?', *The Wire*, 16 May 2018, https://thewire.in/rights/pathalgadi-is-nothing-but-constitutional-messianism-so-why-is-the-bjp-afraid-of-it.

41. Amarnath Tewary, 'The Pathalgadi rebellion', *The Hindu*, 14 April 2018, https://www.thehindu.com/news/national/other-states/the-pathalgadi-rebellion/article23530998.ece.

42. Mohan, 'Inside India's Sham Trials'.

43. Roy, 'India: Intimations of an Ending'.

44. Environmental Justice Foundation, 'Climate Displacement in Bangladesh', ejfoundation.org/reports/climate-displacement-in-bangladesh.

45. P. V. Rao, 'South Asia's retarded regionalism', in *Indian Ocean Regionalism*, eds. Dennis Rumly and Timothy Doyle (London: Routledge, 2016), 37–53; Pratap Bhanu Mehta, 'SAARC and the Sovereignty Bargain', *Himal Southasian* 18:3 (November/December 2005), 17–21.

46. Amulya Leon speech, 20 February 2020, https://www.youtube.com/watch?v=fUOcHVw9Evg.

47. Rohini Swamy, 'Student who shouted "Pakistan Zindabad" on Owaisi stage had praised Modi hours before', *The Print*, 21 February 2020, theprint.in/india/student-who-shouted-pakistan-zindabad-on-owaisi-stage-had-praised-modi-hours-ago/368917; K. P. Sasi, 'Sedition for Peace! The Curious Case of Amulya Leona', *Countercurrents*, 25 February 2020, https://countercurrents.org/2020/02/sedition-for-peace-the-curious-case-of-amulya-leona.

48. D. P. Satish, 'Let Her Rot in Jail, Says Father of Amulya Leona, Arrested For Raising Pro-Pakistan Slogans', *News18*, 21 Feb. 2020, news18.com/news/india/let-her-rot-in-jail-says-father-of-amulya-leon-arrested-for-raising-pro-pakistan-slogans-2509445.html; Manu Kaushik, 'If released, we will kill her in encounter: Ram Sena man offers Rs 10L bounty for Amulya's head', *Times Now*, 22 February 2020, timesnownews.com/india/article/if-released-we-will-kill-her-in-encounter-ram-sena-man-offers-rs-10l-bounty-for-amulyas-head/556634.

49. Raghu Karnad, 'Farewell to Shaheen Bagh, as Political Togetherness Yields to Social Distance', *The Wire*, 24 March 2020, thewire.in/politics/farewell-to-shaheen-bagh-as-political-togetherness-yields-to-social-distance.

50. Pranav Kohli and Prannv Dhawan, 'Covid-19 and India's Hindu-Fascism Outbreak', *Newsclick*, 22 March 2020, newsclick.in/index.php/covid-19-and-indias-hindu-fascism-outbreak.

51. Vidya Krishnan, 'High on talk, low on substance: Modi's speech showed India is ill-prepared for COVID', *The Caravan*, 20 March 2020, caravanmagazine.in/health/high-on-talk-low-on-substance-modi-speech-showed-india-ill-prepared-covid.

Critique without ontology
Genealogy, collective subjects and the deadlocks of evidence

Daniele Lorenzini and Martina Tazzioli

In the past few years, the number of migrant deaths in the Mediterranean Sea has dramatically increased due to the strengthening of border controls and a deliberate politics of migration containment put into place by the EU in cooperation with third countries. In 2018, according to UN Refugee Agency [UNHCR] estimations, an average of six migrants died at sea every day, trying to cross the Mediterranean from Libya.[1] These figures do not take into account the so-called 'ghost shipwrecks', that is, the number of people who died in ships that simply sank without being detected by the authorities. During these years, the Mediterranean Sea as a space of governmentality has been the object of multiple readjustments. Back in 2013 and 2014, within the context of the military-humanitarian operation *Mare Nostrum*, Italian Navy vessels used to patrol the Mediterranean close to Libyan waters; since then, the EU has shifted towards a more pervasive and blatant politics of containment. Thus, the 'good scene of rescue'[2] has been replaced by a generalised retreat of European vessels from the Mediterranean Sea, and since the signing of the *Memorandum of Understanding* between Italy and Libya in March 2017, the work of rescuing, capturing and sending migrants back to Libya has been left to the Libyan coast guard alone.

In the face of this dramatic situation, important civic mobilisations have been organised and many journalistic investigations have been carried out to demonstrate and denounce the states' responsibility, the violation of international law, and to downplay – by providing more informative statistics – the alarmist analyses that constantly warn EU citizens against a 'migrant invasion' and a 'refugee crisis'. Researchers have also convincingly shown that NGOs conducting search and rescue operations in the Mediterranean do not constitute a pull-factor for migrants.[3] More broadly, many scholars have become more and more engaged in producing 'public truth' about states' violations of human rights and the international law, and in providing the kinds of evidence that can help prove such truths. This goal has been pursued by mobilising diverse epistemic approaches. One of these is the forensic method, which consists in 'a mode of public address and a means of articulating political claims using evidence grounded in the built world.'[4] In this case, the production of evidence is mainly conceived in legal terms, even though, as Eyal Weizman aptly contends, it is not limited to law and it also possesses an eminently political significance. By contrast, in mainstream migration scholarship, the production of evidence is mostly oriented towards generating knowledge with a view to governing migration 'better' and more fairly.[5] Within a general migration policy framework, evidence is generated and exposed as part of a problem-solving strategy. By contrast, in what follows we will consider 'evidence' not only in its legal dimension: we will also address its production in terms of both the unveiling and crafting of the truth of (border) violence and numbers (of migrant deaths).

Evidence of migrant deaths at sea has been incessantly produced through circulation in the media of pictures and videos of migrants' bodies ashore, and of migrants detained and tortured in Libyan prisons. To some extent, the sheer exposure of violence perpetrated on migrants mirrors states' blatant violation of international law and human rights. Nevertheless, this *accumulation of evidence*, which is a consequence of the attempt to prove (and expose) the reality of brutal violence against migrants as well as the deadly effects of EU politics of migration containment, is neither limiting nor disrupting the constant rise of racism and xenophobia in Europe.[6] Europe is confronted with a situation that is properly *intolerable*, on both ethical and political grounds, yet most Europeans, with varying levels of regret or distaste, continue tacitly to tolerate it. We will return to Foucault's pertinent emphasis on 'the intolerable' in the penultimate section of this article.

The main aim of this article is to address this theoretical and practical impasse, and to ask, in the context that it continues to define: What is the role of critique today? What does it mean to produce critical knowledge about the aforementioned situation, and many others? Recent literature on post-truth and post-critique avoids finding the answer to these questions in a (new) normative definition of critique. Yet this scholarship generally conceives of the act of bringing evidence – not as something just to discover, but in the constructive sense of 'crafting' and 'building' – as the main ground on which to rely in order to elaborate effective 'critical' practices. More precisely, while it questions the accumulation of evidence as a theoretical and political goal, this literature nevertheless defends an epistemology that aims to augment reality and 'compose' as a way to go beyond a purely negative or debunking critique.

Although we do not want to deny the usefulness of evidence and of epistemic moves to bring evidence in certain contexts, we contend that this strategy alone is clearly insufficient and that it relies on an ontological and genealogical anxiety deriving from a fundamental misunderstanding of the operations of critique – and more specifically of critique as a debunking activity as it is conceived of by Nietzsche and Foucault. Our aim in this paper is to defend, develop and redeploy this specific, Nietzschean-Foucauldian mode of critique.[7] In fact, the idea that (debunking) critique is pointless and that it should be replaced by the task of bringing evidence, with a view to describing (and possibly denouncing) things as they are, risks, we argue, obscuring the crucial role that critique can still play in contemporary society as a movement of contestation of the regimes of truth that govern us – and of transformation of the truth-power-subjects nexus on which they rely.

To better define such a role, we address in turn three fundamental dimensions of what we call the 'laborious work of critique': history, desubjugation and the creation of new collective subjects. Our argument proceeds as follows. First, we emphasise the problematic elision, in post-critical approaches, of the *history* of what is produced and presented as a 'truth' or a 'fact', and we question the way in which certain phenomena and subjects are transformed into 'problems' to be 'solved'. Second, we claim that, far from unveiling hidden truths, critique crucially entails disengaging from and refusing the effects of power in terms of subjection that stem from a given regime of truth – in other words, critique is conceived of here as a 'politics of desubjugation'. Third, we argue that critique is to be addressed specifically in its capacity to create new collective subjects and, at the same time, to problematise the production of a given category of subjects as the 'others' of critique. We conclude by gesturing towards two further points to be addressed in future inquiries: on the one hand, we contend that we should strive to attune critical interventions to the current movements of collective refusal; on the other, that building transversal alliances between EU citizens and those labelled as 'migrants' might prove to be crucial in the years to come.

Ontological anxiety and genealogical critique

In recent years, critique has been widely questioned for its purely negative, debunking or deconstructive nature. Indeed, instead of unmaking and subtracting, the role of humanities and social sciences – we are told – should be to provide us with tools to craft and build, or better, to *compose*. Commenting on Bruno Latour's 'Compositionist Manifesto',[8] Rita Felski argues that 'the idea of composition … speaks to the possibility of trying to compose a common world, even if this world can only be built out of many different parts.'[9] Focusing on composition instead of critique means evacuating 'the uninteresting question of what is constructed or not constructed' in order to raise 'the key question of whether something is well made or badly made.'[10] Similarly, Jonathan Luke Austin gestures towards composition as an epistemic and methodological move that allows one to retain the complexity of reality against critique conceived as suspicion and subtraction.[11] More generally, partisans of post-critique such as Felski and Austin have convincingly challenged both a normative understanding of critique and a neo-positivist conception of evidence – understood as a move from secrecy to transparency, or as a way to 'unveil' what is hidden.

Nevertheless, these attacks on critique rely on what we could call an 'ontological anxiety': the fear that critique, by 'deconstructing and demystifying', will end up making things 'less real by underscoring their social constructedness' – thus leaving us with no solid ground on which to stand, 'however temporarily or tentatively'.[12] This ontological anxiety, we argue, is the correlate of what Amia Srinivasan calls 'genealogical anxiety'.[13] Indeed, in the past three or four decades, and drawing mostly from Nietzsche and Foucault, genealogy has been posited as a basis for social and political critique precisely insofar as it fosters anxiety as to the validity of our shared beliefs and practices.[14] In other words, genealogy has been used for debunking critical aims because it allows us to show that if a belief or practice emerged in a contingent, historical way – and which one did not? – we are justified in criticising or even abandoning it.[15]

In a time that so many are eager to define as one of 'post-truth',[16] ontological and genealogical anxieties end up mutually fostering and reinforcing each other. Postmodernism, we are told, miserably failed – or it brilliantly succeeded, depending on the point of view. The idea that there is no objective truth, that every truth or fact can (and should) be debunked and criticised, has brought us straight to a situation in which it is no longer possible to distinguish truths from lies, in which populism is on the rise everywhere in the world, and nationalism and racism with it.[17] Thus, Latour's claim that 'critique has run out of steam', and his argument about the conundrums of critical theory,[18] have nurtured a wide interdisciplinary scholarship which includes anthropology, sociology, philosophy of science, international relations and critical security studies, among others. Critique, the argument goes, has been conceived as a move away from facts and a perpetual debunking of truths with a view to emphasising the historical and epistemological conditions that contributed to their production. However, 'the question was never to get away from facts but closer to them.'[19] Consequently, Latour argues, we should now turn our attention towards 'matters of concern' and 'transform the critical urge in the ethos of someone who adds reality to matters of fact and not subtract reality from it.'[20]

In order to get out of this vicious circle of (ontological and genealogical) anxieties and be able to concretely intervene in reality, humanities and social sciences – we are told – should concentrate on (and limit themselves to) the task of bringing evidence. Indeed, the injunction to 'get closer to facts' and 'add reality to matters of fact' is generally taken to mean that evidence is the only solid ground on which to rely in order to elaborate effective socio-political practices and fight against the proliferation of rhetorical speech and fake news. Politics has been defined as a struggle 'identifying the creation of new assemblies, or gathering empirical evidence for causal arguments.'[21] This idea has become so widespread that 'fact-checking' is often presented as the most effective (and sometimes the only) critical intervention that scholars and journalists should aspire to make. For instance, in both the Italian press and the scholarly literature, the 'truth of numbers' and the 'reality of facts' have been largely mobilised to undermine the claims by the ex-Minister of the Interior, Matteo Salvini, about a supposed 'migrant invasion' taking place in Europe and to counter the widespread perception of a 'migrant threat'.[22]

Problematising 'post-critique'

To a certain extent, all of the above is correct. Critique should not limit itself to negative, debunking or deconstructive tasks. Indeed, if, on the one hand, unpacking, undoing and problematising are the verbs of what we define here as the 'operations of critique', on the other hand, critique, as a practice, should also consist in enacting and opening up. In other words, critique should also be able to build and produce. Why then should we continue to call it 'critique'? Some prefer to herald the twenty-first century as an era of 'post-critique'.[23] After an epistemological critique preoccupied with defining the limits of our knowledge, as Kant defined it in his *Critique of Pure Reason*, and a genealogical critique occupied in debunking operations, as Nietzsche first conceived of it, the time has come – or so we are told – to do away with critique altogether and replace it with ontology. Indeed, although one can argue that 'the goal of post-critique is not to do away with critique, but to treat it simply as one language game among others',[24] in this recent postcrtical literature a critical attitude is de facto dismissed and reduced to a hermeneutics of suspicion and a series of acts of denunciation. We already conceded that the questioning of critique in this scholarship deserves to be taken seriously, as it exposes the limitations of critical analyses and interventions – as the Mediterranean migration context demonstrates – and helps to reconceive the very meaning and function of critique today. However, the debunking and productive aspects of critique should never be separated. We should thus reject the binary opposition between subtracting and adding reality, as well as the idea that we should do away with critique altogether. Critique and the production of subjectivity and new political spaces should be thought *together*.

Clearly, the act of bringing evidence alone is not enough to prove a case, let alone to make a political difference. Despite the well-intentioned efforts to gather evidence about Europe's scandalous treatment of migrants that we evoked above, according to the polls, Salvini has been gaining more and more support in the past year, and his party, the League, is now the most popular party in Italy. More generally, an increase in the supply of evidence does not seem to be able, in itself, to counter the rise of populism, nationalism and racism in Europe and all over the world. It is not even so sure that the problem is that we (supposedly) live in a 'post-truth' era. As Bernard Harcourt argues, there is no 'reliable evidence, one way or the other, as to whether the strategic use of the post-truth and fake news arguments are effective political weapons.'[25] In this respect, it is also worth mentioning Jacques Derrida's poignant 'History of the Lie'. Critically engaging with lies, he argues, actually pushes us to revisit our notion of truth as an object which is not given in advance, and to reconceive of it by opposing testimony to proof: 'The opposition veracity/lie is homogeneous with a testimonial problematic, and not at all with an epistemological one of true/false or of proof.'[26]

In other words, the problem is not to try to restore a utopian situation in which the truth would be able to impose its law on everybody solely because it is the truth.[27] The 'regime of truth' characterising the socio-political context, differently from the one characterising, for instance, logic or science, does not (and will never) function on the basis of the idea that it is enough to bring convincing evidence supporting a given conclusion in order for everybody to accept it as true.[28] The problem is rather to be aware that there is a multiplicity of different regimes of truth, that is, of ways in which the relations between the manifestation of the truth, the exercise of power in the form of the 'government' of human beings and the constitution of the subject are organised in our society.[29] It is therefore crucial to produce critical knowledge of these regimes of truth – such as the regime of truth associated to the government of migration – which not only tells us how they function, but also opens up the possibility to transform the nexus truth-power-subjects that supports them. These three dimensions being separable only in theory, and never in practice, a critical intervention limiting itself only to one of them – in the hope, to take the case discussed here, that bringing facts and truths would be enough to change the relations of power in place, and the ways in which the subjects are constituted (and subjugated) – is inevitably condemned to fail.

To argue with Foucault that no truth can be manifested independent of a given regime of truth, and therefore independent of a given set of power relations and forms of subjection/subjectivation does not entail, however, the conclusion that truth does not exist. On the contrary, truth is literally everywhere and plays a crucial role in almost every aspect of our life. But truth is always *situated* – that is, it has no intrinsic 'force' allowing it to impose itself to everybody or in every possible circumstance.[30] Donna Haraway has notably proposed a feminist account of objectivity in terms of situatedness and partiality, adding that, however, partiality as such is not enough: it should be coupled with constant critical investigation.[31] Bringing evidence, stating the facts, demonstrating the truth – all these moves can, and should, be part of a critical intervention. But the idea that they are enough in and of themselves is an illusion: truth is not the Truth of critique.

The laborious work of critique

Critique is questioned today for both theoretical and political reasons. We should add to this the appropriation (and capitalisation) of critique by the neoliberal academy – which, despite appearances, contributes to making any genuine practice of critique even harder. Being critical, producing critical knowledge, elaborating critical analyses, far from being presented and perceived by Western universities as uncomfortable and potentially threatening tasks, have become both a sort of (neoliberal) injunction and a 'brand'. From this perspective, the impact-driven approach that dominates today's academy is not far from the quest for evidence and the resulting neutralisation of critique that aims to augment and intervene in, or impact upon, reality. Impact, we are told, 'remains the ultimate test of the usefulness of the critical approach.'[32] Does this mean that any possible space for critique, and for its desubjugating and transformative effects, has been irremediably closed off?

Here, we would like to echo Wendy Brown's considerations on the supposedly anachronistic character of critique. In contemporary society, she argues, we witness 'a common conservative and moralising rejection of critique as untimely': 'It is not the time', we are told.[33] However, it is precisely this untimeliness that renders critique a crucial epistemological and political task. Indeed, critique does not consist in

> making flamboyant interventions, or staging irreverent protests, but rather [in] contest[ing] the very senses of time invoked to declare critique untimely. If the charge of untimeliness inevitably also fixes time, then disrupting this fixity is crucial to keeping the times from closing in on us. It is a way of reclaiming the present from the conservative hold on it that is borne by the charge of untimeliness.[34]

To defend the untimeliness of critique both from those who want to do away with critique, or who treat it as a mere 'language game',[35] and from those who conceive of critique as nothing more than a brand, we will address in turn the three main dimensions that lie at the heart of what we call the 'laborious work of critique': history, desubjugation and the creation of new collective subjects. Our aim is to show that critique rarely stems from an isolated act or the simple gesture of bringing evidence to support the truth of a charge or claim. On the contrary, it almost always requires work over an unspecified period of time and an acceptance of the lack of stable epistemological and political grounds. In this specific sense, we argue, critique has not yet run out of steam.

Let us consider again the case of migration. From what we argued above, it follows that it is paramount to pay attention to the simultaneous processes of redefinition and recrafting of violence as well as of infringement of the law. If, by letting migrants die, states have overtly violated the international law of the sea on many occasions, they have also enacted legal artifices in order not to be held responsible. For instance, instead of undertaking push-back operations on the high seas, EU member states paid the Libyan coast guard to bring the migrants back to Libya. Indeed, conflicting jurisdictional regimes enable states 'to simultaneously extend their sovereign privileges through forms of mobile government and elude the responsibilities that come with it.'[36] Consequently, as Judith Butler points out,

> when law becomes the instrument of violence and administrative power becomes its own form of quasi-legal or extra-legal violence, then the problem is not just the death-dealing power of the sovereign. ... In the Mediterranean, it is precisely through the invocation of sovereignty that international obligations are abandoned and calls for assistance refused.[37]

The blatant exposure of violence and its justification through sovereignty and law are not in contradiction: they take place jointly and reinforce each other. Reconceiving of critique today requires taking into account the problematic nature of the indefinite accumulation of evidence vis-à-vis the growing exposure of violence in the absence of an impartial third party that could bring justice. What kind of critical knowledge would be able to disrupt the normalisation and the threshold of acceptance of migrants' deaths? What forms of critical practice would succeed in countering the saturation of the political space and discourse generated by the proliferation of images of migrants' suffering? While we do not want to dismiss nor downplay the theoretical and political deadlocks of critique, we would like to embrace this disquiet and think through it. Our goal is not to 'rescue' critique as such, nor to advance a normative definition of critique that would be valid once and for all. Instead, we aim to emphasise a series of *practices of critique* as interventions in the present driven by moves of desubjugation resulting in the creation of new collective subjects, as well as by the questioning of accepted conceptual frameworks through which objects and problems are crafted.

Bringing in history

In discussing the current impasses of critique, the first question to ask is: What do we mean by intervening in the present? What does 'intervention' stand for here? This question is inextricably linked to the first crucial dimension of the laborious work of critique – history – but remains almost completely unaddressed in much of the existing scholarship.

Feminist historian Joan Wallach Scott can help us think the pitfalls of evidence and of equating critical intervention with the simple move of bringing evidence to support a claim. When discussing historical approaches that promote the subjects' experience as the ultimate, solid ground on which historical knowledge should rely, Scott criticises the claims to transparency and visibility underpinning this methodological move: the 'metaphor of visibility as literal transparency',[38] she argues, fails to account for the 'constructed nature of experience' and 'precludes critical examination of the workings of the ideological system itself, its categories of representation (homosexual/heterosexual, man/woman, black-/white as fixed immutable identities), its premises about what these categories mean and how they operate, and of its notions of subjects, origin, and cause.'[39] Similarly, Carlo Ginzburg's seminal work allows us to problematise the quest for evidence by showing that the production of truth cannot be detached from the obstacles encountered by the historian in the research process, nor from the way in which she chooses to narrate 'facts'.[40]

Building on Scott and Ginzburg, it is possible to emphasise the problematic elision of the *history* of what is produced and presented as a 'truth' or a 'fact' which sustains post-critical approaches focusing exclusively on the quest for evidence. By contrast, bringing history into critical practices allows us to avoid the 'trap of presentism'[41] which is at the core of problem-solving analyses and imposes on us a specific and monolithic temporality – one that is often conceived in terms of 'crisis'. As Janet Roitman aptly remarks, drawing on the work of Reinhart Koselleck, the notion of crisis 'is always in articulation with the notion of critique', and 'conversely, this involves that critique itself is framed according to the political grammar of the crisis and of crisis moments.'[42] Indeed, if we think about migration, the current practices of critique are structured around and against the taken-for-granted background of the so-called 'refugee crisis' – either by asking how to 'solve' such a crisis or by denouncing the way states address it. By contrast, we argue that it is paramount to develop practices of critique that are detached from the crisis-script, and to avoid the reproduction of the crisis-narrative through our critical knowledge production, thus opening the analysis to multiple and fragmented temporalities.[43] This also allows us to do justice to the 'precarious and fragile history', characterised by a 'confluence of encounters and chances', in the course of which 'the things which seem most evident to us are ... formed.'[44]

Thus, instead of engaging in a normative understanding of critique and providing a new definition of it, we suggest focusing on a questioning of the ways in which certain phenomena and subjects are transformed into 'problems' to be 'solved'. For instance, the crafting of migration as an object of government, even by those who aim to challenge repressive state policies and border closures, necessarily entails a very specific – and problematic – framing of critique: critical interventions de facto end up relying on and taking for granted the nexus between migration and governmentality, instead of questioning it as their first move. By bringing history into critical practices, we aim to problematise not only what is presented as a 'truth' or a 'fact', but also (and in the first place) what is presented as a 'problem' with a view to addressing it according to a problem-solving logic. This obviously entails unsettling and refusing the current modes of defining and crafting 'problems'. Yet the job of critique does not stop there. Indeed, critique should also elaborate new strategies to address specific phenomena and events by reverberating them into the realm of politics with a view to problematising its boundaries, its grammar and its exclusionary mechanisms. Here, we echo Foucault's definition of *problematisation* as the

> development of a domain of acts, practices and thoughts that seem ... to pose problem for politics. For example, I don't think that in regard to madness and mental illness there is any 'politics' that can contain the just and definitive solution. But I think that in madness, in derangement, in behaviour problems, there are reasons for questioning politics.[45]

However, as mentioned above, problematisation should also be extended towards a questioning of what we mean by 'problems' and used to resist the collapse of 'problems' into problem-solving strategies.[46] Indeed, when these two overlap, critique ends up being equated to the mere gesture of bringing evidence and thus turned into a neo-positivist approach. By contrast, problematisation, as we conceive of it drawing on Foucault, consists in constantly questioning the acceptability of current regimes of truth and engaging in *transformative* – and not solution-based – practices. It entails the epistemological-political task of unpacking what is deemed to be a 'problem', and it mobilises specific subjects and events in order to question the mechanisms of subjugation at play in our society. Thus, problematising critique rejects all the approaches that focus solely on the act of bringing evidence while leaving untouched the framing of – and the objectivation of phenomena and subjects as – 'problems'. Without a prior work of problematisation, we argue, any augmentation of reality risks doing nothing but intensifying the existing power relations.

In *Reassembling the Social*, Latour argues for 'deployment' against critique,[47] claiming that 'sticking to the description protects against the transmission of explanations' and that 'to deploy simply means that ... the number of actors might be increased; the range of agencies making the actors act might be expanded; the number of objects active in stabilising groups and agencies might be multiplied.'[48] Hence, deployment and description are presented by Latour as weapons in the struggle against what he calls a 'deficit in reality'.[49] Yet augmenting reality and multiplying connections do not, in and of themselves, equip us with analytical, political and ethical tools for refusing and disengaging from mechanisms of domination and forms of subjection. As Foucault argues, a genuine critical intervention in the present 'does not consist in a simple characterisation of what we are but, instead – by following lines of fragility in the present – in managing to grasp why and how that which is might no longer be that which is.'[50] Consequently, he concludes, 'any description must always be made in accordance with these kinds of virtual fracture which open up the space of freedom understood as a space of concrete freedom, that is, of possible transformation.'[51]

As we show below, this becomes even more glaring when addressing phenomena that add a further layer to critique and problematisation, namely, what we call the 'others' of critique (in our case, those labelled and racialised as 'migrants'), thus pushing us to reconceive of the collective subjects of critical interventions. In particular, claims for an 'applied critique' aiming at '*designing, crafting, building* and *distributing* concrete things'[52] risk leading to a mere problem-solving approach, as they consider the 'deficit in reality' as the main or even the only obstacle to overcome, while disregarding the question of desubjugation. Hence, if we cannot but approve of the fact that Foucault's non-normative definition of critique is widely mobilised in current post-critical approaches, we argue that their fundamental methodological move – reassembling critique and critical interventions as 'action' – ultimately risks neutralising the political purchase of his analyses by getting rid of the crucial nexus between critique, desubjugation and the politics of truth.

Politics of desubjugation

Latour's famous 'critique of critique', or better, as he corrects himself, his claim for a 'critique acquired second-hand – so to speak – and put to a different use',[53] hints at a concept of critique as a movement of unveiling and making visible what is hidden. Critique would thus enable us to see the true reality obfuscated by ideology: 'With critique, you may debunk, reveal, unveil, but only as long as you establish ... a privileged access to the world of reality behind the veils of appearances.'[54] Such a concept of critique is actually very different from Foucault's definition of critique, or of 'critical attitude' as 'the art of not being governed like that and at that cost ... the art of not being governed quite so much.'[55] More precisely, for Foucault, critique can never be detached from a movement of desubjugation: 'the movement by which the subject gives himself the right to question truth on its effects of power and question power on its discourses of truth', thus attempting to produce his or her own desubjugation 'in the context of what we could call ... the politics of truth.'[56] Far from unveiling hidden truths, the critical attitude entails, then, disengaging from and refusing the subjugating effects of power which stem from a given regime of truth.[57] This constitutes the second main dimension of what we call here the laborious work of critique.

What we want to emphasise and put at the heart of our analysis is precisely the fundamental connection between critique and practices of desubjugation. In addition to informing critique in political terms, this connection qualifies the political relevance of critique in specific ways, as Linda Zerilli has recently observed, arguing that critique as a '*politics* of desubjugation' should not conceive of the latter as a purely individual act of the will, but (also) as a collective experience.[58] Indeed, desubjugation does not mean negative subtraction. In recent years, some feminist writers have foregrounded the centrality of desubjugation as a mode of *active refusal* that defines and enacts critique.[59] In this literature, following Foucault, critique is thus conceived as an activity that involves transformative practices: 'The critique of what we are is at one and the same time the historical analysis of the limits that are imposed on us and an experiment with the possibility of going beyond them.'[60] If the core of critique is constituted by a series of practices of desubjugation, the subjects themselves cannot but be incessantly transformed through the critical activity.

This element of desubjugation is crucial for genealogical critique as well. Indeed, for both Nietzsche and Foucault, debunking beliefs and values is, first and foremost, a debunking of the subject.[61] In other words, genealogy is relevant for our account of critique insofar as it focuses on 'the emergence and transformations of forms of subjectivity related to power', with a view to questioning the latter and open up the possibility of future transformations.[62] By contrast, in coming to grips with the limitations of critique, post-critical approaches have generally elided the question of the subject(s) of critique and expunged desubjugation, refusal and resistance from the politics of truth. While questioning a normative understanding of critique, these approaches ultimately re-propose an a-historicised conception of subjectivity. Moreover, they seem more interested in freeing 'the matters of fact from their reduction by "Nature"' and in liberating 'objects and things from their "explanation" by society'[63] than in creating new possibilities for *subjects'* practices of freedom.

Consequently, it is crucial, we argue, to resist this move and, instead of refusing the debunking aspects of critique (as suggested by post-critical scholars), emphasise – with Nietzsche and Foucault – that debunking operations should concern first and foremost subjects themselves. Critique can be effective only if it does *not* leave its subjects untouched: far from removing the solid ground under the feet of given and fixed subjects, critique proceeds by transforming the subjects themselves and their way of thinking and being. Thus, the laborious work of critique cannot be reduced to moments of pure debunking, of simple desubjugation and refusal. As mentioned above, its effects are transformative in a *positive* sense: critique, as we conceive of it, is creative of new modes of subjectivation. However, moving beyond Foucault, who never systematically conceptualised notions of collective action and resistance, we contend that these effects of critique should be explored specifically in relation to their capacity to create new *collective* subjects.

The 'we's and the 'others' of critique

Critique is always situated and requires an analysis of the specificities of the present, of what makes it different from the past. Therefore, the current social and political situation pushes us to ask: How should we reconceive of critical knowledge and practices in order to address the features of the present in which we live? In order to answer this question, not only do we have to take seriously the conundrums of critique emphasised in the scholarly debate discussed above. We must also deal with the new power dynamics and forms of violence currently at play. Thus, when mobilising authors such as Foucault, Scott or Butler, we do not want to suggest that their ideas could or should be directly 'transposed' into our present to legitimise and defend the use of critique. On the contrary, these authors are helpful precisely because they insist on the need to constantly reconceive of critique in the light of specific configurations of power relations, new modes of subjection and, we contend, different *subjects of critique*. If we think of the Mediterranean context, it is clear – albeit rarely remarked – that the production of critical knowledge and the elaboration of critical practices should not be detached from the question of the 'we' or the collective subjects of critique: Who are the subjects of critique in this case? And how does the 'we' engaged in a critical intervention relate to what we call here the 'others' of critique, that is, the migrants who are left dying at sea?

As Butler points out, the question "'what are we to do?" presupposes that the "we" has been formed and that it is known, that its action is possible, and the field in which it might act is delimited.'[64] By contrast, the 'we', or, better, the 'we's that critique should contribute to the creation of are not predetermined nor stable; they are never defined once and for all, but fluid, heterogeneous, multiple and structurally open. Foucault famously claims that the main (political) problem is 'to make the *future* formation of a "we" possible' (a 'we' that 'would also be likely to form a community of action'), because 'the "we" must not be previous to the question; it can only be the result – and the necessarily temporary result – of the question.'[65] Thus, far from being a purely negative or debunking endeavour, critique necessarily entails a creative process of 'we-making'.[66] This is the third main dimension that lie at the heart of the laborious work of critique.

Our focus on the Mediterranean scene of death pushes us to further problematise the nexus between critique, desubjugation and we-making. Indeed, the subjects of critique, that is, those who elaborate critical interventions, are not in this case directly affected by the deadly politics of migration containment. 'We' – EU citizens, scholars, human rights activists or journalists – criticise state policies and police measures, the violations of international law, as well as the unjust laws through which individuals labelled and racialised as 'migrants' are left dying in the Mediterranean and at other borders of Europe.[67] As we argued above, desubjugation might in fact be conceived as a refusal of the policies that states implement (a refusal to be complicit with them), or it might take the form of a radical questioning and ultimate non-acceptance of the narratives about the so-called 'refugee crisis' and of the 'minimalistic biopolitics'[68] centred on migrants as 'black' bodies to be rescued. Yet this does not exempt us from asking: What about the 'others' of critique? What about those in whose name 'we' give voice to *our* critique of the EU's politics?[69]

In this case, as in many others, one cannot raise the question of critique without addressing at the same time the issue of the desubjugation of the subjects of critique *and* of the 'others' of critique – the migrants. Ultimately, we concur with Judith Revel in thinking that the 'questioning of the present state of things which can produce an interruption concerns not only our knowledges and our practices; it also immediately includes the question of the subject-form itself in its collective inflection ("we"), namely, also in its political dimension.'[70] However, the focus on migration highlights that the question of the constitution of a 'we' as the outcome of the practices of critique is inextricably connected to that of the 'subjects-objects' of critique who, in this case, do not speak. By this, we do not mean to deny migrants' agency or the reality (and strategic importance) of their multiple struggles constantly forcing state authorities to invent new strategies of capture. But since we are specifically addressing the production of critical discourses on and contestations of migration policies, as well as the analyses currently developed about migrants' deaths at sea, we find it necessary and urgent to ask: How would it be possible to craft a 'we' (of critique) without foreclosing other potential 'we's and, at the same time, without transforming migrants into mere objects of 'our' critical discourse on border violence?[71]

Our tentative answer is that the current problematisation of critique should be taken as an invaluable occasion to problematise and recraft the 'we's of critique as well. For instance, when questioning deadly migration policies, the 'we' that is implicitly assumed echoes the 'we, citizens of Europe',[72] and thus de facto corroborates a Euro-centric and Euro-driven approach to migration

– which is too often presented as a strictly 'European question'.[73] Instead, we argue that critique should be conceived and practiced as an experimental terrain for the creation of *other* collective subjects, of different and plural 'we's[74] More concretely, it is crucial to emphasise that, in the European public debate, opposition to the EU's deadly politics of migration containment is often shaped in a way that ignores the presence of active citizen mobilisations on the Southern and Eastern shores of the Mediterranean Sea. However, while in Europe grassroots organisations were actively trying to counter the states' retreat from search and rescue operations, in Tunisia fishermen were saving migrants who were about to drown in their attempt to reach Italy. Tunisian fishermen, much like many EU citizens who provided infrastructure to support migrants across Europe, have been systematically criminalised and accused by state authorities of smuggling migrants to Italy.[75] This is why we argue that building Mediterranean transversal connections is a crucial aspect of the laborious work of critique.

The question of how and for which purposes one is to produce a critical discourse on existing mechanisms of domination and, at the same time, of how to connect this discourse to concrete political practices, was at the heart of the activities of the *Groupe d'information sur les prisons* (GIP) at the beginning of the 1970s.[76] In that case, the elaboration of a critical intervention (questioning the institution of the prison) was tightly linked to what Foucault calls 'the intolerable' and the will not to accept it anymore. The intolerable stands at the crossroads of ethics and politics. It entails a movement of refusal, and emphasises the unacceptability of the mechanisms of domination:

> The prison should no longer be left in peace, nowhere. … Let what is intolerable – imposed, as it is, by force and by silence – cease to be accepted. We do not develop our inquiry in order to accumulate knowledge, but to intensify our intolerance and make it an active intolerance.[77]

Yet it is important to emphasise the *collective* dimension of the intolerable that Foucault and the GIP gesture towards, claiming that 'we have to transform individual experience into collective knowledge; that is to say, into political knowledge.'[78] Hence, the production of the intolerable and its unacceptability should be clearly distinguished from (political) emotions such as resentment or indignation. Indeed, far from being purely negative, the intolerable is essentially connected to the positive triggering of practices of resistance. In this sense, the emergence of a (temporary) 'we' of critique is always linked to the production of a *common* intolerable, and the will to challenge the asymmetries between the subjects of critique and the 'others' of critique.

Conclusion

In 'History-Writing as Critique', Scott claims that critique should not be confused with 'an endorsement of objectivity'.[79] Critique, she argues, building on Foucault, entails destabilising accepted norms and retracing the historical and political conditions through which specific power dynamics became naturalised, with a view to engaging in transformative socio-political practices. Indeed, according to Scott, critique is predicated upon an ethical commitment which, far from defining in advance the political outcomes of one's actions and the evidence one has to bring, consists in 'staying open to the future.'[80] However, this structural openness should be combined with discursive and non-discursive practices actively oriented at de-objectifying and de-racialising the 'others' of critique, and at creating new 'we's – different from the taken-for-granted subjects of critique. As Claudia Aradau contends, critique 'builds upon an understanding of what produces differences and inequalities, power asymmetries, violence and injustice.'[81] In this sense, it 'can be a site of politics' – at least so long as it challenges the production of degrees and 'categories of being human and non-human',[82] subject and object.

By warning against the quest for evidence in the humanities and social sciences, and arguing for the need to reconceive of critique, its subjects and its 'others', we have taken seriously the conundrums of critique that post-critical scholars have recently emphasised. But instead of advancing a new normative definition of critique, we insist on the crucial role that practices of de-subjugation play in relation to any critical intervention within the context of what Foucault calls a politics of truth. Moreover, we have sought to draw attention to the current practices of knowledge-production and questioned the ways in which these craft 'critical' discourses or present themselves as 'critical'. In a time during which, when dealing with sheer border violence, there seem to be 'no tribunals to address',[83] critique is not an anachronistic intellectual practice detached from reality, nor a task to be confined to problem-solving endeavours. This is particularly evident when we consider the states' overt violations of international law, on the one hand, and their ability to play with the law, on the other. In the face of this situation, conflating critique with a mere accumulation of evidence has generated a saturation of the political space without being able to produce any 'common intolerable'. Thus, the laborious work of critique aiming to unmake the effects of power associated with any given regime of truth should not be replaced with a series of claims for more reality, more facts or more truths.

By focusing on the Mediterranean scene of death, we hope to have shown the urgent need to refuse the terms in which this 'problem' is currently framed and to question the very fact of thinking of migration as a 'problem'. Instead, it is paramount to shift our attention to the constant, albeit often invisible, racialisation of migrant lives as 'black' bodies to be saved. Indeed, the differential labelling and the racialisation of lives which sustain the government of a category of subjects called 'migrants' should be taken not only as a fundamental target of critique, but also as the starting point for a new problematisation of the subjects of critique. If 'immanent critique' can be defined as a 'kind of critique that does not involve the adoption of a privileged position with respect to the object of critique',[84] the concept of critique that we defend here is *doubly immanent*, since it also strives to problematise its own position with respect to the subjects of critique.

To conclude, we would like to mention two further issues as possible orientations for future inquiries.

First, the current (theoretical and political) conjuncture of the conundrums of critique clearly indicates the impossibility of detaching critical interventions from 'the fabric of social struggles',[85] and the intellectual and practical necessity to ground critique in those contestations. The appropriate response to critical practices that turn out to be ineffective is not an impact-driven or problem-solving approach. On the contrary, we should strive to attune critical interventions to the movements of collective refusal that are currently in place. One of the main methodological principles that one can draw from Foucault's work is that 'where there is power, there is resistance, and yet, or rather consequently, this resistance is never in a position of exteriority in relation to power.'[86] To be consistent with this principle, when revealing the role of historically constituted power/knowledge formations in the shaping of our current beliefs, practices, institutions and of our own selves, critique must also reveal the multiplicity of points of resistance that played 'the role of adversary, target, support or handle' for the emergence and concrete functioning of those formations.[87] Thus, critique should never be separated from concrete movements of desubjugation and resistance. In other words, 'the historical and theoretical analysis of power relations, institutions and knowledge' should always be coupled with 'the movements, critiques and experiences that call them into question in reality.'[88]

Second, as our analysis of the Mediterranean context has shown, raising and problematising the issue of critique, of its subjects and objects, also entails questioning its main hinge: the (re)production of racialised mechanisms of capture and asymmetries of lives, as well as of the 'others' of critique, might make it necessary, within migration studies itself, eventually to reorient critique away from an exclusive focus on migration as such, or from a 'containerisation of critique'.[89] Striving to build transversal alliances between EU citizens and those labelled as 'migrants' to fight against current rights destitution strategies and deadly politics of precarisation is a route worth exploring.

Daniele Lorenzini is Assistant Professor of Philosophy at the University of Warwick and author of La force du vrai *(2017). Martina Tazzioli is Lecturer in Politics and International Relations at Goldsmiths, University of London, and a member of the editorial collective of* Radical Philosophy. *Her books include* The Making of Migration *(2019).*

Notes

1. UNHCR, 'Desperate Journeys' (2018), accessed 31 August 2019, https://www.unhcr.org/desperatejourneys/
2. Martina Tazzioli, 'The Desultory Politics of Mobility and the Humanitarian-Military Border in the Mediterranean: *Mare Nostrum* Beyond the Sea', *REMHU: Revista Interdisciplinar da Mobilidade Humana* 23 (2015), 61–82. See also Maurice Stierl, 'A Fleet of Mediterranean Border Humanitarians', *Antipode* 50:3 (2018), 704–24.
3. Matteo Villa, 'Sea Arrivals to Italy: The Cost of Deterrence Policies', *Italian Institute for International Political Studies* (2018), accessed 31 August 2019, https://www.ispionline.it/en/publication/sea-arrivals-italy-cost-deterrence-policies-21367

4. Eyal Weizman, *Forensic Architecture: Violence at the Threshold of Detectability* (New York: Zone Books, 2017), 65.

5. Alexander Betts and Paul Collier, *Refuge: Transforming a Broken Refugee System* (London: Allen Lane, 2017); Heaven Crawley et al., 'Destination Europe? Understanding the Dynamics and Drivers of Mediterranean Migration in 2015', MEDMIG Final Report, 2016, https://www.compas.ox.ac.uk/wp-content/uploads/PR-2016-MEDMIG_Destination_Europe.pdf

6. Roberto Beneduce, *Archeologie del trauma: Un'antropologia del sottosuolo* (Roma–Bari: Laterza, 2010).

7. We do not want to suggest, however, that such a mode of critique constitutes the *only* legitimate way in which critique can be conceived of and practiced today. We do not discuss, for instance, the fruitful critical resources that the Marxist tradition provides us with to address the issues that we raise here.

8. Bruno Latour, 'An Attempt at a "Compositionist Manifesto,"' *New Literary History* 41:3 (2010), 471–90.

9. Rita Felski, 'Introduction' to the special issue 'Recomposing the Humanities with Bruno Latour', *New Literary History* 47:2–3 (2106), 221.

10. Ibid., 221–2.

11. Jonathan Luke Austin, 'A Parasitic Critique for International Relations', *International Political Sociology* 13:2 (2019), 215–31.

12. Felski, 'Introduction', 221.

13. Amia Srinivasan, 'Genealogy, Epistemology, and Worldmaking', *Proceedings of the Aristotelian Society* 119:2 (2019), 127–56.

14. Raymond Geuss, 'Genealogy as Critique', *European Journal of Philosophy* 10:2 (2002), 209–15; Martin Saar, *Genealogie als Kritik: Geschichte und Theorie des Subjekts nach Nietzsche und Foucault* (Frankfurt-am-Main: Campus, 2007); Colin Koopman, *Genealogy as Critique: Foucault and the Problems of Modernity* (Bloomington: Indiana University Press, 2013).

15. Mark Bevir, 'What is Genealogy?', *Journal of the Philosophy of History* 2:3 (2008), 263–75; David Couzens Hoy, 'Genealogy, Phenomenology, Critical Theory', *Journal of the Philosophy of History* 2:3 (2008), 276–94.

16. See for example Daniel J. Levitin, *Weaponized Lies: How to Think Critically in the Post-Truth Era* (New York: Penguin Random House, 2016); Lee McIntyre, *Post-Truth* (Cambridge, MA: The MIT Press, 2018).

17. Roberto Mordacci, *La condizione neomoderna* (Tornio: Einaudi, 2017).

18. Bruno Latour, 'Why Has Critique Run out of Steam? From Matters of Fact to Matters of Concern', *Critical Inquiry* 30:2 (2004): 225–48.

19. Ibid., 231.

20. Ibid., 232.

21. Rita Felski, *The Limits of Critique* (Chicago: The University of Chicago Press, 2015), 171.

22. Elias Steinhilper and Rob Gruijters, 'Border Deaths in the Mediterranean: What We Can Learn from the Latest Data', *Border Criminologies* (2017), accessed 31 August 2019, https://www.law.ox.ac.uk/research-subject-groups/centre-criminology/centreborder-criminologies/blog/2017/03/institutional

23. See, for example, Laurent De Sutter, ed., *Postcritique* (Paris: Presses universitaires de France, 2019).

24. Jesper Aagaard, 'Striving for Experiential Resonance: Critique, Post-Critique, and Phenomenology', *Qualitative Studies* 5:1 (2018), 32.

25. Bernard E. Harcourt, 'The Last Refuge of Scoundrels: The Problem of Truth in the Twenty-First Century', unpublished manuscript.

26. Jacques Derrida, 'History of the Lie: Prolegomena', in *Without Alibi* (Stanford: Stanford University Press, 2002), 61.

27. Michel Foucault, *On the Government of the Living: Lectures at the Collège de France, 1979–80*, ed. Michel Senellart (Basingstoke: Palgrave Macmillan, 2012), 95–6.

28. Daniele Lorenzini, 'What is a "Regime of Truth"?', *Le Foucaldien* 1:1 (2015), https://foucaldien.net/articles/abstract/10.16995/lefou.2

29. Foucault, *On the Government of the Living*, 82, 93–4.

30. Ibid., 100–1.

31. Donna Haraway, 'Situated Knowledges: The Science Question in Feminism and the Privilege of Partial Perspective', *Feminist Studies* 14:3 (1988), 575–99.

32. Richard Wyn Jones, 'The Test of Practice: An Interview with Richard Wyn Jones', in *Critical Theory in International Relations and Security Studies*, eds. Shannon Brincat, Laura Lima and Joao Nunes (London: Routledge, 2012), 100.

33. Wendy Brown, *Edgework: Critical Essays on Knowledge and Politics* (Princeton: Princeton University Press, 2005), 4.

34. Ibid., 4.

35. Felski, *The Limits of Critique*, 29.

36. Charles Heller and Lorenzo Pezzani, 'Ebbing and Flowing: The EU's Shifting Practices of (Non-)Assistance and Bordering in a Time of Crisis', *Near Futures Online*, 2016, accessed 31 August 2019, http://nearfuturesonline.org/ebbing-and-flowing-the-eus-shifting-practices-of-non-assistance-and-bordering-in-a-time-of-crisis/

37. Judith Butler, 'Critique, Crisis, and Violence', lecture delivered at the University of Bologna, 2017, accessed: 31 August 2019, https://www.youtube.com/watch?v=peVgdUK5qAQ

38. Joan W. Scott, 'The Evidence of Experience', *Critical Inquiry* 17:4 (1991), 776.

39. Ibid., 777–8.

40. Carlo Ginzburg, *Il filo e le tracce: Vero, falso, finto* (Milano: Feltrinelli, 2006).

41. William Walters, 'Foucault and Frontiers: Notes on the Birth of the Humanitarian Border', in *Governmentality: Current Issues and Future Challenges*, eds. Ulrich Bröckling, Susanne Krasmann and Thomas Lemke (London: Routledge, 2011), 138–64.

42. Janet Roitman, *Anti-Crisis* (Durham, NC: Duke University Press, 2013), 3.

43. Lisa Lowe, *The Intimacies of Four Continents* (Durham, NC: Duke University Press, 2015).

44. Michel Foucault, 'Structuralism and Post-Structuralism', in *Aesthetics, Method, and Epistemology*, ed. James D. Faubion (New York: The New Press, 1998), 450.

45. Michel Foucault, 'Polemics, Politics, and Problematizations: An Interview with Michel Foucault', in *The Foucault Reader*, ed. P. Rabinow (New York: Pantheon Books, 1984), 384.

46. On this point, see also Verena Erlenbusch-Anderson, *Genealogies of Terrorism: Revolution, State Violence, Empire* (New York:

Columbia University Press, 2018), 163. For a similar point, see Claudia Aradau, Presentation delivered at the 44th Annual Conference of the British International Studies Association, London, 12–14 June 2019.

47. Bruno Latour, *Reassembling the Social: An Introduction to Actor-Network-Theory* (Oxford: Oxford University Press, 2005), 136.

48. Ibid., 137–8.

49. Ibid., 92.

50. Foucault, 'Structuralism and Post-Structuralism', 449–50.

51. Ibid., 450.

52. Jonathan Luke Austin, 'Towards an International Political Ergonomics', *European Journal of International Relations* 25:4 (2019), 980.

53. Latour, 'An Attempt at a "Compositionist Manifesto"', 474.

54. Ibid., 475.

55. Michel Foucault, 'What is Critique?', in *The Politics of Truth*, ed. S. Lotringer (Los Angeles: Semiotext(e), 2007), 45.

56. Ibid., 47.

57. Daniele Lorenzini, 'From Counter-Conduct to Critical Attitude: Michel Foucault and the Art of Not Being Governed Quite So Much', *Foucault Studies* 21 (2016), 7–21.

58. Linda Zerilli, 'Critique as a Political Practice of Freedom', in *A Time for Critique*, eds. Didier Fassin and Bernard E. Harcourt (New York: Columbia University Press, 2019), 36–51.

59. Brown, *Edgework*; Butler, 'Critique, Crisis, and Violence'; Chandra T. Mohanty, *Feminism without Borders: Decolonizing Theory, Practicing Solidarity* (Durham, NC: Duke University Press, 2003); Saba Mahmood, *Politics of Piety: The Islamic Revival and the Feminist Subject* (Princeton: Princeton University Press, 2011).

60. Michel Foucault, 'What is Enlightenment?', in *The Foucault Reader*, ed. P. Rabinow (New York: Pantheon Books, 1984), 50.

61. Jesse J. Prinz, 'History as Genealogy: Interrogating Liberalism Through Philosophy's Past', unpublished manuscript.

62. Martin Saar, 'Understanding Genealogy: History, Power, and the Self', *Journal of the Philosophy of History* 2:3 (2008), 312.

63. Latour, *Reassembling the Social*, 109.

64. Judith Butler, 'What is Critique? An Essay on Foucault's Virtue', *Transversal*, 2001, https://transversal.at/transversal/0806/butler/en

65. Foucault, 'Polemics, Politics, and Problematizations', 385. On this point, see Judith Revel, *Foucault avec Merleau-Ponty: Ontologie politique, présentisme et histoire* (Paris: Vrin, 2015), 53.

66. Daniele Lorenzini, 'On Possibilising Genealogy', *Inquiry: An Interdisciplinary Journal of Philosophy* (2020), https://www.tandfonline.com/doi/full/10.1080/0020174X.2020.1712227

67. Nicholas De Genova, 'The "Migrant Crisis" as Racial Crisis: Do *Black Lives Matter* in Europe?', *Ethnic and Racial Studies* 41:10 (2018), 1765–82.

68. Peter Redfield, 'Bioexpectations: Life Technologies as Humanitarian Goods', *Public Culture* 24:1 (2012), 157–84.

69. For a similar question, see Michel Foucault and Gilles Deleuze, 'Intellectuals and Power: A Conversation between Michel Foucault and Gilles Deleuze', in Michel Foucault, *Language, Counter-Memory, Practice: Selected Essays and Interviews*, ed. Donald F. Bouchard (Ithaca: Cornell University Press, 1977), 205–17.

70. Judith Revel, '"What Are We at the Present Time?" Foucault and the Question of the Present', in *Foucault and the History of Our Present*, eds. Sophie Fuggle, Yari Lanci and Martina Tazzioli (Basingstoke: Palgrave Macmillan, 2015), 20.

71. Saidiya V. Hartman, *Scenes of Subjection: Terror, Slavery, and Self-Making in Nineteenth-Century America* (Oxford: Oxford University Press, 1997).

72. Étienne Balibar, *We, the People of Europe? Reflections on Transnational Citizenship* (Princeton: Princeton University Press, 2003).

73. Nicholas De Genova, 'The European Question: Migration, Race, and Postcoloniality in Europe', *Social Text* 34:3 (2016), 75–102.

74. Martina Tazzioli, *The Making of Migration: Biopoltics of Mobility at Europe's Borders* (London: Sage, 2019).

75. Lorenzo Tondo, 'Tunisian Fishermen Await Trial after "Saving Hundreds of Migrants"', *The Guardian*, 2018, accessed 10 November 2019, https://www.theguardian.com/world/2018/sep/05/tunisian-fishermen-await-trial-after-saving-hundreds-of-migrants

76. Philippe Artières et al. (eds.), *Le Groupe d'information sur les prisons: Archives d'une lutte, 1970–72* (Caen: IMEC Éditeur, 2003).

77. Michel Foucault, '(Sur les prisons)', in *Dits et écrits II, 1970–75*, eds. Daniel Defert and François Ewald (Paris: Gallimard, 1994), 176.

78. Michel Foucault, 'Enquête sur les prisons: brisons les barreaux du silence', in *Dits et écrits II, 1970–75*, eds. Daniel Defert and François Ewald (Paris: Gallimard, 1994), 178.

79. Joan W. Scott, 'History-Writing as Critique', in *Manifestos for History*, eds. Keith Jenkins, Sue Morgan and Alun Munslow (London: Routledge, 2007), 23.

80. Ibid., 25.

81. Claudia Aradau, 'Technology, Agency, Critique: An Interview with Claudia Aradau', in *Technology and Agency in International Relations*, eds. Marijn Hoijtink and Matthias Leese (London: Routledge, 2019), 196.

82. Ibid.

83. Butler, 'Critique, Crisis, and Violence'.

84. Robert Guay, 'Genealogy as Immanent Critique: Working from the Inside', in *The Edinburgh Critical History of Nineteenth-Century Philosophy*, ed. Alison Stone (Edinburgh: Edinburgh University Press, 2011), 169.

85. Mohanty, *Feminism without Borders*. See also Sandro Mezzadra, 'European Citizenship and the Place of Migrants' Struggles in a New Radical Europe: An Interview with Sandro Mezzadra', *LeftEast* (2013), accessed 31 August 2019, http://www.criticatac.ro/lefteast/european-citizenship-and-the-place-of-migrants-struggles-in-a-new-radical-europe-a-talk-with-sandro-mezzadra/

86. Michel Foucault, *The History of Sexuality, Volume 1: An Introduction* (New York: Pantheon Books, 1978), 95.

87. Ibid.

88. Michel Foucault, 'Politics and Ethics: An Interview', in *The Foucault Reader*, ed. P. Rabinow (New York: Pantheon Books, 1984), 374.

89. Tazzioli, *The Making of Migration*, 156.

Centre for Research in Modern European Philosophy

ANALYZE – CRITICIZE – CONSTRUCT

Apply now to join our postgraduate community in autumn 2020

MA Modern European Philosophy

MA Aesthetics & Art Theory

MA Philosophy and Contemporary Critical Theory

MPhilStud Philosophy (2 years)

Research degrees: MRes/MPhil/PhD

STAFF TEAM
Étienne Balibar   Howard Caygill
Peter Hallward   Catherine Malabou
Peter Osborne   Stella Sandford
Peter Woodford

Kingston University London

www.kingston.ac.uk/crmep

Masses, class and the power of suggestion

Andrea Cavalletti

1. I will attempt here to reflect on three major themes, 'masses, class, suggestion', with the hope that, by doing so, I will also indirectly bring to light the relevance of Gabriel Tarde's thought today. One may wonder why my title does not include – perhaps in place of the term 'class', which is not central to Tarde's toolkit – the concept of 'public', which, as is well known, Tarde (in 'The Public and the Crowd' [*Le public et la foule*], 1901) distinguishes from that of the 'crowd', giving to the latter an opposite and by no means positive meaning. Yet it is precisely this distinction that leads us back to the range of relations that bind together 'masses, class and suggestion'. In turn, it is only in the light of this that such distinction becomes intelligible. Why, then, these three terms? What is the nature of the bond that unites them?

'Masses' – this word, as we will see, immediately clings to the last one: 'suggestion'. It clings to it by virtue of another term that we have not yet mentioned: that is, 'prestige' [in the French: *prestige*]. In fact, in Tarde's time, prestige defined the leader's force of attraction, and thus produced effects of mass suggestion. If my title does not feature 'prestige' but rather 'class', it is because class stands precisely there, between the masses and suggestion, as an element of articulation, a sort of hinge. And rightly so: indeed, as we shall see, one of the primary, fundamental meanings of the word 'class' correlates precisely to such a function.

However, one could insist: this word appears in place of the other thanks to an elision; 'class' surfaces and makes room for itself between 'masses' and 'suggestion' by replacing 'prestige'. Indeed, if understood in a sense that perhaps diverges from its primary meaning, class does not unite but separates 'masses' from 'suggestion', and it does so by covering up and eliminating prestige.

Where there is no prestige, and therefore no mass suggestion, there class is. Or at least, there 'class' takes on another and very different meaning, as I will endeavour to explain.

2. Why should the word 'masses' – as I said – cling to 'suggestion' by recalling immediately a third term, that is, 'prestige'? The question is at the very least legitimate and an answer can be found in Freud's famous 1921 essay *Group Psychology and the Analysis of the Ego* [*Massenpsychologie und Ich-Analyse*]. This is of course an answer in psychoanalytical terms to the first important texts of social psychology, mainly associated with the French school, among which the most renowned is certainly still Gustave Le Bon's *The Crowd: A Study of the Popular Mind* [*Psychologie des Foules*] (1895). At the beginning of the essay's fourth chapter, a quick overview of the key authors of mass psychology – or, we should rather say, crowd psychology, since the German *Masse* translates precisely the French *foule* – introduces Freud's critique of Hippolyte Bernheim and the so-called Nancy School. It is a decisive passage that marks (once again and in the clearest way) Freud's distance from the theorists of suggestion. It reads:

> what we are offered as an explanation by authorities upon Sociology and Group Psychology is always the same, even though it is given various names, and that is – the magic word 'suggestion'. Tarde [1890] calls it 'imitation'; but we cannot help agreeing with a writer who protests that imitation comes under the concept of suggestion, and it is in fact one of its results [R. Brugeilles, *L'essence du phénomene social: la suggestion* (1913)]. Le Bon traces back all the puzzling features of social phenomena to two factors: the mutual suggestion of individuals and the prestige of leaders. But prestige, again, is only recognisable by its

capacity for evoking suggestion.¹

Whether masses form by imitation or contagion, suggestion always plays the decisive role, and, in Freud's reading, is in turn an effect of prestige. Freud's intention is to snatch this problem from the theory or wizardry of suggestion, so as to locate and solve it on the field of the analysis of the Ego.

Although here we are concerned not with Freud but Tarde, the same tenet is still valid. Tarde himself places 'prestige at the foundation and origins of society'.² Well before Max Weber read Rudolph Sohm and, drawing inspiration from the notion of *charis* in early Christianity, coined the concept of charismatic leadership, both Tarde and Le Bon had termed this suggestive force 'prestige'. The leader is first and foremost the subject gifted with prestige, and the hypnotic effects of power originate precisely from his (or her) prestige. When Tarde compares the social man to a sleepwalker, he clarifies that the magnetiser – *meneur* – has no need to terrorise in order to secure passive obedience: his prestige will suffice.

3. Tarde wrote these words in his 1884 essay, 'What is society?' [*Qu'est-ce qu'une sociéte?*], published in Théodol Ribot's *Revue philosophique*. Two years later, the same journal featured one of Henri Bergson's first works, entitled 'On Unconscious Simulation in States of Hypnosis' [*De la simulation incosciente dans l'état d'hypnotisme*], which was devoted not accidentally to the theme of hypnosis. This was by no means a unique case. Tarde himself quotes articles by Charles Féré, Richet and Bertrand, which were also published in the *Revue philosophique* at about the same time. As Pierre Janet later recalled, 'in those years, from 1880 to 1895, there was a lot of discussion about suggestion: all psychology and medicine books were filled with studies on this seductive topic, and the *Index medicus* published every year several thousand articles on hypnotism, suggestion and related problems.'³

Janet, Freud's great antagonist, pronounced these words in November 1926, during a conference at the Congress of Psychiatry in Zurich. A few months earlier, Thomas Mann had endured that 'tragic vacation experience' in Forte dei Marmi, Italy that would inspire soon after his famous novella *Mario and the Magician* (written in 1929 and published in 1930). Almost ten years later, in 1935, Hermann Broch started writing his novel, *The Spell* (*Die Verzauberung*), that is, *The Spellbinder* (*Der Versucher*).

The idea of the leader as magician, and of political suggestion or prestige, the idea of crowds following their figurehead as if in a state of trance, as Le Bon put it, has thus (if we are to use Walter Benjamin's terminology) a 'pre-history' and an 'after-history' – and, in this Tardian context, we may say a '*histoire future*' (a future history) also.

4. The after-history of this idea in the twentieth century, that is, the popularity of the concept of suggestion in the age of plebiscites, mass media and totalitarianisms, is well known: it is not related only to Freud, of course, but is inevitably affected by Freud.

Recall that Reich's *The Mass Psychology of Fascism* was published in 1933. In this famous study, the father of Freudian-Marxism challenged the socio-economic interpretation in favour of a sexual-economic one, revealing a close correspondence between social structure and the individual's psychological structure and thus identifying the generative moment of the totalitarian system in the repression of primary drives [*pulsioni*]. Equally famous is *Crowds and Power* [*Masse und Macht*], Elias Canetti's 'lifework', published in 1960 but first conceived in the early 1920s, when Canetti's long and rather intense dialogue with Le Bon and Freud began.

Canetti had in mind the monumental and incomplete project *Massenwahntheorie*, which his friend and contemporary Broch had committed himself to around 1942. Here, the nineteenth-century idea of the dangerous mob of sleepwalkers is moulded into a new philosophical, Husserlian and Scherlerian form. In 1914, Broch, while attending an event for the proclamation of the Republic in Vienna, felt horrified at the sight of 'the aggregate of mouths, noses and bellies that we call masses.'⁴ Later, during his American exile, he studied the crowds of totalitarianism, kept in a sleepwalking state through the 'magic religion of enslavement', and glimpsed a possible escape route in the conversion (*Bekehrung*) to a kind of crepuscular wisdom (that is to a systematic devalorisation of the myths of victory, race, etc.) that would liberate the masses from their leader and, in turn, the individuals from the masses.

These are just some of the most famous works. I don't have space here to elaborate further on this brief review, nor to dwell on Canetti's discussion of Le Bon's and Tarde's texts (especially the latter's *The Public and the Crowd* [*Le public et la foule*]), nor, earlier still, on Wilhelm Reich, Hermann Broch or, among others, Robert Ezra Park. I will however mention the primary advocate of philosophical anthropology Helmuth Plessner. In 1924, Plessner in his famous study *The Limits of Community: A Critique of Social Radicalism* offers an incisive and acute definition of 'prestige'. The reason why I single this out is because it links prestige to two other terms: security [*sicurezza*] and aura. Prestige, Plessner writes, is what gives power an auratic effect, endowing it with a certain halo, *ambiance* or *Nimbus*. ('*Sicherungweise des Nimbuseffekt ist das Prestige*', or, the nimbus effect is guaranteed by prestige,) But how is this halo or *Nimbus* to be defined? How can we explain, Plessner continues, something that is supposed to exist and be effective, without however being 'there' at all ('*etwas ... das da sein und wirken soll, ohne "da" zu sein*').[5]

The term 'prestige', that magic word of mass psychology – and the term 'crowd' itself, as Tarde wrote in 1901, exudes a prestigious attraction – acquires then a precise meaning; it designates a peculiar displacement: it is by withdrawing into a strange 'not here' that something is capable of exerting its power here. A personality becomes prestigious by way of alluding to something elusive, by way of talking about something that is never completely here. It is thanks to such a withdrawal that we have a *Gewalt des Nimbus* (Violence of the Nimbus): that is, the power, authority, force or violence of the aura, or *ambiance*.[6]

5. Prestige: such is the name we give to our illusions, the attribute of what appears to be something that it is not. As Jean Fallot wrote in his critique of science (*Prestiges de la science*, 1960), 'the illusionist with his tricks will make appear a snake where there's only a rope. Certainly, there's something at work behind prestidigitation, only not what one thinks.'[7]

To understand the aura, secret and strength of political prestige, we have therefore to focus on the dark background from which it originates. To understand the currency of prestige and suggestion, we should consider their pre-history. In particular, we should investigate the specific biopolitical and security-obsessed origins of the modern concept of society.

Philosopher Maine de Biran, one of Gabriel Tarde's mentors, wrote in his *Journal* of 1817 (10-18 July): 'In society I am like a sleepwalker'.[8] We should bear in mind that at the time 'electricity', 'magnetism', 'somnambulism' and 'imitation' were all seen as near synonyms, and since the time of Anton Mesmer, with his theories of mesmerism or animal magnetism, these terms had defined a field of hardly distinguishable phenomena which, in the following century, would have been designated by expressions such as 'hypnosis' or 'suggestion'. In 1773, Holbach could say that: 'man in society is electrified'.[9] Earlier still, in 1756, Antonio Genovesi, a Neapolitan author, wrote in his *Economia Civile* that social man is an 'electric being' who acts by imitation and sympathy.[10]

I mentioned above Anton Mesmer. The arc of his life is well-known: the Parisian fame, the stratospheric ascendency and the rapid, at least apparent, fall. In 1784, the Royal Commission, comprising Bailly, Le Roy, Benjamin Franklin and Lavoisier, expressed its famous condemnation of mesmerism. In the proceedings, the scientists maintained that the universal magnetic fluid allegedly discovered by Mesmer in fact did not exist at all, but – they added – the effects of that phantom over the imagination and imitation were nonetheless real, highly contagious and socially harmful. The exercise or rather the monopoly of the forces of suggestion emerged thus as a crucial question, directly affecting the sovereignty and structure of the power system. After all, Mesmer was the first to recognise the role and strength of imagination: meticulously attentive to scenography, he staged his therapy sessions like an actual living theatre, while dedicating his intellectual efforts to the elaboration of a universal 'theory of imitation' [*théorie imitative*] well before Tarde. To understand the aura, secret and strength of prestige, we should therefore ask why and in which way does man 'in society' [*dans la société*] imitate and become electrified by entering into a field of suggestive energy.

6. It is in exactly this same period that the notion of *energy*, as pointed out by Michel Delon, enters the scene, taking on a crucial role in political theory (earlier than in science) and, remarkably, at the same time in art theory and aesthetics as well. Let's consider for instance the entry for 'Expression' in the *Encyclopedie*, which adds something essential to the seventeenth-century

Cartesian dogma of clarity: a good composition, it reads, can endow artistic expression with an 'aesthetic energy that affects understanding and strikes the mind'.[11]

This idea of an energy or electrical-social atmosphere in which art participates by virtue of its capacity to transmit, suggest or arouse feelings and ideas was widespread. Hence, the tendency to privilege both the initial and final stages of the work of art: the fragment or the sketch, namely, the cursory drawing that communicates a force and asks to be completed, awakening an image in the viewer; as well as the ruin, which brings the work of art back to its initial condition of simple outline. An energetic topology of the arts will be developed by Jean-Georg Sulzer: an artwork may surprise or enhance the representative faculty by communicating its own energy to the viewer's mind; another will instead transmit its energy to human passions and moral sentiments, turning feelings into action...

Always already immersed in an energy field, art is then not only useful to politics (as it has been over the centuries) but becomes the preferred testing ground and main paradigm for the exercise of power: in the visual arts and the dramatic arts, as well as in the '*architecture parlante*' [speaking architecture], social energy is in fact harnessed, strengthened and transformed into a flow that is truly capable of liberating actions by working on feelings.

In this respect, we may trace a precise genealogical line of the aesthetic-political notion of 'character'. According to the eighteenth-century definition, character is what ensures consistency between impulse and action. Those who understand character control the play of imagination: they can transmit certain forces to achieve the desired effects. In architecture – as Étienne-Louis Boullé, Le Camus de Mezières and Claude-Nicolas Ledoux teach us – the Ionic order or character, for instance, is congruent with the spirit of a theatre, while both the Corinthian and Ionic order would not be appropriate for the martial character of barracks or the severe austerity of the *barrière*, which require in its place the Tuscan order. It is clear that such 'consistency' manifests already in itself a precise political tenor (the fact that barracks instill a feeling of reverential respect is of course the result of a long and severe *dressage* [training]).

7. In much the same way that 'from 1880 to 1895, there was a lot of discussion about suggestion', and that, in those same years, the leading eighteenth-century theme of animal magnetism, which had never completely disappeared, once again surged to prominence in the medical and social sciences, so neurologists returned to the problem of character, together with that of habit and automatism, through a perspective which was both original and faithful to the older Enlightenment inheritance.

For the doctor, neurologist or hypnotist, to define a patient's character meant to understand how s/he reacts, what s/he will be able or unable to do, which orders s/he will execute and how; it meant to recognise her/his resistances so to identify a coherent link between impulse and action. Or, in other words, to assert one own's agency and force over the other's inertia, so as to stir and guide her/his actions. Taking up in his own way a commonplace of the then current debate, Tarde described in a similar vein suggestion as the ability to grasp and arouse in the sleepwalker a potential power, which, albeit dormant, has not disappeared.

Right at the end of the century, hypnosis, like the eighteenth-century theories of energy and character, entered fully into the domain of aesthetics, for instance via Bergson in the first chapter of *Time and Free Will: An Essay on the Immediate Data of Consciousness* (1888) and Paul Souriau in *L'hypnotisme et la suggestion dans l'art*, published in 1909 but conceived twenty years earlier. In the moment of suggestion's triumph, the artist's technique itself was seen as a technique of suggestion, an exercise of power whose primary aim is not so much to express feelings but, as Bergson writes, to impress them on us (and 'character' means indeed imprint).[12] Understood in such a way, perhaps the work of art neither opens a world, nor keeps 'the openness of the world open', but at least unlocks the doors of society to those who are fascinated by it. Like Tarde, Bergson was also an admirer of Maine de Biran.

8. What is then society? Modern society, as Foucault taught us, is constituted as a biopolitical apparatus for the control of human life and for the continuous division of such a life between what appears as normal or pathological, safe or dangerous, from the point of view of the state and the government. Biopower ensures, takes responsibility for and takes hold of the living conditions of the population. In taking charge of the population, as Italian authors such as Genovesi, Cesare Beccaria and Jacopo Ortes observe, biopower marks the difference between a 'right population' or 'true population' and a 'false or apparent population', the latter of which will gradually be excluded from the beneficial effects of power so that ultimately its life, to use Foucault's expression, is 'disallow[ed] to the point of death'.[13] 'Right population' designates here a certain standard of living, a certain proportion between number of inhabitants and territory (i.e. the wealth, food provisions and assets available in that territory). Therefore, it is not a fixed group (since these resources may alter, in the same way as climatic conditions, markets or the value of currency also change), but rather a sort of primary density or positive intensity that certainly affects the arrangement of the state while depending on it and being always connected to governmental techniques, balances of power and their constant variation.

To govern [*governare*] means then to engender a certain condition, to induce a certain desirable and safe behaviour by projecting relative fears and insecurity. As the story of mesmerism illustrates, it is clear that the role of imagination and imitation becomes essential to this aim. To govern, as Genovesi argued, does not mean to educate the population by eliminating false myths and errors, but on the contrary to educate them by selecting or even inventing and nurturing useful prejudices, without which 'the beautiful principle of energy would languish' and 'people, families and civil bodies would waste away.'[14]

To govern [*governare*] is thus a truth game that makes the figure of the 'right population' appear by animating the threatening spectre of the 'false or apparent population'. In other words, the primacy of the governmental function lies with the negative polarity: it is poverty that defines wealth, fear that defines security, the false that determines truth; it is pain, as both Genovesi and Verri said, that is the 'mainspring', the 'triggering principle' and 'first motor' of the art of government. If it is true that the government must take responsibility for the living conditions of the population – as Joseph von Sonnenfels said, resolving a theoretical impasse which had marked the birth of cameralism [*Scienze camerali*] – this does not mean that it must first of all ensure its well-being, but on the contrary that it must work such that the population will desire this. But how to do so? Precisely by exercising the pressure of threat, pain and fear. To govern means to foster a behaviour or form of life congruent with the power of the state under the continuous pressure of a more or less latent threat that of course the state must nurture and control (the monopoly of the government over states of alertness is pivotal to such a system). Such is the principle of the modern security state, which has changed over the centuries, has been updated and refined, so that it still rules us today – as we know first-hand.

If we examine closely eighteenth-century texts, we discover that by conceiving society as an field of energy that develops between the opposites of pleasure and pain or suffering, it was possible to define a 'true', 'right' population – precisely consistent with the government's own aims – and so to draw a division between the right or true population, on the one side, and the false population, on the other. Biopolitical society includes the broad spectrum of the population's ways of life, running the gamut of pleasure and pain, from comfortable to less pleasant conditions. To govern this society means to guide the individual's conduct within a space of freedom defined by the polarity of fear and desire: that is, to ensure that a certain fear arouses a certain desire, and that a desire reveals a definite anxiety, so that, from both the former and the latter, clear tendencies, consistent with the government's own ends, arise. Not only has the happy condition of the state, as is obvious, nothing to do with a general chimerical happiness, but it coincides with a precise and useful individual un-happiness (or in-security) which is constantly nurtured and needs therefore to be carefully defined.

At the risk of going off topic, I stress once again the novelty of this system: whereas, in Hobbes's rigorous theory, the sovereign is the one who offers to his subjects security (which does not exist outside the state), and were he to fail he would cease to be a sovereign, the modern biopolitical system is instead a security-obsessed order – which is interested in the (right) population's conditions of life, and therefore organises schools, builds hospitals, treats newborns, sets urban hygiene regulations, etc. – and is based on insecurity itself, according to a paradox that is merely apparent. The subject is now inscribed in a relation of sovereignty on the basis of the fear that internally animates his or her security, making the latter unequivocally desirable. As I will attempt to clarify later on, the sovereign in this system will not cease to be such if he fails or is unwilling to ensure the peace and tranquility of his subjects. On the contrary, as is clearly evident today, he may even announce a future of terror (while blatantly arranging the conditions for this prophecy to come true). The war, which Hobbes had placed outside the state, coincides for us with the civic condition itself. We have become so used to applying or enduring such war against civilians that the real fight between soldiers seems a mere pretext or disguise.

9. Let us return to our main theme: to govern is an exercise that develops between the poles of security and insecurity through the control of suggestive drives [*spinte suggestive*]. However, the spectres of pleasure and pain are not themselves imaginary but palpable, imprinted on the same human multitude. Not only will each member of such a multitude – of this field of energy – shift his or her behaviour from one pole to the other, possibly fleeing pain and desiring pleasure, but they will also be electrified in a negative or positive sense (that is, their living conditions will be desirable for some, fearsome for others).

In society, thus, each individual becomes electrified: s/he acquires a certain electrical charge that conditions or leads her or his actions, exerts or suffers a certain attraction, can reject or be rejected. Each individual will be, at the same time, actor in and spectator of a show that features her or his own social galvanising. Simultaneously both magnetiser and magnetised, no one can escape this all-encompassing game or show, not even the rulers. Here – where each subject becomes, in both senses of the word, public – spectacular (or theatrical) and social demeanour [*tenore*], aesthetic and political demeanour cannot be separated.

It is in this fully public dimension, in this electrified atmosphere, that the halo of prestige shines through the ages, from Mesmer to Le Bon. Its effect is powerful and violent, since it is congruent with the action of the security apparatus, with the control and regulation of behaviour, with the brutal partition between right and false population, between normal and abnormal, with practices of disciplining, exclusion or reclusion of those who are deemed dangerous. This is the violence of the aura or, to use Plessner's expression, the *Gewalt des Nimbus* Plessner's definition is illuminating: the suggestive or electrical-social force derives from a certain lack, from the happiness we do not have but nonetheless believe in under the pressure of our current malaise, from the insecurity which defines security as such, in other words from what is 'not here', from the potential fears that make us accept the current situation, from the evident threat and possible evil that make a living condition appear comfortable. 'Here', then, spontaneous ideas and actions do not exist, but only, in Tarde's own words, suggested ideas and actions.

10. The eighteen-century theory of characters, as we saw, was meant to establish a coherence between impulse and action: it turned buildings into speaking architecture, so that a church or courthouse would not provoke hilarity or derision. However, when centres of suggestion [*centri di suggestione*] multiplied and disseminated amongst the population itself, the definition of character became a never-ending task, whose peculiar difficulties would remain for a long time puzzling, unanswered even in the following age by the luminaries of a new science or in the pages of the *Revue philosophique*. Meanwhile society tendentially transformed itself into an utterly messy field of suggestive effects, in which everyone is subject to an indefinite number of attractions and repulsions: a simple aggregate of strangers and rivals that risks encroaching upon the domain of the 'right' population. The contagious power of imitation and the pervasive force of imagination therefore had to, once again, be brought back to order. The elemental partitions of pleasure/pain, normal/abnormal, true/false population remained an active paradigm but required a second model to back it up. To master the game of power, it was necessary to identify its regulatory postulate, its principle of intelligibility. Class division is the principle of intelligibility of biopower as a suggestive and electrifying power.

Let us focus on the term 'class' and its modern history. Introduced by so-called economists or physiocrats such as Mirabeau and Quesnay in the dictionary of the art of government in the 1760s and 1770s, it played a precise and indispensable function in their system. It is thanks to this concept that the phenomenon of 'population' could be grasped as a 'natural' element in the eighteenth-century sense of the term, that is, in Foucault's words, as 'accessible to agents and techniques of transformation ... [that] are at once enlightened, reflected, analytical, calculated and calculating.'[15] Any governmental venture, as well as any political economy, could then fashion and refashion itself precisely on the basis of such an effect of naturalness.

Marie-France Piguet has traced the physiocratic origin of the concept of *class*, which Joseph A. Schumpeter had already pointed to in his *History of Economic Analysis* (1954).[16] One should only add to this that the innovation introduced by the *économistes* was combined with a dynamism, an instability to which we are now fully accustomed. The government of such a class society and the achievement of its perfect balance involve a constant and gradual process of adjustment. The new concept of class is thus flanked by the idea of *civilisation*, another concept coined in the physiocratic forge. Regarding the concept of civilisation, as we know, a glorious tradition of studies exists: from the first essays by Joachim Moras, Lucien Febvre, Marcel Mauss, Émile Tonnelat, Alfredo Niceforo, Louis Weber (1930), to the equally famous contribution by Émile Benveniste (1954) and the opening chapter of Jean Starobinski's book *Blessings in Disguise, or, the Morality of Evil* [*Le remède dans le mal*].[17] What is important for the purpose of our discussion is the fact that the word *civilisation* – whose suffix *-isation* (as demonstrated by Benveniste) expresses the idea of movement, the slow advance of education and progress – conjures up the division of society into classes: indeed, the two are mutually embroiled.

Merged into an indistinguishable hendiadys, civilisation (or education) and classification provide thus the ordering principle for the play of imagination. The biopolitical system for partitioning (into true and false, normal and abnormal) and classifying the population can thus be defined, using Carl Schmitt's expression, as an immense psychotechnical apparatus of mass suggestion. The most cogent articulation of such a deceptive, spectacular and theatrical aspect can be found in Marx, when he explains how in a class society men and things become character masks (*Charaktermasken*) of power relations.

11. The object of the art of government is now the 'right' population as divided and orderly. It is a historical-natural being provided with an internal dynamic – the antagonism, the class struggle that, as Marx learned from Guizot, animates civilisation – endowed with a principle that turns it from a lifeless entity into a living being, into shimmering, excitable movement, able to react to certain prods, which can be corrected or balanced over time. What happens then to the 'false' or 'apparent' population? In the context of a conventional society organised into classes, and of the process of civilisation, what is properly abnormal or pathological?

What is considered socially abnormal – or 'false', 'apparent' – is that phenomenon or being that upsets and interrupts the regular progress of educational time, that muddles any partition or class division: a being whose appearance coincides with the instantaneous and violent suspension of the normal time of civilisation.

Half a century separates Guizot's *General History of Civilisation in Europe* from Gustave Le Bon's *The Crowd: A Study of the Popular Mind*. Half a century had to pass before the biopolitical theory of class divisions and civilisation developed its particular counterpart in the visions of Le Bon, Gabriel Tarde or Scipio Sighele: that is, the theory of the dangerous and criminal crowd, of the collective and irresistible suggestion, of the heterogeneous – that is, unclassifiable – crowd that forms and spreads at once by a simple contagion, which is as powerful as it is sudden. A much older figure, the dissolved multitude that Hobbes excluded from the state, now seems to reappear within society wreaking havoc on the orderly process and design of *civilisation*.

However, we should clarify that the crowd – this primary, feral, heterogenous, instinctive entity – is both the *enemy and specific product* of the same apparatus of classification of the social body. The suggestive drives [*tensioni suggestice*], in fact, prove to be irreducible because precisely the classification of individuals, which should limit them, produces their peculiar effects: material effects, to be sure, and therefore, in turn, suggestive. There is then a continuous excess of suggestion, which, sooner or later, will result in a dangerous eruption, a convulsive mass crisis.

It follows from this that to govern, at a deeper level, means also to stir up the masses, to provoke them at the right time, to trigger riots before their uncontrollable outbreak, or, better still, if possible, to keep the crowds in a state of vulnerability and frightened paralysis. In short, it is a matter of promptness and good timing; a technique of infiltration and a management of fears and worries, which, however, does not avoid but rather promotes the spread of terror. Constitutively unable to exclude the latter, biopower must necessarily attest to a phenomenon of hallucinatory paroxysm. Yet, it is certain that this new exercise will in turn spin out of control and that the development of biopolitical rule or civilisation will wrap itself into an endless spiral.

As Hermann Broch clarified, it is a question of directing the madness of the crowds, that is, of stabilising it, however tragically paradoxical this task may seem. It's a question of building a State on the 'movement' (*Bewegung*) of the crowd, by perpetuating – in the form of a mandatory rally [*adunata obbligatoria*] – that crucial moment when the crowd comes to life. In other words, the structure of government has to be adjusted on the basis of such an elusive object, so as to maintain class divisions in spite of everything.

Although its signs have long been evident, this epochal shift can only be as sudden, instinctive and violent as the crowd itself. Le Bon's book becomes thus the guiding text, while the figure of the ruler comes to coincide with that of the star or leader of a multitude of passive followers [*una moltitudine gregaria*]. With the advent of totalitarian regimes, the abrupt leap from the eighteenth-century prehistory to the post-history of suggestion takes place, and, I would add, this post-history is not confined only to the twentieth century.

12. In order not to remain at the level of suggested opinion, however, it is necessary to openly ask the question: is this figure still relevant today? Or, more pessimistically, we could ask: did we ever come out of this end of century nightmare? Did we rid ourselves of the appeal of the twentieth century?

One may observe that even the way out of a nightmare can be in fact just a stage of the dream. It should be clear by now that the appearance of the crowd is internal to biopower's spectacle of suggestion. This means that the crowd appears first of all to itself, its criminal sneer and frightened wince, as belonging to the same face; the expression 'fear of the crowd' should be read in both the two senses of the genitive as the fear that the crowd feels towards itself. Such a 'product', therefore, stands at the centre of the system endowed with a constitutive power: that is, the image of the 'right' population – namely, the non-pathological incarnation of a mass with diametrically opposed, positive and desirable attributes – is produced by a specific and positive projection of the crowd.

Gabriel Tarde himself, who had stared intently at the face of the stupid and dangerous multitude, unified through immediate contact and lacking the ability to invent, would envision (in 'The Public and the Crowd') the image of a spiritualised mass, that is, of a *public* that instead communicates at a distance and is therefore, unlike the *foule*, intelligent and capable of invention. In a host of popular, lowbrow publications by minor authors issued at the start of the twentieth century, the nightmare could tip over into a mirage: 'Goodness is a crowd-process', one could read for instance in a sociologically-inspired best-seller released in the United States in 1913. It is well known that the idea of the democratic and inventive power of the multitude is a long-lasting myth. Indeed, it would be straightforward even to interpret the great spectacular and psychotechnical apparatus put in place in the twentieth century and never so much developed as in our day – the apparatus that invests and controls the entire social dimension – as a set of devices able to put us in contact and keep us in touch, each time connecting the Tardian figure of the public to that of the crowd at the precise moment in which it pretends or at least promises, according to a specular dynamic, to turn the crowd into a public.

Thus, the true question is: can we overcome the biopolitical magic of prestige? That is: are we able to disarticulate and block the apparatus of suggestive classifications?

13. The (right, true) population was a 'natural' element for the physiocratic authors. The crowd, on the other hand, 'really is a spectacle of nature [*Naturspiel*] – if one may apply the term to social conditions.'[18] These words by Walter Benjamin can be found in his 1938 essay 'The Paris of the Second Empire in Baudelaire'. In a famous letter, written two years earlier on the 18th of March 1936, Theodor W. Adorno presented a number of rather harsh critiques concerning Benjamin's essay 'The Work of Art in the Age of its Mechanical Reproducibility'. Yet, Adorno added: 'I cannot conclude, however, without telling you that your few sentences about the disintegration (*Desintegration*) of the proletariat as "masses" ("*Masse*") through revolution are among the profoundest and most powerful statements of political theory that I have encountered since I read *State and Revolution*.'[19] It is in these sentences written by Benjamin (in fact a long footnote), and so admired by Adorno, that we can discover that second, new meaning of the term 'class' at which I hinted at the start.

'The Work of Art in the Age of its Mechanical Reproducibility', as is well known, concerns the decline of aura (or *nimbus*). In this essay, Benjamin, in order to define the revolutionary class, does not refer in the first place to the domain of Marxist studies but, in what may seem a curious move, to the authors of nineteenth-century social psychology. He explains that the model of this crowd described by mass psychology is the multitude of customers randomly gathered by the market: a simple aggregate of individuals, namely consumers, who have nothing in common but the fact of all being animated by their own private interests. It is precisely these heterogenous, unruly masses that the totalitarian state forges into a 'people's community' [*Volksgemeinschaft*], by offering each individual a way to rationalise in terms of race, blood and soil the disturbing randomness that brings them together, and at the same time providing them with a reliable leader, a spellbinder to follow. The specific 'performance' (*Leistung*) of such a political leader, as Benjamin elaborates, is the same as that of a movie star: both must feel comfortable before a camera, remain there to be admired by others, win over the crowds by steering the suggestive drives [*le spinte suggestive*] in a precise direction.

For this reason, a revolutionary politics – that is, a specifically non-fascist politics – for Benjamin, consists in an opposite technique, capable of destroying the aura of the leader by loosening the bonds of suggestion. Revolutionary is she who succeeds in not being a leader, not pulling along the crowd, even if again and again she loses herself in the masses. Alien both to the cult of the star and its correlate, the cult of the masses, revolutionary politics is thus an anti-suggestive technique. Once again, as logic suggests, the arts, that is, cinema and earlier still theatre, will be the battlefield and field of experimentation of such a technique. Brecht's epic theatre, as is widely known, was central to Benjamin's thought in this period.

What is then the revolutionary class? It is an *Auflockerung*, Benjamin says, a loosening up of the tensions that excite the crowd, made possible by solidarity. The best definition of this loosening up (and thus of solidarity) can be found in his writings on Brecht's theatre.

As Benjamin explains, when the director of epic drama stages a renowned story, he *loosens* its links, its internal and customary connections, just like the dance teacher loosens the dancers' joints to make them perform unimaginable pirouettes. Where spectators of classical theatre – who follow the unfolding of events on stage in an almost hypnotic state – would expect a plot twist, there epic drama interrupts the representation, exposing the story to detached examination and discussion. By loosening and dissolving with the aid of critique dramatic suspense, epic drama shows how nothing is predetermined and how everything could have gone otherwise. Even the theatre audience, then, changes, or rather loosens itself in turn; it is transformed from a reactive crowd in thrall to the actor into a plurality, both relaxed and active, of collaborators aware of their social situation: that is, it becomes class. This is the new meaning of the word that, as I said earlier, can slip into the space between 'masses' and 'suggestion': a meaning which is no longer biopolitical and which emerges where the aura and prestige of the star is dissolved.

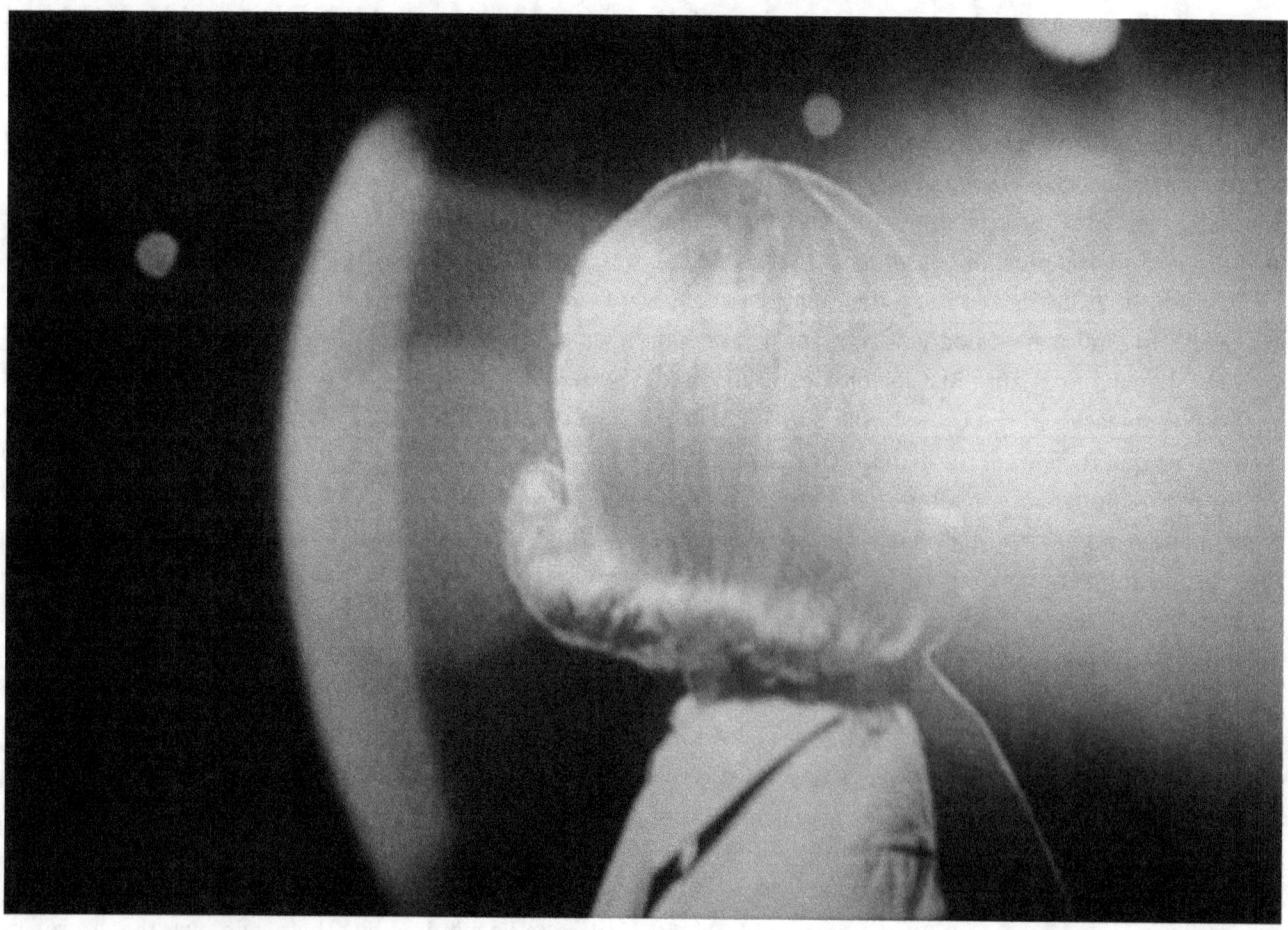

As Benjamin taught us, politics is a technique: modelled after the example of Brechtian theatre, it becomes capable of a revolutionary operation (*Leistung*), by virtue of which the masses neither recognise nor follow any leader. In fact, there can be no leader, magician, or spellbinder with the act of loosening up: no psychosomatic subject is allowed to fashion itself as the centre of attraction.

14. Still caught under the spell of 'prestige', Tarde may surely appear very distant from this perspective. But one must be fair to Tarde. At the start, I quoted Freud and, I think, it was precisely Freud who understood the key aspect of Tarde's thought when he compared the author of *The Laws of Imitation* to Hippolyte Bernheim, as the one who had converted and developed into a political and social key the theory of suggestion.

It is well known that the birth of psychotherapy was marked by the controversy, about a decade long, between the Paris school, or school of the Salpêtrière, and the Nancy school; that is, between the theory of suggestion and the theory of hypnotism, between the method of Bernheim and that of Jean-Martin Charcot. The latter had built his scientific paradigm on the neat partition between wake and sleep, or – to put it in classical, Aristotelian terms – between activity and passivity; so that, at the Salpêtrière, the diagnosis and treatment of hysteria were articulated, consistently, on the hierarchical division of roles: the doctor's role (healthy, male) who acts (awake) and commands, and the patient's role (hysterical and, therefore, female) who takes orders (passively, that is, in a state of sleep).

Bernheim's hypothesis unsettled this system. In Nancy, suggestion served as an explanation for everything, while hypnosis was considered only a special case of a relationship that existed even during the waking state. Any partition between activity and passivity had to falter, while the relationship between doctor and patient was revealed to be a mutual and complex game of suggestion and counter-suggestion.

These two positions were so diametrically opposed and conflictual that a fierce battle (fought with no holds barred, especially by Charcot's clique) was inevitable. This battle was long indeed, and would become even harsher after the publication in 1886 (again in the *Revue philosophique*) of Joseph Delboeuf's essay 'De l'influence de l'imitation et de l'éducation dans le somnambulisme provoqué' [On the influence of imitation and education in induced somnambulism]. This is a dispassionate but all the more merciless analysis of Charcot's laboratory, which appears here, in some ways, very similar to that of a sideshow hypnotist. In Delboeuf's eyes, the Salpêtrière was after all only a theatre where hysteria was staged according to a technique very close to that used, for instance, by the magnetiser Donato: a suggestive technique, based on imitation (the young patients witnessed the crisis of their older peers) that produced the canon of hysteria by projecting onto the scene the masks of the doctor and the patient, the healthy man and sick woman.

Delboeuf was close to Bernheim, and Tarde was Delboeuf's friend. But what was Tarde's position exactly? Certainly, he was not a partisan; but his position was not ambiguous either, and over the years it became clearer and more explicit. In 1890, in a footnote to *The Laws of Imitation*, he claimed for instance to have introduced six years earlier 'the idea of a universal social suggestion, an idea which has since been so strongly emphasised by Bernheim and others'.[20] In 1893, in the pages of *Monadology and Sociology*, once again raising the question 'What is a society?' that he had already asked in 1884, Tarde replied that it is 'each individual's reciprocal possession ... of every other'.[21] Even though the first fascination, which establishes a relationship with the 'vital element', is unilateral, this later develops and is socially diluted into universal possession or reciprocal imitation. This means that the centre of attraction of imitation (what Tarde calls 'genius'), despite appearances, can never be reduced to the circumscribed identity of a psychosomatic individual. Since society encompasses everything, this very identity is already caught in the game of imitations and differences.

In the context of universal suggestion, 'to exist is to differ', or, to use a lesser-known formula (drawn from the notes for '*Essentiel pour les bases du système*']), in society 'at all times I differ from myself and I will never be again the self that I am right now'.[22] This entails that prestige, in Tarde's use of the term, exceeds the Ego's individuality, and is not consistent with the definition of the subject (through character) but rather with the radical removal of the subject from any stability. In this sense, prestige is not a magic trick that exchanges the 'here' with the 'not-here' through the action of the latter on the former, because everything differs and nothing and nobody is here any longer.

The critique of biopower (which is, I would say, the true critique of the crowd) is a critique of the principles of the art of government – such as the partition between right and false population, and divisions into classes – which are principles of intelligibility (or truth), stabilisation models, control systems, at times violent, with imponderable and even more pernicious effects. We should recognise that this critique involves the destruction (or loosening) of the subject's unity or identity,[23] and therefore can only move forward along the path of universal imitation and reciprocal possession, following the sign laid out by Tarde, Delbouef and Berhheim: everything is suggestion.

Translated by Elisa Adami

Andrea Cavalletti is Professor of Aesthetics and Contemporary Literature at the IUAV University of Venice. He is the author of Class *(Seagull Books, 2019), as well as of* Suggestione *(2011) and* La città biopolitica *(2005).*

Notes

1. Sigmund Freud, *Group Psychology and the Analysis of the Ego*, trans. James Strachey (London: Hogarth Press and Institute of Psychoanalysis, 1945), 34.
2. Gabriel Tarde, *The Laws of Imitation*, trans. Elsie Clews Parsons (New York: Henry Holt and Company, 1903), 79.
3. Pierre Janet, 'Rapport sur la suggestion (présenté au Congrès de psychiatrie de Zurich le 27 novembre 1926)', in *Archives Suisses de Neurologie et de Psychiatrie* (Archiv für Neurologie und Psychiatrie) 20:5 (1927), 5.
4. Hermann Broch, *Die Straße* (December 1918), in *Briefe 1913-1938*, KW 13/1, ed. Paul Michael Lützeler (Frankftur a. M.: Suhrkamp, 1981), 31.
5. Helmuth Plessner, *The Limits of Community: A Critique of Social Radicalism*, trans. Andrew Wallace (New York: Prometheus Books, 1999), 135.
6. I will not expand on the internal displacement of the expression *Dasein* in Plessner's text, nor on the implicit deductions that we could draw from it with regards to the relationship between the *Nimbuseffekt* and Husserl's concept of *Erlebnis* or Heidegger's idea of *Faktizität*.
7. Jean Fallot, *Prestiges de la science* (Neuchâtel: Éditions de la Baconnière, 1960), 11.
8. Maine de Biran, *Journal, II, 1er 1817- 17 mai 1819*, ed. Henri Gouhier (Neuchâtel: Éditions de la Baconnière, 1955), 55.
9. Paul Heinrich Thiry (Baron) d'Holbach, *Système social, ou, principes naturels de la morale et de la politique*, tome premier (London: 1773), 204.
10. Antonio Genovesi, *Lezioni di commercio o sia d'economia civile*, I (Napoli: Fratelli Simone, 1765), chap. 2 & 6, 41.
11. Michel Delon, *L'idée d'énergie au tournant des Lumières (1770-1820)* (Paris: Presses Universitaires de France, 1988), 109.
12. Henri Bergson, *Time and Free Will: An Essay on the Immediate Data of Consciousness*, trans. F. L. Pogson (London: George Allen & Unwin, 1950), 51.
13. Michel Foucault, *The History of Sexuality, Volume 1: An Introduction*, trans. Robert Hurley (London: Penguin, 1990), 138.
14. Genovesi, *Lezioni di commercio o sia d'economia civile*, I, Chap. 2 & 10, 44.
15. Michel Foucault, *Security, Territory, Population: Lectures at the College de France 1977-78*, trans. G. Burchell (New York: Palgrave Macmillan, 2009), 71.
16. Marie-France Piguet, *Classe: Histoire du mot et genèse du concept des Physiocrates aux Historiens de la Restauration* (Lyon: Presses universitaires de Lyon, 1996); Joseph A. Schumpeter, *History of Economic Analysis* (London: Taylor & Francis, 2006).
17. Émile Benveniste, 'Civilisation: A Contribution to the History of the Word', in *Problems in General Linguistics*, trans. Mary Elizabeth Meek (Coral Gables: University of Miami Press, 1971); Jean Starobinski, *Blessings in Disguise, or, the Morality of Evil*, trans. Arthur Goldhammer (Cambridge, MA: Harvard University Press, 1993).
18. Walter Benjamin, 'The Paris of the Second Empire in Baudelaire', trans. Howard Eiland, in *Selected Writings, Vol. 4, 1938-1940*, eds. Howard Eiland and Michael W. Jennings (Cambridge, MA: The Belknap Press of Harvard University Press, 2002), 36.
19. Theodor W. Adorno et al., *Aesthetics and Politics* (London: Verso, 2007), 126.
20. Tarde, *The Laws of Imitation*, 76.
21. Gabriel Tarde, *Monadology and Sociology*, trans. Theo Lorenc (Melbourne: re.press, 2012), 51.
22. '*Je différe à chaque instant de moi-même. Je n'ai été, ni ne serai jamais le moi que je suis en ce moment*', in Gabriel Tarde, *Essentiel pour les bases du système* (1873-79), Juillet 1878, ed. Filippo Domenicali, *I castelli di Yale* I:2 (2013), 351.
23. Benjamin introduced the concept of a 'loosening of the self (*Lockerung des Ich*)' in his 1929 essay on Surrealism. See Walter Benjamin, 'Surrealism: the Last Snapshot of the European Intelligentsia', trans. Edmund Jephcott, in *Selected Writings, Vol. 2, 1927-1934*, eds. Howard Eiland, Michael W. Jennings and G. Smith (Cambridge, MA: The Belknap Press of Harvard University Press, 1999), 207–221.

Hegel's natural assumption
The first sentence of the *Phenomenology of Spirit*
Hammam Aldouri

The 'Introduction' to the *Phenomenology of Spirit* has enjoyed a long and rich critical reception in the history of Hegel scholarship.[1] Distinguished from the famous 'Preface' in that it introduces the particular ambitions of the *Phenomenology* as opposed to Hegel's philosophical enterprise as a whole, the opening section of the 1807 work has been understood as the exposition of a paradoxical structure of philosophical science (*Wissenschaft*): the path of philosophical science emerges from out of the analysis of the immanent dialectical unfolding of an introduction to this same philosophical science. Hegel acknowledges this paradoxical relation between the path *to* and the path *of* philosophical science at the end of the introductory section to the *Phenomenology*: 'the way to philosophical science is itself already philosophical science.'[2]

A crucial element of this internally paradoxical conception of philosophical science within the *Phenomenology* – that it is simultaneously the introduction to philosophical science and always already a part of that science – is a preliminary dialectical critique of the limits of modern theories of cognition. As the memorable opening passage of the Introduction makes clear, the problem with modern epistemology is that it tries to know the mode of knowing most appropriate for comprehending the truth of the absolute – the truth of what is – before any step is taken into the philosophical knowledge of truth as such:

> It is a *natural assumption* that in philosophy, before we start to deal with its proper subject-matter, viz. the actual cognition of what in truth is, one must first of all come to an understanding about cognition, which is regarded either as the instrument to possess the Absolute, or as the medium through which one discovers it.[3]

[*Es ist eine* natürliche Vorstellung, *daß, ehe in der Philosophie an die Sache selbst, nämlich an das wirkliche Erkennen dessen, was in Wahrheit ist, gegangen wird, es notwendig sei, vorher über das Erkennen sich zu verständigen, das als das Werkzeug, wodurch man des Absoluten sich bemächtige, oder als das Mittel, durch welches hindurch man es erblicke, betrachtet wird.*]

Before one gets into the work of philosophy, one must first learn to philosophise.[4] Much ink has been spilt in explicating *why* it is that Hegel starts his Introduction to his 1807 book with this 'natural assumption'. Above all else, Hegel is said to be positioning his phenomenological study in relation to the distinctive problems of modern epistemology, principal among which is the presumed separation of the subject of knowing and the object known via the instrumentalisation of cognition. But *how* did the 'natural assumption' appear? How did it become a predominant form of philosophical proceduralism? What are the processes that allowed it to manifest in such a manner that Hegel was able to deploy it as the starting point of his *Phenomenology*? Are those processes intra-epistemological or broader socio-historical ones? Without answering these questions, any exposition of the 'natural assumption' is in danger of being itself naturally assumed as a simple manifestation of the limits of theories of cognition when, in fact, something significantly more complicated is taking place.

This essay aims to protect against such an ironic fate by offering an alternative account of the first sentence of the Introduction. It will provide an exposition of the presupposed processes that render the 'natural assumption' possible as a hypostatised cultural form that could be immediately mobilised by Hegel as the starting point of the *Phenomenology*. I will show that, more than simply a critique of modern theories of cognition, the 'natural assumption' expresses a complex historical abstraction that constellates both the concealed impositions of institutionalised academic philosophical production, and the mediation of the private property relations that dominate modern civil society. By abstraction I mean the process of the interconnection of elements that constitute a phenomenon but which are not empirically observable on its surface. The abstraction of the 'natural assumption' is that it contains and expresses social and historical processes – the mechanisms and apparatuses of the social space of philosophical production within the late eighteenth- and early nineteenth-century university system and the general structural presuppositions of private property relations in modern Prussian life – but does not display those processes at the level of its formal characteristics. Specifically, I will seek to show that Hegel's critique discloses the social imbalance that posits philosophical cognition as a product of the specific form of ethical substance that dominates early nineteenth-century life: the system of private property relations constitutive of civil society.

In order to develop this claim, I provide a detailed commentary on a number of terms that appear in the opening sentence of the Introduction but have yet to be explored in greater detail: 'before' (*vorher*), 'necessity' (*notwendig*), 'philosophy' (*Philosophie*), 'one' (*man*) and 'possession' (*bemächtigen*). These terms are the clues to disinterring the processes that, I argue, render the natural assumption possible as a cultural form.

The imposition of propaedeutics

As was noted above, the dominant understanding of the starting point of the Introduction to the *Phenomenology* is that it presents an immanent critique of the basic presupposition of modern theories of cognition.[5] Modern epistemology separates the subject of knowing from the object known, thus inaugurating a whole series of assumed divisions: subjective certainty is cut off from objective truth; the method of philosophising is disconnected from philosophical knowledge; the infinitude of truth is irreducible to the finitude of subjective reflection; and so on. As important as this focus is, however, one consequence has been a misconstrual of the opening passage in terms of the staged, explicit relation to existing modes of philosophising crystallised in particular systems of thought. In other words, the Introduction is not simply an interrogation of modern epistemology, but a personification of modern epistemology in a particular system. The most dominant point of reference indicated in the Introduction is, according to Hegel scholarship, Immanuel Kant's conception of transcendental critique.

The 'natural assumption' is said to personify the standpoint of Kantian philosophical critique understood as an investigation into the conditions of possibility of *a priori* knowledge of the concepts, principles and criteria of metaphysics. What this investigation produces is a discourse on the nature and limits, and thus legitimacy, of knowledge free of experience (reason). As a result of the delimitation of reason, the *limits* of knowing are known, whereas the *boundaries* of reason can only be thought (since they are 'beyond' experience).[6] As a consequence of this distinction between the known limit and the thought boundary, Kantian philosophy produces a separation between the knowing subject (the limits of subjective reflection) and the unknowable object of thought (reason as that which *burdens* humans with necessary questions that cannot be answered).[7]

The Kantian problematic of the presupposition of a subjective dogmatism that is hidden within the transcendental critique of objective legitimacy, has been well explicated by Hegel himself as well as by secondary literature. Yet, nowhere is Kant explicitly referenced in the Introduction. This, of course, does not mean that Kant's critical method is not *implied* – it clearly is since the whole problematic of the opening passage concerns the elaboration of the nature and limits of the correct cognition of the truth of the absolute. The purpose here is not to contest this. Rather, I take the absence of direct reference to Kant as an invitation to reconsider the function and the presuppositions of the first sentence. In fact, the character of the opening sentence – which is said to establish the whole issue of the critique of modern epistemology – is far too general a proposition for it to provide, as Ludwig Siep reminds us, 'an exacting critical engagement … with Kant.'[8] Indeed, Hegel's generalisation is so general that it is remarkably difficult to identify a particular philosophical system as the *specific* target of the Introduction's opening passages. Although certain references to Descartes, Locke, Kant, Jacobi and Reinhold can no doubt be discerned if one follows an 'iconological' impulse (a search for sources), this preoccupation with past philosophical systems as providing some determinate content to the standpoint of the natural assumption is, I would argue, misleading in that it particularises the general.⁹ As such, it is, I think, precisely the status of generalisation embodied by the natural assumption that should be analysed if we are to have an alternative understanding of its status.

In fact, as I will suggest below, the generalisation of the natural assumption could be construed as a determined effect of a historical process that, in specific institutional fields of knowledge production, converts particular modes of philosophical orientation into a fixed, generalised code or convention of philosophical practice. In the case of the Introduction to the *Phenomenology*, this specific institutional field is that of the discipline of philosophy within the modern German university system, usually periodised as beginning in the early 1700s with the emergence of the University of Göttingen. The institutional determination of a generalised philosophical convention can be discerned in at least two interrelated ways in the opening sentence: first, by the imposition of propaedeutics as what comes 'before' (*vorher*) philosophy; and second, by an abstract power of the 'necessity' (*notwendig*) of propaedeutics.¹⁰

What allows the natural assumption to be perceivable and deployable as a generalised starting point of philosophical practice is, therefore, the sense in which what it signals is the convention of propaedeutics – that is to say, the preparatory studies required for individuals to enter into specific disciplines. The Introduction consciously stages a confrontation with the mechanisms and demands of general *introductory* knowledge (*pro*-paedeutics). Propaedeutics are, then, a general introduction to a particular knowledge that aims to provide students with some basic theoretical content (concepts, ideas, systems, methods, bibliographies, etc.). In Hegel's time, the status of propaedeutics were, generally speaking, governed by institutionalised education, and Hegel knew the character of this pedagogical form well. Not only was he part of the university system throughout his life – albeit in a highly uneven way – but he also produced a philosophical propaedeutic whilst teaching at a *Gymnasium* in Nuremberg.¹¹

Propaedeutics, according to one of Hegel's letters, are the *enforced* educational condition that assures 'that empty minds are filled with thoughts' so that the 'natural peculiarity of thought – i.e., accident, caprice, oddness in matters of opinion – is driven out.'¹² In this context, Hegel is referring to the education of school children, which is obviously different to the situation staged in the opening of the *Phenomenology*. Nevertheless, the latter is marked by a certain demand that philosophical work begin first by subjugating thinking to the order of a learned practice; or, put another way, of a practice that demands that the individual would-be philosopher fill in his or her philosophical mind by an established convention of orientation. It insists that before one does philosophy, one needs to *learn* how to philosophise. Propaedeutics is, from this perspective, in-built into the very substance of philosophical knowledge of which it is thus an integral part.

The necessity of the conjunctural relation of propaedeutics and philosophy within philosophical work was, for Hegel in Jena, an absurdity. The absurdity is formalised in a nice gnomic attack on Kant's notion of philosophising in the so-called 'Aphorisms of the Wastebook' (1803/4-1806). Kantian philosophising aims to teach philosophy prior to doing philosophy. It is, as Hegel puts it somewhat brutally, 'as if someone could teach carpentry but not how to build a table, a chair, a door, a cabinet, etc.'[13] 'Carpentry' in this notebook entry is understood as the generalised logic of the practice and teaching of making things made out of wood without actually making things made out of wood. It is an infinitely repeatable order of practice that can be mapped onto all who wish to enter the practice, but done so without actually entering into the practice of philosophy. Or, to recode the metaphor into the language of epistemology, it means to know the faculty of knowing without knowing anything. Hegel takes this point up again in his lectures on the history of philosophy. This time he draws attention to the 'old story' of the σχολαστικός (*scholasticus*) – that is to say, the institutionalised subject of competent scholarship.[14]

This reference, together with Hegel's earlier attack on the internal contradiction of Kant's philosophy in the 'Wastebook' notes, can be said to work analogically to the hidden presupposition of the natural assumption: the latter is produced within an order of institutionalised philosophical practice that elaborates externally-imposed instruments of philosophical practice that organise philosophical work prior to any philosophical knowledge. Philosophy within the university system, as the institution that dominates (although not *absolutely*) the practice of philosophy in Prussia in the eighteenth and nineteenth centuries, produces in this way a meta-philosophical injunction – a kind of academic categorial imperative – that precedes philosophical knowledge and that, crucially, polices the passage into philosophy. It is not insignificant that Hegel notes the *necessity* (*notwendig*) that animates the natural assumption: to do philosophy, one *must* first follow the proceduralism of propaedeutics in so far as it is the latter that structurally presuppose philosophy.[15] The matter is an imperative; and the imperative precedes philosophy but has no determinate philosophical content since it is not premised on the knowledge that one is always already within the element of philosophising the absolute by virtue of the unity of the latter with *ourselves*.[16]

Hegel's concerns in the opening of the *Phenomenology*, then, are not simply limited to the problem of modern epistemology. They take issue with other latent processes that condition the *possibility* of doing philosophy in a given moment. But this is only one aspect of the natural assumption. The meta-philosophical imperative emerges as a duty that is *taught* in such a way that it gets fully *internalised* by the subject of the natural assumption – namely, the one who carries it out as if it were totally natural. The agent of the natural assumption is a subject of the acquisition of competency – a kind of 'student-subject', as I would define it, who is shepherded into a process of philosophical practice that rests on a certain academic-institutional consensus that philosophical work begins first by a propaedeutics on cognising cognition. Interestingly, Hegel's opening sentence ascribes an abstract status to this student-subject that is subjectivised by the necessity of a particular order of philosophical production. The sentence makes note of this subject as 'one'.

The 'one' as abstract subject

For the natural assumption to have appeared as immediately perceivable form of thought, there must have been a process of imposition that gets internalised by a subject in such a way that it becomes a habit or reflexive second-nature that is manifested in institutionalised conventions of philosophical practice. The opening of the Introduction suggests this sense of the reflexive character by posing an unjustified mode of philosophical orientation as if it were fully justified. In other words, the standpoint of the necessity of propaedeutics arrogates to itself the position of philosophical beginnings. We can develop a deeper and more precise understanding of this hidden process of the institutional formation of philosophising by considering the strange abstract subject that punctuates the opening sentence – the 'one' [*man*].

It should be noted at this point that the subject of the 'natural assumption' is not *solely* a student-subject. Functioning beyond the strict limits of schematised education, the 'natural assumption' is a constitutive feature of philosophical production *per se* in Hegel's present. In other words, it points to a broader social issue, one animated by the question of how philosophy in any given historical moment is produced at a general level. Thus, the generalisation of philosophical practice is semantically registered by a generalised subject, an abstract 'one'. This subject is an agent that is represented, at first blush, as if it is stripped of any determinate socio-historical content. Regardless of context, the 'one' simply carries out the task of how to philosophise. But as I already suggested, this generalisation is an abstraction of what is nonetheless also a determinate institutional field and set of practices (the university). The abstract character of the 'one' is, accordingly, abstract in an internally contradictory sense: it can be described as formally abstract only in so far as its concrete content is concealed from it. *That* the 'one' is required to blindly follow the regulations of a prescribed schema of transition into philosophical knowledge, reveals the determinacy of the subject's structure as being threaded through by the mechanisms that organise, produce and reproduce the schema. The indeterminacy of the 'one' is, paradoxically, the determination of institutionalised philosophical production raised to the level of generalised architectonic logic.

Unfortunately, not only has the historical and philosophical status of the 'one' in Hegel's opening passage received little analysis in Hegel scholarship, but it has often been (albeit unconsciously) covered over. Take, for example, Adris Collins' preliminary presentation of the basic structure and posited goal of the opening sentence of the Introduction to the *Phenomenology*: 'It seems "natural", to assume, Hegel says, that we must understand the nature and limits of the instrument or medium through which we discover the truth before we become involved in actual knowing.'[17] Collins here immediately collapses the 'one' into a 'we'. That is to say, she substitutes an abstract, individuated subject for an abstractly collectivised social subject.[18] Within the context of the *Phenomenology*, this substitution is highly charged: the 'we' constitutes, as is well-known, the very centre of Hegel's notoriously complex concept of spirit as defined, for the first time in the 1807 work ('I that is We and We that is I').[19] Although it enters into Collins' exposition somewhat precipitously, the reference to the 'we' is, according to the salience of the 'we' in Hegel's thought, not without some justification.

Spirit only finds its initial point of philosophical description in the fourth chapter of the *Phenomenology* within the context of the formal definition of self-consciousness as mutual recognition, but it already appears in the Introduction by way of the philosophical dissolution of the separation between cognition and the absolute. As Hegel will try to show, the absolute is not an object to be epistemologically won by cognition, but is, rather, the process of a subject's reconstruction of itself from out of its dynamic externalisation and reintegration of its objective otherness – that is, of spirit that comes to know the result of its negation, differentiation and alienation of otherness, and as the very subject that knows itself as the process of negation, differentiation and alienation of otherness as its own act and substance. That is to say, as a subject that knows that it is *in itself* the negation of the object, and as the subject that knows that it is the negation of that knowing in a higher order experience of ontological unity with the object – or, a subject that knows that it has the in itself as something *for itself*.

Within the context of the Introduction, this dialectical process of the in-self as becoming fully appropriated by the for-itself of spirit results in the identification of the absolute with nothing less than *ourselves* since the knower is not extrinsic to the object known, but is a dynamic processual unity (a spiritual unity) of the two. In other words, in so far as *we* are the subjects of knowing, we are the absolute. The *Phenomenology* is, understood thus, the introduction and first part of a systematic presentation of speculative philosophy raised to the order of social ontology.[20]

However, Hegel refrains from identifying the subject of the opening sentence of the Introduction with the subject of the 'we', in order to begin to disclose the sense in which theoretical propaedeutics are *obstacles* in the passage toward grasping the truth of the absolute as the truth of who and what we are. To immediately posit that *we* are the subject of natural assumption is to socialise a phenomenon (regardless of how formal or abstract it is) that is, for Hegel, *de-socialised* within the order of the demands made by philosophical propaedeutics (since it posits abstract, anonymous individuals, the mere 'one'). The process of de-socialisation consists of the misrecognition of the social character of the 'we' as the absolute – a subject that articulates the recognition of its collective status as dialectically particular and general. (The chiastic form of the 'I' and 'we' in the famous formulation cited above registers this.) This process of spirit's actualisation as the collective social 'we' is, crucially, determined by spirit itself. Spirit is the name of a 'subject' that produces its own subjectivity, thus *both* its status as subject and substance. It is ontologically identical to processuality – it *is* process (and thus cannot be reducible to either subject or substance). As Hegel notes in a remarkable proposition in the 1803/04 'First Philosophy of Spirit', the ontological processuality of spirit consists of '*bringing itself* to birth'.[21]

It is the task of philosophical science to expose spirit's self-parturition at the level of its most adequate form of expression. This means that philosophical science is the form in which spirit unfolds itself as the *free* subject of its own formation, which of course means, by extension, that philosophical science is the most developed manifestation of freedom. It is for this reason that Hegel's philosophical enterprise aims to achieve the status of being presuppositionless; spirit must express itself from out of its own determinate content. It is spiritual freedom expressed as spiritual freedom. Or, put another way, the collective 'we' must form its freedom from out of its own activity.

In the opening of the *Phenomenology*, philosophical thinking is imposed upon by an extrinsic schema of theoretical progress, one that misshapes progress for inert regression since it bars us from a passage into philosophy by locking thinking into an interminable struggle of working out how to enter. The 'one' is the kind of subject that emerges in this relation of externality, of an abstract, indeterminate particular that is ignorant of its own particularity. More importantly, the 'one' is a hypostatised agency that is, ironically, barred access to the substance of philosophical knowledge by being forced to remain within an illusory expanse of superficial logical and epistemological concerns.

The Reinholdian distinction between the passage into philosophy and the passage of philosophy – allegorised by Hegel in the figures of the 'spacious vestibule' of pseudo-scientific philosophising and the 'temple' of philosophy – is an element of the processes that give sense to how the natural assumption became a natural assumption. The architectural allegory that represents the division, however, does not simply draw attention to two modes of intellectual orientation – of a passage into philosophy that, because of the 'bad infinity' of its practice, never gets into philosophy, and the passage of philosophy.[22] It also underlines the mediation of the *social* division operative within the spaces that determine philosophical production: the spaces that either permit or forbid entry into the temple of philosophy. In *The Difference Between Fichte's and Schelling's System of Philosophy* Hegel mockingly refers to the Reinholdian orientation, which reduces reflection – thus anticipating the more memorable element of instrumentalisation in the opening sentence of the Introduction to the *Phenomenology* – to an appropriable skill, 'a kind of handicraft, something that can be improved by newly invented turns of skill.'[23] It is the task of philosophy to provide access to this handicraft. Thus, '[Reinhold] seems to think of this task as the finding of a universally valid and ultimate turn of skill such that the work [of philosophical cognition] completes itself automatically for anyone who can get acquainted with it.'[24]

Interestingly, philosophy is, within the Reinholdian disposition, presented as a 'representation of philosophy' instead of philosophical work as the development of its own immanent unfolding.[25] What I think is more significant in Hegel's devastating critique of Reinhold is the hidden *social* division and asymmetry that structures the abstractly open passage into the acquaintance with philosophical cognition – anyone can do it, so long as they are appropriately initiated – and the fact that the reduction of philosophical cognition into a learnt skill is itself socially reproduced as a set of 'mental exercises' of 'big brains'. A disciplined subject of philosophy as produced and reproduced under the auspices of the university system knows how to enter into philosophy since they know how to obediently perform its exercises. It is a subject that already knows how to be in a given order of philosophy by way of the recurrence of such exercise. For it to have appeared as a natural assumption, the form must thus have been slowly internalised by way of the *repetition* of exercises in a given social field. And for the repetition to be repeated, the convention must have been abbreviated into a relatively accessible and assimilable – repeatable – schema. Something that can be learnt by rote and never be forgotten.[26] This learning by rote – what Hegel will refer to as 'mechanical memory' in his *Philosophy of Spirit* – is internalised by way of social inclusion and exclusion within the production of philosophy. The university system is a social context in which the would-be philosopher learns how to cultivate the illusory image of intellectual self-organisation. Or, more precisely, the student comes to know that he is the subject of philosophical knowledge production when he learns how to order his own thoughts according to the internalised rules of academic work.[27] Philosophical disciplinarity is self-incurred obedience.

This notion of a disciplined university subject offers us one way, then, of understanding the peculiar reference to philosophy – *Philosophie* – in the opening sentence of the Introduction. The reference is strange for the simple fact that it is noted in the very first sentence only to be used again in the sparest of ways. The 'Preface' of the *Phenomenology* already provides us with one reason as to why it is that Hegel dissolves the notion of *Philosophie*, preferring instead *Wissenschaft*. What the 1807 work tries to develop is the passage into actual knowledge of the truth of the absolute and not, as Hegel has it, the mere '*love of knowing*' – that is to say, a classically-orientated mode of philosophical production that is marked by an unbridgeable internal distance from the knowledge of the truth of the absolute since it rests on the fundamental presupposition of modern theories of knowing – namely, that truth is an object to be known by a knowing subject.[28]

What is perhaps more interesting about the first sentence is, however, the sense in which the philosophical proceduralism of the natural assumption operates *within* philosophy (*in der Philosophie*). That is to say, philosophy is not conceived as a limit to be overcome by actual scientific knowledge, but it is posited as the space – the 'spacious vestibule' – in which disciplinarity is produced and reproduced. This suggests that *Philosophie instrumentalises* the natural assumption and recodes it, ideologically, as if it were something pertaining to philosophy as such – that is to say, philosophy as a historical task and not simply a university discipline.

Hegel does not try to rescue philosophy from this ideological imbroglio. He will, rather, disclose the way in which the abuses of philosophy as institutionalised mode of intellectual production are immanent, determinate aspects of the historical unfolding of philosophical science (*Wissenschaft*). This brings us to another significant point that Hegel explores in his critique of Reinhold in 1801 – one which I would tentatively suggest may imply that another presupposition of the natural assumption is the tacit representation of philosophical reflection as an instrument whose historical specificity can be construed as an effect of *private property* relations in particular.

Private property relations

Hegel's critique of the 'mental exercises' that '[keep philosophy] busy with analysis, with methodology and with storytelling, so that it saves itself from taking the step [into philosophy] altogether', is that this not only restricts philosophy to the level of an infinitely repeatable schema of cognising cognition, but it also extracts philosophy from the broader realities of social life.[29] It makes it 'deaf to all demands' of existence at a given historical-social moment.[30] More specifically, as a result of the mediation of the relations of civil society, philosophy is not simply a way of knowing cognition but it is reduced to being the 'private possession of a few individuals.'[31] In the critique of Reinhold in 1801, then, what appears as something formally accessible to all is, in reality, a socially ordered and institutionally reproduced possession of a particular group of institutionalised educators. In this sense, the distinction between the 'one' and the 'we' – of an abstractly produced and reproduced subject of philosophical production that is ignorant of the imposition of the given ethical substance and the concrete complex processual spirit that produces its own life from out of itself – is overdetermined by the historical moment. By pointing to instrumentality, of a *thing acquired*, Hegel is, I argue, underlining the structural features that determine that moment.

The critique of the instrumentalisation of cognition

as pure means of acquisition of the knowledge of the truth of the absolute is, as I have already noted, a well-documented episode in *Phenomenology* scholarship. *That* the 1807 work begins within the socio-ethical order of acquisition – that the absolute is an object to be *possessed* (*bemächtige*) and that cognition is a thing to be acquired – has however, like the previous two points I have explored, received little attention.[32] This is surprising. From his earliest writings in Bern to his mature works, Hegel was extremely attentive to the private property relations that defined modern civil bourgeois society.[33] For example, his fragmentary writings on 'love', composed while in Frankfurt, offer an allegorical image of social union in which private property is superseded into a higher order unity of true relationality (thus anticipating, to some extent, the logic of mutual recognition that constitutes the general character of spirit within the *Phenomenology*).[34] Significantly, this 'true union' of love is articulated by Hegel according to a preliminary passage through its negative formation. Prior to such union, love appears as the process of the direct consumption of the object of desire. The loved object is *owned* by the lover. Hegel uses the figure of the prostitute to render this point more pronounced; and money appears as the mechanism that insures exclusive right of access to the object. Love, under the conditions of civil society, leaves lovers in an insurmountable impasse: they experience each other only as objects to be acquired. As Hegel puts it, such love is, in truth, 'loveless' 'hostility' that yields only a relation conditioned by the defense of its 'right, its property'.[35]

Despite their energetic commitment to thinking the unified social totality, what these Frankfurt writings cannot account for, however, is the manner in which the very instrument of the construction of new images of social unity – namely, the instrument of philosophy – is itself an object alienated from historical-social life, itself an object of the civil society it criticises and aims to negate. It is only when Hegel moves to Jena that he begins to understand the way in which *philosophy* comprises a privately possessed object that structures the legal and ethical modalities of exclusive access and alienation. When Hegel notes that the source of the need of speculative philosophy is the diremption of social life in its given, modern conjuncture – the divisions of society as *atomistic* bourgeois individuals who lose their connection to the collective life of their ethical substance – he not only, then, reflects on why it is that civil society needs philosophy, but he also underscores what philosophy itself needs for it to be understood as the ideal reflexive form of knowing the totality of ethical substance as the truth of spirit.[36]

The atomistic individual of civil society concretises as such the ostensibly abstract 'one' who appears as the first named subjectivity of the *Phenomenology*. I would argue this 'one' is not a free-floating entity but rather the subject of civil society in the early nineteenth century. As a consequence of this atomisation of philosophical practice, the subject of that practice can only connect himself to the order of institutionalised philosophy or the practical demands of the civil service since it is in that social space that one acquires (or becomes 'acquainted' with) the instruments of philosophical knowledge.[37] At the beginning of the nineteenth century, universities were no longer spaces of scholastic and religiously orthodox tutelage of things disconnected from everyday life. Rather, they had become spaces of knowledge that augmented practical studies for a student body made up of nobles and the middle classes that passed through universities so as to be professionalised according to the demands of the state, which is to say, to work as civil servants.[38] To philosophise in the first years of the nineteenth century according to the conventions of the university system was thus to be mediated by a complex set of social processes that structured that system. Hegel felt the effects of this system directly – for many years he lived a highly precarious economic life, finding it difficult to make ends meet because of the shift in labour relations in universities. When Hegel moved to Jena he quickly became part of a radically expanding class of teachers known as *Extraordinarien* (inexpensive instructors that held the rank of 'associate professor').[39] His thought developed within a changing labour market which was itself a part of an uneven history of university reforms that was controlled by the conjunctural relation upheld by German institutions with the state. This relation tried to manage particular crises involving the financial situation of universities, the rising rate of qualified individuals in the professional realm of a civil service that had only a finite number of positions, the problem of the socio-ethical responsibility of universities as formally open to all but in reality servicing only those who could afford it, and so on.

Importantly, philosophy in the university system of the eighteenth century was not simply a discipline that taught the history of systems of thought traditionally transmitted as 'philosophical', but it was a site of different processes, crises and social practices overdetermined by the relations of private property in civil society. The natural assumption contains elements of this overdetermination in so far as it operates on two orders of *givenness*: first, that of the pre-given status of metaphilosophical proceduralism, a schema of production that dictates how it is that one is to start philosophising from the standpoint of institutionalised philosophy; and second, that cognition as a means is given as an object to be *acquired*, a possession that can be used to instrumentally manipulate the absolute according to its own form. Taken together, these two orders of the given allow us to perceive that a distinctive presupposition of the natural assumption – of what allows the natural assumption to appear – is that it constellates processes of *appropriation* that disappear from within the generalisation of proceduralism into a self-evident, naturally assumable, order of philosophical knowledge.

Philosophical production according to the natural assumption, then, starts with an appropriation of a metaphilosophical practice of propaedeutics that has been internalised to the level of reflexive second nature – metaphilosophical in so far as it assumes certain methods, criteria and borrowed theoretical approaches instead of tarrying with the philosophical problem of what it means to be a philosophical science that, if rigorously philosophical, cannot start with a blind confidence of those methods, criteria or borrowed models of theoretical construction.[40] The infamous 'way of despair' that Hegel notes later in the Introduction is precisely that path in which one not only does not know the way in which it will develop, but that also has to be constructed, somewhat paradoxically, by being pursued.[41] What is proper to philosophy – its subject-matter – is, then, nothing that can either be appropriated by an extrinsic non-scientific thought or be appropriated as such (since it is produced by spirit as spirit's own production). The starting point of the *Phenomenology*, the natural assumption, is the start that unfolds both the critique of the limits of the use of extrinsic mechanisms, and the fact that one must start with what presents itself as the most culturally dominant way of starting to philosophise – which, for Hegel, is the codified form of philosophical production in the university system that is internalised, as if it were truth and not representation, by the subject of philosophy.

This sense of the natural assumption as an appropriated mode of thinking overdetermined by private property relations suggests, once again, that we cannot therefore simply explicate the opening of the *Phenomenology* as a theoretical critique of the presuppositions of modern epistemology but, rather, that it should also be understood as a constellated, overdetermined phenomena that contains within itself, although in abstracted form, the mediation of the critique of epistemology by the private property relations that structure modern civil society.

Conclusion

A structural presupposition of the reflections set out in this essay has been to take seriously – to the point of exaggeration – an important caveat and proviso of the reading of the *Phenomenology* that Hegel makes in his prefatory remarks to the book: 'Impatience demands the impossible, to wit, the attainment of the end without the means. But the length of this path has to be endured, because, for one thing, each moment is necessary; and further, each moment has to be *lingered* (*verweilen*) over.'[42] I have tried to linger over the natural assumption by inquiring into what mediates its mode of appearance – what allows it to 'come on the scene' (*Auftreten*), as Hegel likes to put it in the *Phenomenology* – as construed from the standpoint of a concept of history as an ensemble of relational social processes (institutions, practices, etc.).[43] I have tried to do this so as to offer an alternative perspective from which to reflect on the opening of Hegel's celebrated 1807 work.

Crucial to this, as I have argued, is the way in which the relations of private property that structure civil society overdetermine the sense in which cognition, as a result of the natural assumption, emerges as a means (instrument/medium) through which one possesses the absolute. In so far as the absolute is the higher order dialectical unity of ourselves as subject and object (of spirit in a moment of its self-formation) the absolute is something that can be neither privately owned (as it is an expression of the totality of spirit) nor publicly distributed (as this still presupposes a social asymmetry of access, acquisition and alienation since it assumes a subject that carries out the distribution and one who receives it).

This allows us to consider the ways in which the natural assumption in the Introduction to the *Phenomenology* is an expression of a socio-historical phenomenon that is considerably more complicated than the narrower epistemological concerns with which it is usually associated. Philosophical cognition, and the problem of how to start to philosophise, is not a uniquely theoretical problem concerned with the possibility of knowing the mode of knowing most adequate to knowing the absolute. It is also, for Hegel, a constellated problematic of other social processes and practices that render its appearance possible – processes that allow it to emerge as a phenomenon that has crystallised in such a way that it can be immediately deployed as a starting point. In other words, Hegel's *Phenomenology* does not start solely from the premise of an idealised interrogation of modern theories of cognition – idealised by assuming a historical body of knowledge that one could totalise as 'modern epistemology' – but also from a socially and historically and specific object, one that contains within itself the processes that allow it to appear as an ideal, isolatable, generalised form.

Hammam Aldouri holds a PhD from the Centre for Research in Modern European Philosophy, Kingston University. He teaches at Moore College of Art and Design and Temple University, Philadelphia.

Notes

1. I would like to thank Stephen Howard for his valuable suggestions, critical insights and unwavering encouragement. Special thanks also to Peter Osborne, who guided much of the work presented here when it was in germinal form.
2. G.W.F. Hegel, *Phenomenology of Spirit*, trans. A.V. Miller (Oxford: Oxford University Press, 1977), 56; G.W.F. Hegel, *Phänomenologie des Geistes* (Frankfurt am Main: Suhrkamp, 1983), 80. The English pagination of the *Phenomenology* will henceforth be followed by the German when direct reference to the German is noted.
3. Hegel, *Phenomenology*, 46, 68. Emphasis added and translation of *bemächtige* as 'to get hold of' amended, see note 32.
4. Hegel famously presented this problematic in later works by way of an allegory of 'learning to swim' without getting into the water. See G.W.F. Hegel, *Lectures on the History of Philosophy, Volume 3*, trans. E.S. Haldane and Frances H. Simson (Lincoln and London: University of Nebraska Press, 1995), 428; and G.W.F. Hegel, *The Encyclopedia Logic*, trans. T.F. Geraets, W.A. Suchting and H.S. Harris (Indianapolis: Hackett Publishing Company, 1991), 34 and 82.
5. For example, see Robert C. Solomon *In the Spirit of Hegel: A Study of G.W.F. Hegel's Phenomenology of Spirit* (Oxford: Oxford University Press, 1983); Kenneth Westphal, *Hegel's Epistemological Realism: A Study of the Aim and Method of Hegel's Phenomenology* (Dordrecht: Kluwer Academic Publishers, 1989); Terry Pinkard, *Hegel's Phenomenology: The Sociality of Reason* (Cambridge: Cambridge University Press, 1994); Tom Rockmore *Cognition: An Introduction to Hegel's Phenomenology of Spirit* (Berkeley: University of California Press, 1997); and Karin de Boer, 'Hegel's Conception of Immanent Critique: Its Sources, Extent and Limit', in *Conceptions of Critique in Modern and Contemporary Philosophy*, eds. Karin de Boer and Ruth Sonderegger (Basingstoke: Palgrave MacMillan, 2012), 83–100.
6. The distinction between the limits of cognition and the boundaries of reason are perhaps rendered most clear in the difference between the *immanent* ('within the limits of possible experience') and *transcendent* ('those that would fly beyond these boundaries') use of principles of reason. Immanuel Kant, *Critique of Pure Reason*, trans. Paul Guyer and Allen Wood (Cambridge: Cambridge University Press, 1998), 385.
7. This sense of the 'burden' of human reason is a reference to the first sentence of the preface to the first edition of the *Critique of Pure Reason*. See Kant, *Critique of Pure Reason*, 99.
8. Ludiwg Siep, *Hegel's Phenomenology of Spirit*, trans. D. Smyth (Cambridge: Cambridge University Press, 2014), 63.
9. Siep claims that Hegel perhaps had Jacobi in mind since the latter 'thought it essential to insulate the faithful intuition of God from all concepts of the understanding.' Siep, *Hegel's Phenomenology*, 64. Ardis Collins offers us an alternative reference point. She notes that perhaps Hegel had Reinhold in mind in the Introduction since the latter, according to Hegel's devastating critique of his work in the 1801 *Differenzschrift*, posits the absolute as if it were an immediately known and objective philosophical result that simply needs philosophically reconstructing. See Ardis Collins, *Hegel's Phenomenology: The Dialectical Justification of Philosophy's First Principles* (Montreal and Kingston: McGill-Queen's University Press, 2013), 176. Evangelia Sembou gives us a broader reference point: Hegel's Introduction is concerned with the 'tradition' of modern epistemology that runs from Descartes to Kant. See Sembou, *Hegel's Phenomenology and Foucault's Genealogy* (Farnham: Ashgate, 2015), 14. In an older text, Werner Marx notes, in his excellent study of the 'Preface' and 'Introduction' to the *Phenomenology*, that the 'Cartesian principle of self-consciousness was among the "self-evident truths" of the "culture" of Hegel's day.' Werner Marx, *Hegel's Phenomenology of Spirit: A Commentary Based on the Preface and Introduction*, trans. P. Heath (Chicago: University of Chicago Press, 1975), 2. I borrow the notion of 'iconology' from Erwin Panofsky's exposition of the idea in his major work *Studies in Iconology* (Oxford: Oxford University Press, 1939).
10. Kant described his *Critique of Pure Reason* as a propaedeutic. Kant, *Critique of Pure Reason*, 123, 133 and 149.
11. G.W.F. Hegel, *The Philosophical Propaeduetic*, trans. A.V. Miller (Oxford: Basil Blackwell, 1986).
12. G.W.F. Hegel, *Hegel: The Letters*, trans. C. Butler and C. Seiler

(Bloomington IN: Indiana University Press, 1984), 280.

13. G.W.F. Hegel, *The Miscellaneous Writings of G.W.F. Hegel*, ed. J. Stewart (Evanston IL: Northwestern University Press, 2004), 252. Hegel allegorises the separation of learning to philosophise from philosophical knowledge by another mode of artisanal work (that of the leather shoemaker) in the *Phenomenology*. See Hegel, *Phenomenology*, 41, 63.

14. Hegel, *Lectures on the History of Philosophy, Volume 3*, 428. On a critical sociological account of the social field of academic work within the European university complex, see Pierre Bourdieu, *Homo Academicus*, trans. P. Collier (Stanford: Stanford University Press, 1988).

15. This notion of institutionalisation as enforced condition of philosophical practice that gets internalised by a subject as if it constituted the true mode of philosophical production could be systematically reconstructed in light of Hegel's earlier notion of 'positivity'. The latter is, according to Hegel's first major Bern writing, the reconfiguration of Jesus' 'virtue religion' into an authoritarian doctrine of moral obligation by way of the power of the Church-State. See G.W.F. Hegel, *Early Theological Writings*, trans. T.M. Knox (Philadelphia: Pennsylvania State University Press, 1975), 75–86.

16. Hegel, *Phenomenology*, 47.

17. Collins, *Hegel's Phenomenology*, 173.

18. Perhaps one reason for Collins' immediate turn to the 'we' is that it appears in Miller's translation of the opening sentence. Michael Inwood's peculiar recent translation completely covers over the reference to the 'one'. Instead, he renders the sentence as follows: 'It is a natural idea that in philosophy, before we come to deal with the Thing itself, namely with the actual cognition of what in truth is, it is necessary first to come to an understanding about cognition, which is regarded as the instrument by which we take possession of the absolute, or as the medium through which we catch sight of it.' G.W.F. Hegel, *Hegel: The Phenomenology of Spirit*, trans. M. Inwood (Cambridge: Cambridge University Press, 2018), 35. Both J.B. Baillie's somewhat forgotten translation as well as Terry Pinkard's new edition offer us a more precise rendition of the German: 'It is a natural supposition that in philosophy, before one gets down to dealing with what is at issue, namely, the actual cognition of what, in truth, is, it is first necessary to come to an understanding about cognition, which is regarded as the instrument by which one seizes hold of the absolute or as the means by which one catches sight of it.' G.W.F. Hegel, *The Phenomenology of Spirit*, trans. T. Pinkard (Cambridge: Cambridge University Press, 2018), 49. 'It is natural to suppose that, before philosophy enters upon its subject proper – namely, the actual knowledge of what truly is – it is necessary to come first to an understanding concerning knowledge, which is looked upon as the instrument by which to take possession of the Absolute, or as the means through which to get a sight of it.' G.W.F. Hegel, *Phenomenology of Mind*, trans. J.B. Baillie (New York: Harper and Row, 1967), 131.

19. Hegel, *Phenomenology*, 110.

20. This is a central concern of two recent collections of essays: Italo Testa, ed., *I that is We, We that is I: Perspectives on Contemporary Hegel* (Leiden: Brill, 2016); and Heikki Ikäheimo and Arto Laitinen, eds., *Recognition and Social Ontology* (Leiden: Brill, 2011). For a conception of Hegel's social ontology that that does not situate his thought in relation to pragmatism, see Georg Lukács, *The Ontology of Social Being: Hegel*, trans. D. Fernbach (London: Merlin, 1978).

21. G.W.F. Hegel, *System of Ethical Life and First Philosophy of Spirit*, trans. H.S. Harris (Albany NY: State University of New York Press, 1979), 228.

22. Hegel's critique of Reinhold's reduction of philosophy to philosophical logic that, when viewed historically, accounts to nothing more than the image of philosophical systems as idiosyncratic views bolted onto a preexisting image of the history of philosophy as the endless aggregation of those views anticipates the concept of the 'spurious infinite'. See G.W.F. Hegel, *Science of Logic*, trans. A.V. Miller (London and New York: Routledge, 2010), 139.

23. G.W.F. Hegel, *The Difference Between Fichte's and Schelling's System of Philosophy*, trans. H.S. Harris (Albany NY: State University of New York, 1977), 86.

24. Hegel, *Difference*, 86. Interestingly, Reinhold's commitment to universalising philosophical logic so as to be universally valid is a politico-ethical injunction that Hegel retains in his own work. The promise of raising philosophy to the standpoint of universalised cultural language is made note of in Hegel's famous unsent letter to the German classicist J.H. Voss in 1805. Hegel, *Letters*, 107.

25. Hegel, *Difference*, 86. (Translation slightly modified.)

26. The practice of repetition finds its most ironic formalisation in Hegel's analysis of the emptiness of consciousness as emptiness of being in the repetitive practice of the Vedic *Om*. Hegel, *Science of Logic*, 97.

27. It should be noted that university students were almost exclusively male in the eighteenth and nineteenth century Germanophone context. For an excellent study of this history, see Patricia Mazón, *Gender and the Modern Research University: The Admission of Women to German Higher Education, 1865-1914* (Stanford: Stanford University Press, 2003).

28. Hegel, *Phenomenology*, 3.

29. Hegel, *Difference*, 88. On 'diremption', see *Difference*, 89-90.

30. Ibid., 88.

31. Hegel, *Phenomenology*, 7.

32. Miller's translation of the verb *bemächtigen* as 'to get hold of' somewhat downplays the more aggressive socio-political connotations of the expression. Baillie and Pinkard come closer to it when they translate it as 'to take possession' and 'seizes hold of', respectively.

33. This attentiveness to private property relations is no doubt due to his interest in Rousseau's thought (in particular, of the *Second Discourse*, in this context). The Genevan was, as a school friend of Hegel's once noted, the latter's 'hero ... whose works he continually read.' Cited in H.S. Harris, *Hegel's Ladder, Volume 1: The Pilgrimage of Reason* (Indianapolis and London: Hackett, 1997), 2.

34. On the relation of Hegel's writings on love to the concept of recognition in his mature writings, see Robert R. Williams, *Recognition: Fichte and Hegel on the Other* (Albany NY: State University of New York Press, 1992), 74-80.

35. Hegel, *Early Theological Writings*, 302–308.

36. On the 'atomism' of civil society, see G.W.F. Hegel, *Encyclopaedia of Philosophical Sciences: Philosophy of Spirit*, trans. A.V. Miller (Oxford: Oxford University Press, 2003), 256–257. On 'the need of philosophy', see Hegel, *Difference*, 89–93.

37. The following historical and sociological remarks draw heavily from Charles E. McClelland's excellent social history of the modern German university system. See his *State, Society, and University in Germany: 1700-1914* (Cambridge: Cambridge University Press, 1980). On the context of the development of universities in Prussia after 1806, see R. S. Turner, 'The Prussian university and the university imperative, 1806 to 1848', unpublished PhD Thesis (Princeton: Princeton University, 1972). (I am grateful to Ryan Dahn for this reference.) For more expansive analyses of the European university system in the early modern period, see also Hilde de Ridder-Symoens, *A History of the University in Europe, Volume II: Universities in Early Modern Europe, 1500-1800* (Cambridge: Cambridge University Press, 1996).

38. But this transformation of the university into finishing schools for bureaucrats was radically uneven throughout the eighteenth century for a number of interconnected reasons: wars, the tensions among principalities and the state, the consistent decline in student numbers, financial mismanagement, a slow but relatively steady attack on the institution by public opinion, and so on.

39. To be more precise, the rate of pay of the 'extraordinaries' was seldom enough to make a living. Thus, most had to augment their income by other means (private tutoring, writing journalistic articles, etc.). See McClelland, *State, Society, and University*, 81.

40. This is why the Introduction to the *Phenomenology* quickly turns into an posited examination of the philosophical lexicon one immediately deploys when one philosophises – 'absolute', 'cognition', etc. Hegel, *Phenomenology*, 48.

41. Ibid., 49.

42. Ibid., 17, 13. Martin Heidegger offers us a model of the imperative of patience. His essay 'Hegel's Concept of Experience' is one of the most protracted philosophical interpretations of a single moment in Hegel's thought. See Martin Heidegger, *Off the Beaten Track*, trans. J. Young and K. Haynes (Cambridge: Cambridge University Press, 2002), 86–156. In a recent work, Rebecca Comay and Frank Ruda exacerbate Hegel's injunction by focusing on Hegel's use of the non-linguistic semantic notation of the dash, a mark that appears at the end of the *Phenomenology* and in the opening sentence of Hegel's exposition of being in the *Science of Logic*. See Rebecca Comay and Frank Ruda, *The Dash – The Other Side of Absolute Knowing* (Cambridge MA and London: MIT Press, 2018).

43. Hegel, *Phenomenology*, 48, 71.

---

independent thinking from polity

A Left that Dares to Speak Its Name
34 Untimely Interventions
Slavoj Žižek

With irrepressible humor, Slavoj Žižek dissects our current political and social climate, discussing everything from Jordan Peterson and sex "unicorns" to Greta Thunberg and Chairman Mao. This wide-ranging collection of essays provides the perfect insight into the ideas of one of the most influential radical thinkers of our time.

PB 978-1-5095-4118-8 | March 2020 | £14.99

Violence and Political Theory
Elizabeth Frazer & Kimberly Hutchings

"This excellent book offers a very careful, systematic and immensely readable introduction and analysis of the intersection between violence and politics, from Machiavelli to the present day."
Vittorio Bufacchi, University College Cork, Ireland

PB 978-1-5095-3672-6 | April 2020 | £15.99

Migrants and Militants
Alain Badiou

Writing with the rigor, clarity, and polemical flair that have made him one of the world's most influential philosophers, and drawing on a rich body of material including contemporary poetry and the words of an anonymous migrant, Badiou develops a powerful riposte to those who have stoked the fear of migrants and exploited the migration question for political ends.

PB 978-1-5095-4246-8 | March 2020 | £9.99

The Black Register
Tendayi Sithole

"Tendayi Sithole is one of the most generative thinkers of his generation, in any hemisphere. A bold and sublime meditation on how key black thinkers have confronted the ongoing catastrophe of anti-blackness, The Black Register builds on the past to enact a new form of Black political resistance."
Robin D. G. Kelley, author of *Freedom Dreams: The Black Radical Imagination*

PB 978-1-5095-4207-9 | March 2020 | £17.99

Order your copy now:
free phone 0800 243407 | politybooks.com

 @politybooks 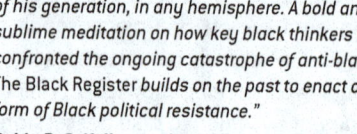 facebook.com/politybooks

Dare to think!

ROBERT BERNASCONI
BRENNA BHANDAR
FRANÇOISE COLLIN
SIMON CRITCHLEY
PENELOPE DEUTSCHER
MEENA DHANDA
HARRY HAROOTUNIAN
PAULINE JOHNSON
CHRISTIAN KERSLAKE
PHILIPPE LACOUE-LABARTHE
KOLJA LINDNER
JOSEPH McCARNEY
ANDREW McGETTIGAN
PETER OSBORNE
ROSA & CHARLEY PARKIN
STELLA SANDFORD
LYNNE SEGAL
ALBERTO TOSCANO

ÉRIC ALLIEZ
ARIELLA AZOULAY
ÉTIENNE BALIBAR
BORIS BUDEN
HOWARD CAYGILL
SIMON CRITCHLEY
PHILIP DERBYSHIRE
ANNA-SABINE ERNST
PETER HALLWARD
AXEL HONNETH
GERWIN KLINGER
LYNDA NEAD
OMEDI OCHIENG
PETER OSBORNE
ANSON RABINBACH
JONATHAN RÉE
BILL SCHWARZ
JOHN SELLARS
CORNELIA SORABJI

a new series of books from radical philosophy archive

EDITED BY AUSTIN GROSS, MATT HARE & MARIE LOUISE KROGH

PAPERBACK 400 pages UK£14.99/US$22.00
ISBN 1 978-1-9162292-0-4 2 978-1-9162292-2-8
DOWNLOAD www.radicalphilosophyarchive.com

The philosophical disability of reason
Evald Ilyenkov's critique of machinic intelligence
Keti Chukhrov

Present theories of computation and artificial intelligence often claim that philosophy should either discard its principal modes of gnoseology (that is, its theories of knowledge and cognition) and anthropomorphic genesis, or declare philosophical speculation obsolete altogether, since it fails to provide any precise knowledge regarding the most significant contemporary scientific and technological concerns. If post-structuralism doubted the power of philosophy because of its proximity to the sciences and their own discrete discourses, contemporary 'post-philosophies', by contrast, refuse philosophy because of its insufficient knowledge of science and technology.[1]

Two principal contemporary post-philosophical tendencies stand out in this regard. The first is found in cognitivist theories, which posit philosophy as an obsolete cognitive practice, a quasi-mythological narrative that produces fictitious non-scientific notions such as transcendentality, metaphysics, idea, dialectics, the universal or truth. This tendency can be represented by the likes of Thomas Metzinger and Marvin Minsky, as well as cybernetic scholars who argue that mathematical logic should supersede a dialectical one. Others, like the media engineer and theorist Benjamin Bratton, simply describe the sensorics of machinic intelligence without even trying to consider this in relation to any broader context of the humanities.[2]

Another tendency is more subtle and interesting. It posits algorithimic creativity itself as a philosophical procedure. Reclaiming philosophical thought, it confines it mainly to the body of computation. It states that reason itself has drastically changed its intentionality, epistemology and motives with modern scientific and technical breakthroughs. Here, in the works of Luciana Parisi and Reza Negarestani, among others, we come across a series of elaborate standpoints for reconstituting the tasks of philosophy after and as a result of computation.

In this article I intend to consider the premises of thought grounded in computation theory (Negarestani, Parisi) in order to show how in a similar situation – when, in the Soviet 1960s, cybernetic studies were claimed as *the* new philosophical discipline – a communist thought, exemplified here by the writings of Evald Ilyenkov, developed its own militant postulates of what reason is, and why its algorithmic emulation would be impossible.

Reason as functionality

In their recent writings, both Negarestani and Parisi search within the mind, human as it is, for a *function* that would be 'non-human', and which would have no cognitive continuity with the dimension of mind and thought inscribed in human experience, consciousness, history or mortality. Such treatment of the inhumanness of thought, and accompanying theories of autonomous autopoetic intelligence,[3] is not concerned with expanding the human mind towards something cognitively supreme, but rather insists on an entire reconsideration of mind as an inhuman capacity.[4] Referring to Alan Turing, for example, Negarestani argues that there is nothing in the human that could not be abstracted and computationally realised.[5] Not only is a human able to become other in the long run of evolution, but it is able to regard its historical human-ness as other than human.[6]

For Negarestani, mind should thus become first and foremost an exertion of *functions*. Consequently, it is possible to find an appropriate algorithmisation for concept formation, or thought's intentionality, as well as for the application of any meaning. The senses, perception and intentionality, which were hitherto considered inaccessible to machinic intelligence, can now also be inscribed into the machine and algorithimic computation. Indeed, such functionalism, Negarestani insists, was already present in the philosophical tradition in works by Plato, the Stoics, Hegel, Kant, Sellars, and so on.

Negarestani blames modern continental philosophy precisely for what created philosophy – doubt and the articulation of the incapacities of human reason in the face of the Absolute. Indeed, philosophy, throughout its history from Kant to Derrida, has often emphasised the limits of mind in its striving towards the Absolute and the unthinkable horizons of the ineffable. For Negarestani, however, the ineffability of thought is not about its complexity, in a way which questions the instrumentalisation and optimisation of thought, and therefore chooses to become unthinkable; it is simply mind's failure. As Negarestani argues, philosophy in its critique of metaphysics has only ended in limiting thought with 'arguments about various *disabilities*'.[7] According to this view, what makes human thought significant can thus be realised by different individuating discrete properties, inputs, outputs and realisers. Consequently, it is precisely with 'algorithmic intelligence' that a truly productive speculation and thinking can begin.

In her various writings, Luciana Parisi goes even further and disavows the stereotype according to which cybernetics is confined to mere computation.[8] This stereotype has traditionaly been a motivation for doubting the thinking potentialities of computation on the part of philosophy and the humanities in general. However, the principal condition of computation, Parisi insists, is much more complex and is based on the premise of *the incomputable*; a term borrowed by Parisi from the media theorist Gregory Chaitin. The principal presumption in this apology for computation is that, according to Parisi, unlike the cybernetics of the 1950s (first-order cybernetics), which was based on prearranged units, second-order cybernetics (and all the more so, present forms of automation) has changed: it can precisely analyse and compare. As Parisi argues, 'automation can be dynamic and not dependent on a prescribed set of calculables'. Such is the case with algorithms for the second generation of cybernetics, where things 'can run their course with no apriori prior set of rules determining them'.[9] The principal proof for this, according to Parisi, is that, in any computational process, output is greater than input and not necessarily tied to it: 'Between input and output entropic transformation of data occurs. This number of incomputable is infinite'. Incomputability (and generally the algorithimic mode of thought) 'is not simply a break from reason, but reason expanded beyond its limits to involve the processing of maximally unknown parts that have no teleological finality'.[10]

In this new alien mode of thought, as opposed to the old, 'organic' and critical one, incomputable infinities proliferate within (and simultaneously with) the computability of algorithms, and are able to change initial conditions. These incomputable infinities, not prescribed by any input, can express ends that do not match the finality of organic thought. What is 'new' here is that 'in this dynamic processing of infinities, results are not contained in the logical premises of the system'.[11] Incomputability as the crucial function of reason (which is in fact nothing but the probability of contingency, I would argue) has entered the automated infrastructure of cognition as a new *episteme* and is termed by Parisi a 'soft' thought. This new soft thought – the thought generated by 'undecidable propositions within logic' – aligns, according to Parisi, with Goedel's conception of infinity far better than does a so-called organic, critical thought, which is predictable in its provisions of logic.[12]

In her *Contagious Architecture*, Parisi considers 'autopoiesis' and the incomputable nature of algorithmic proliferation at even greater length. Here she manages to show that the autonomy of incomputable algorithmic probabilities is not simply an abstraction extracted from reality, in the vein of, for example, Felix Guattari's a-sygnifying semiology.[13] The autonomy of algorithmic probabilities has lost its epistemic bond with abstract logic and meta-semiology. By contrast, Guattari's abstract logic and meta-semiology – even when they happen to be *detached from reality*, and despite forming contingent and autopoietic series, extracted from reality – retain a correlation with that reality. In other words, Guattari's a-sygnifying semiology still preserves a certain connection with reality even in the act of its disjunction from reality (the signified). Here, abstraction as the act of detachment and autonomisation from reality is evident and explicit. By contrast, in the case of algorithmic probabilities, the very act of disjunction from reality is lost and redundant. The generative realm of algorithms is pure creativity without any analogy, or *any act of detachment* from reality. Parisi is therefore right when she says that the incomputable loops of algorithmisation can engender 'realia', which have no connectivity whatsoever with the organic world, life, human being, 'organic' thought, and so on.

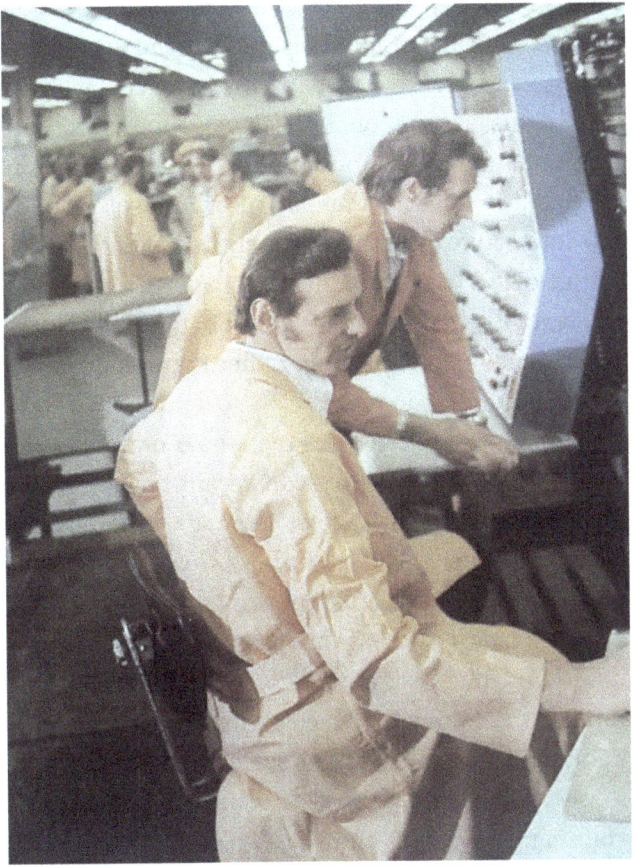

To put this another way, what is created in algorithmic design is not an alternative picture of the world, or a gesture of denial of this world, or a transformation of it; it is just a soft or liquid chain of objecthoods engendered almost *ex nihilo*. It is worth noting, then, that the immanence of abstract units in Guattari cannot be smoothly translated into the type of immanence of algorithimic generativity that Parisi describes, because Guattari's mathematical, virtual and semiological abstractions continue to be logical essences.[14] (That is to say, Guattari's alternative semiology and its distinctive terminology – rhizome instead of structure, abstract machines instead of phonocentric enunciation, asygnifying diagrammes instead of signification chains – still presuppose references to the realm of logic.) The algorithmic realm, conversely, is a set of directives, prescriptions, functions and feedbacks; its functional role is epistemically something other than logic and abstraction. This is why Parisi constantly reiterates the extent to which *prehension* and *pre-emptiveness* are important for this mode of production. In this case, what is created in algorithmic generativity precedes any world, or any word and reflection on it. Such pre-emption randomly abducts the potentialities of a world, which could have been eventually formalised by logic a posteriori. The semantic potentialities are pre-emptively abducted, withdrawn and algorithmisised, before any reflection on the world, life and reality takes place. The proper case of such pre-emption is the agency of incomputable algorithms, in so far as they create bubbles of self-sufficient creative redundancies. In order for this quasi-creative 'vicious' infinity to acquire any creative sense, one has therefore to defy human subjectivity and reason, as these self-generative algorithmic immanences precisely *cannot be* creativities for human imagination and reason.[15]

Parisi's focus on the randomness of final outcomes and outputs – outcomes and outputs which are not projected in inputs – might remind one of, for example, Deleuze's treatment of the event, or his poetics of the throw of dice. Yet for Parisi the incomputable, despite being infinite, should remain completely discrete and countable, even when it is only a potentiality. In *Contagious Architecture*, she seeks to demonstrate how the incomputability of algorithms is nevertheless a discrete unity and 'always corresponds to a quantity'.[16] The incomputable is not, then, 'the unthinkable'. It does not imply any stoppage of 'the machine' or its fatal error, as is the case with Deleuze's speculations concerning a halt inscribed in the machine.[17] The incomputable is simply the still unapplied options of data which have a chance to be generated without being prescribed in the input. Arguably, the fact that computables potentially contain incomputable infinities, which are even immanent to the computables, does not, then, make that very 'incomputable' a confirmation of a philosophical paradox. Parisi's 'incomputable' does not exceed the *discreteness* of reversible, incompressible data. 'The incomputable' is simply the potential data not yet engaged, but implied as the capacity of the algorithmic input to generate unpredicted infinite chains of data, which, despite not being prescribed, can still emerge contingently and autopoetically and be at work, potentially or actually.

In fact, this disjunction between input and output, as generating incomputable infinities within the network, was already revealed by Warren McCulloch and Walter Pitts in the early 1940s. When trying to deduce 'how we know what we know', they suggested getting information about the inside of the brain in order to emulate the neural diagram of how perception evolves. As Slava Gerovich relates, McCulloch and Pitts constructed for this an artificial neural network that could represent logical function, and where, conversely, any logical function could be translated into a neural network. By this they wanted to prove that knowledge has a neural construction and that any logical function can be implemented in formal neural networks. In a nutshell, they sought to deduce the brain's input, the 'black box' (the imprint of facts about external world inside the brain), from its outputs (our perception). Yet, the epistemological ambition of their project failed. As Gerovich writes, McCulloch and Pitts were thus forced to acknowledge that 'from the perceptions retrieved from one's memory, it was not possible to deduce the "facts" that caused those perception'.[18] Nonetheless, McCulloch and Pitts continued to deny this failure. Instead, they simply contended that 'the limitations of their formal model of the brain confirmed fundamental limitations of our knowledge of the world'. Meanwhile the only discovery obtained through the experiment was that 'even if we cannot know the world, the nervous system can at least compute infinite numbers as a universal logical machine'.[19]

We see in this experiment how the epistemological failure to compute knowledge and cognition, i.e., the incommensurable incomputability of thought (the inability to compute input from output), was ultimately ignored and simply superseded by the capacity to produce infinite and contingently produced data at the output *irrespective of input*; this infinitely produced autopoetic data is the very *incomputable* described by Parisi, and it is nothing but infinite number potentially circulated and emitted by the neural network.

Reason's disability

As Paolo Virno points out in his *Multitude Between Innovation and Negation*, a human being, unlike animals, is destined to *neoteny*;[20] that is, the retention of protective capacities for surviving in natural environments – a condition in which the existence of the human species is grounded. This insurmountable neoteny of the human species provides the motivation to produce a second nature – culture, language and intelligent and technological worlds – as the form of inherent incapacity and weakness of the human as an animal. From this perspectice, a human being, then, is a deficient species unable to adapt to its natural environment within and by means of its own morphology of species being. A consequence of such disability is the demand for thought to be general and to evolve in concert and dependence with others, in common. Hence, the young Marx's idea that communism cannot but be a necessity for nature inhabited by a deficient human species, unable to integrate into nature by means of merely its own morphology. In this case, a projection of the universality of human existence is a necessity deriving from the phylogenetic weakness of a human being, rather than, as it is often read, a pretension to power.[21]

In his text, 'Where does the Mind Come from', Soviet philosopher Evald Ilyenkov recalls how Alexander Suvorov (a pupil at the Zagorsk Internat for the blind and deaf,[22] who later graduated from Moscow University and defended his PhD dissertation in psychology) was giving a speech before students and was asked the following question: 'Your case contradicts the old premise of materialism, according to which all that gets into mind is necessarily developed and provided by senses. If your senses are damaged, if you can not hear or see, how could your mind develop?' The question was transmitted to Suvorov via dactile alphabet, and he answered into the microphone: 'and why do you think that we do not hear and see? We are not blind and deaf, we see and hear by the eyes of all our friends, all people, all humankind'.[23]

We see in this example an argument for the early Marx's idea that the human emerges only after privatisation and selfhood are surpassed in favour of generic being or *Gatungswesen* – which is often translated as species-being but which, in fact, implies the condition of the *non-self being* producing the potentiality for the generic. (I will return in a moment to the ways in which, I think, this category of the *non-self being* is connected with the speculative tools of generalisation as against formal abstraction.) Ilyenkov's example of the deaf and blind thinker who sees, hears and even thinks via an other's sense, brains and thinking provides an example of how in fact the gravest deficiency enables development of thought through socially-based, mutual activity:

in this case, the lack in the self entails, for Ilyenkov, the necessity for the other-self, and hence establishes the principle of an other-determined non-self being that grounds the generic being.

Evald Ilyenkov developed his own philosophical gnoseology from the late 1960s when the discoveries of quantum physics and cybernetics were much occupying the minds of a Soviet intelligentsia, and were promising, like today, to resolve numerous issues concerning sociality, politics and ontology. Since his arguments dispute the pretension of 'post-philosophies' either to dismiss philosophy or to promote post-philosophical premises as the 'new' or proper philosophy, they acquire, I want to argue, a new relevance today, in the light of contemporary tensions between critical theory across the humanities and the new post-philosophic theories that have sought to ground themselves in the hard sciences or in cybernetics.

In the Soviet 1960s and 1970s a new generation of mathematical logicians and cybernetic scholars – some from neurophysiology and some from linguistics and economics – tried to endow cybernetic discoveries with the political stakes of Marxist philosophy.[24] The main strategic method for claiming cybernetic theory and informatics as philosophy was in positing systemic theory and computation as dialectical procedures; cybernetics had to acquire, that is, a broader philosophical conceptualisation than simply being an applied field of computation. Veniamin Pushkin and Arkady Ursul in their *Informatics, Cybernetics, Intellect* (*Informatika, Kibernetika, Intellekt*, 1979) discuss the attempt of cybernetic scholars, in this vein, to claim information as the attribute of matter, as its principal reflection (*otrajenie*) and not simply matter's systemic feature among many other features. In this effort one can clearly discern, in the context of a Soviet academia for which only philosophy could have a proper social and ideological influence, the striving to endow cybernetic research with philosophical authority. If Dmitry Pospelov and Modest Gaaze-Rappoport's book *From the Amoeba to a Robot* (1987),[25] for example, was only a study of systemic isomorphism between biophysics, neurophysiology, robotics and social psychology – between reflexological behaviour and the systematisation and modeling of information – Pushkin and Ursul's book already attempts to inscribe informatics (or a theory of cybernetics) into a broader field of philosophical gnoseology.

In fact, despite stating that philosophy and cybernetics have different goals of generalisation, Pushkin and Ursul nonetheless argue very strongly in favor of positing cybernetics as an epistemic part of Marxist ideology and materialist dialectics. In this respect, they make three convincing points to counter the taboo against considering algorithmic intelligence as a form of thinking reason.

First, cybernetics, along with the control and management of systems, presupposes self-development (*samorazvitie*) and self-regulation (*samoreguljazia*), becoming self-learning in computation and cybernetics. From this point of view, self-development (or self-regulation) of matter, and generally any form of self-regulated material immanence – for example, blood circulation – is *already* a mode of cybernetics; in as much as the autopoesis of biological organisms is considered isomorphic with the autopoesis of systems and networks. Consequently, if one assumes that development is synonymous with dialectics, then the cybernetic coding of various forms of development can also be considered dialectical.[26]

Second, if consciousness is no longer a psychic category in its Marxist conceptualisation, but is determined by material processes and social environment, then cybernetics can help to undermine the principal arguments concerning the supposed impossibility of automating consciousness and of translating it into an algorithmic modeling. This is because, in the long run of evolution, consciousness has developed into a socio-neural system. Consequently, if an individual is part of the social system, then the system can regulate or model consciousness as its product.[27]

Finally, cybernetics is able to undermine the main argument on the part of philosophy that mathematical logic and the hard sciences only engage an instrumental rationality (*Verstand*), rather than the complexity of reason (*Vernunft*). Pushkin argues that, in its dialectical connection with ratiocination, reason over time inevitably becomes formalised and hence develops into ratiocination; in this case ratiocination is merely a former reason; consequently, by denying ratiocination the right to count as thought we limit thought itself.[28]

It is such premises that the communist arguments developed by Ilyenkov in his four texts written on machinic intelligence and philosophy – the two pamphlets 'The Mystery of the Black Box' (1968) and 'The Notes of the Bezumtsev' (1978), the didactic essay 'Machine and the Human: Cybernetics and Philosophy' (1966), and his seminal book *Lenin's Dialectics and Metaphysics of Positivism* (1980) – are intended to counter.

First, Ilyenkov argues, it is true that all biological internalities, blood circulation and digestion are self-regulated developing systems; but they cannot be regarded as dialectical only on the grounds of self-development. This is because dialectics implies a relation with the phenomena external to self-developing systems. Interestingly, Pushkin himself acknowledges that the autonomy of systemic self-regulation, on the one hand, and Pushkin's own emphasis on the priority of the human subject in navigating neural networks, on the other, don't go together. If dialectics implies a constant dis-identifying junction between the self and the non-self, then self-regulated systems and their self-developing autonomous immanences cannot be regarded as dialectical.

Second, even though Pushkin acknowledges the social dimension of consciousness, he nevertheless treats it as an evolutionary development of the brain, that is, still determined by reflexes, and the source of which, despite all its social extentions, remains in the brain. By contrast, according to the Marxist interpretation of consciousness (for example, in Vygotsky's psychology, or in Ilyenkov's own dialectical logic), consciousness is non-individual, external and generic/general by definition, i.e., the brain has always been a secondary, applied organ, both for consciousness and language.

Third, reason and ratiocination do not form a unit guaranteeing a necessary transmission of one into another. Thinking does not necessarily entail ratiocinating formalisation, and rationalising formalisation might not necessarily lead to any new intuitive leap of a thinking mind. Consequently, even if ratiocination remains reason in its formalised variation, within this formalisation ratiocination qualitatively changes to the point where it is no longer a thought procedure and its automatic reversibility into thought is not possible.

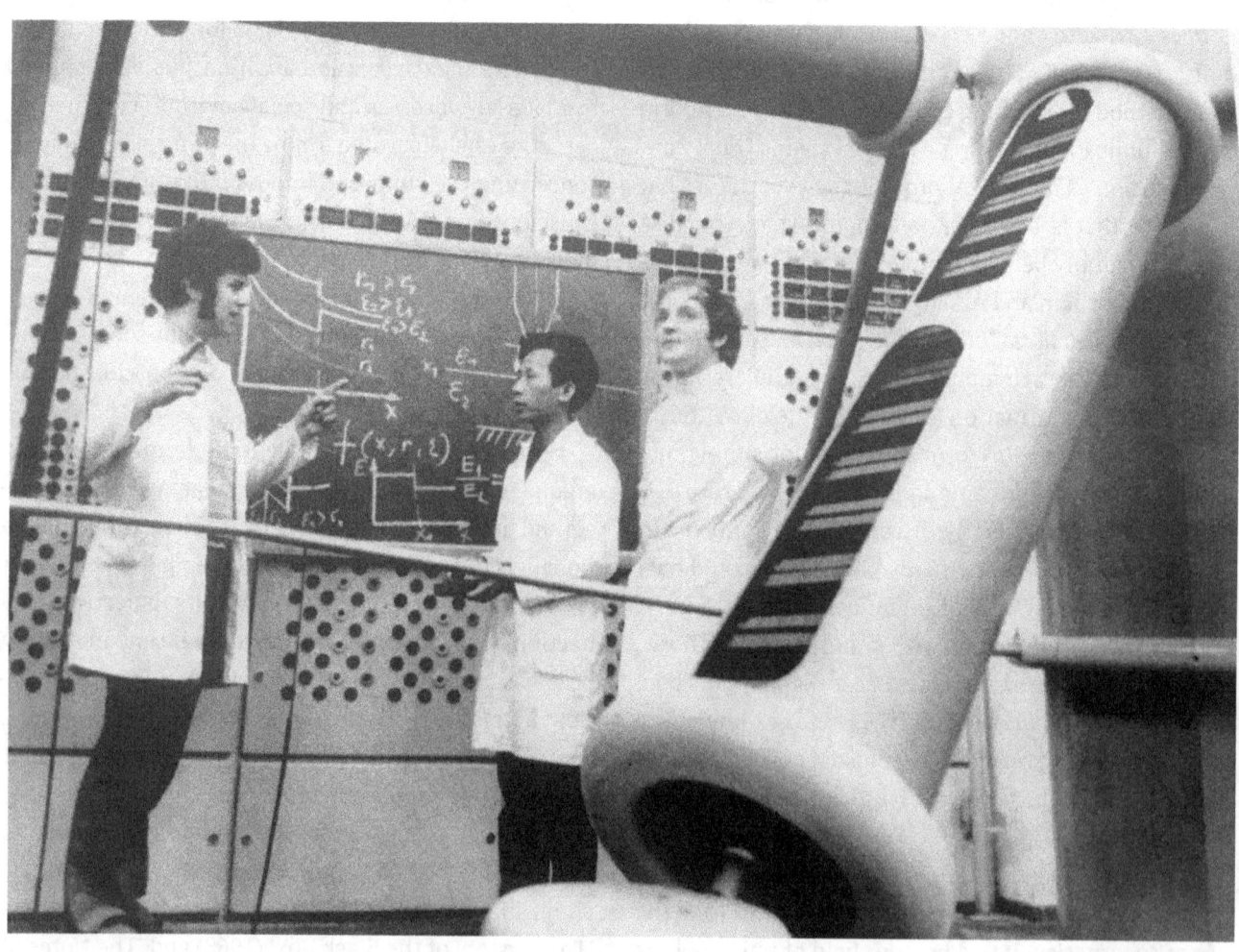

Even in his last book *Lenin's Dialectics and Metaphysics of Positivism* (1980),[29] Ilyenkov, referring in particular to Lenin's 1908 *Materialism and Empiriocriticism*, continued to reiterate his arguments as to why philosophy should not simply be identified with the hard sciences. As he argues, mere data cannot be cognised without gnoseological means of generalisation—and generalisation always entails dialectical contradiction. From this point of view, dialectical tension between the abstract and the concrete cannot be resolved via techno-naturalist isomorphisms; moreover, there can be no isomorphisms between cybernetic, biological, physical laws and their application to social life.

The context in which Ilyenkov was writing the above-mentioned texts was one of anxiety that philosophical gnoseology might well be superceded by intelligence programs and computational algorithms. Indeed, by the time of his pamphlet, 'The Notes of Bezumtsev', in 1978, numerous leading bureaucratic positions in Soviet academic philosophy and the humanities were occupied by former physicists, engineers and scientists.[30] Importantly, Ilyenkov's concern was thus not grounded in any obscurantist refusal of research into artificial intelligence, which for him was an indispensible technical complement to thought; but in his fears that dialectics as the principal philosophical method indispensible for a *communist* society was being displaced by positivist, discrete methods of quantification that were more applicable to the society of bureaucratic capitalism.

'The Notes of Bezumtsev' are written on behalf of a parodic character, a PhD of 'any' sciences, who is bored by all existing scientific fields, and who, in search of a new discipline, decides to combine canine expertise with cinematic theory (kino) to construct a new meta-theory of kinologia (*kinologia*). The science of kinologia would generalise not only dogs but those who generalise dogs in relation to another discipline: cinema. Ultimately, Ilyenkov's fictional pseudo-scientist lists several academicians he intends to collaborate with, which happen to be the distorted names of some of the most renowned Soviet cyberneticians of the 1970s: Victor Glushkov and Mikhail Rutkevich.[31] The main character's name in the pamphlet is Upriamzev (the obstinate); a direct reference to Boris Ukrainzev, an engineer and constructor who took charge of the Philosophy Institute of Academy of Sciences in 1974. As Andrei Maidansky writes in his foreword to *Ilyenkov's Philosophy and Contemporaneity*, Ukrainzev took up a career in philosophy after holding several party positions, including as head of one of the ideological sectors of the CPSU Central Committee. Having become the director of the Philosophy Institute, Ukrainzev founded and headed there the section devoted to the philosophical problems of cybernetics. According to Maidansky, 'for Ilyenkov appointing Ukrainzev as the Philosophy Institute director had devastating consequences. Ukrainzev was an embodiment of all Ilyenkov hated – ideological dictatorship combined with militant philosophic ignorance, justified by the newest achievements of contemporary science'.[32]

Similarly, in *The Mystery of Black Box*,[33] a pamphlet published in 1968, Ilyenkov created a technocratic dystopia in which there is a total supercession of reason and thought by machinic intelligence. The text is readable as seeking to reveal those parameters of dialectical logic that cannot be hijacked by algorithmic ratiocination. *The Mystery of Black Box* touches, in this way, upon some of the most crucial issues which are at stake today, I would argue, in the inquiry concerning what reason is. What are those components of human reason that cannot be emulated by any machinic intelligence? Is machinic intelligence able to become a sovereign autonomous autopoetic Subject, the epistemic nature of which is different from the human mode of speculation, or does it remain a complement of human reason? In other words, precisely those questions that Negarestani and Parisi claim to answer in their recent texts.

In the story told in Ilyenkov's 1968 pamphlet, a cybernetic scholar Adam Adamich decides that the human brain possesses no essential differences from machinic computation. Being sure that a machine has more chances to augment its intelligence than the very slowly developing mind of man, he invents an artificial intelligence intended to accelerate thinking processes. It emulates thinking more efficiently than the human brain. All those arguments about the qualitative difference of human intelligence from machinic intelligence, as represented by such categories as reason, will, the ideal or the sublime, are rejected by Adam Adamich as so much obsolete mythology; a mythology which was once mistaken for philosophy. The machine of augmented intelligence created by the scholar gradually proliferates into a broader neural system, allowing each machine to acquire the capacity to autonomously implement self-learning and self-improvement.

A problem however arises when one of the most advanced machines – 'a thinking ear' – reaches its ultimate goal: it 'learns' to hear everything on the planet; but since there are no sounds in the cosmos, its further perfection becomes unnecessary, whereas the algorithm of amelioration inscribed in its coding incessantly instigates the machine to develop further. This situation creates a contradiction: perfection is an unending capacity of an artificial intelligence, but there is no need in it. Eventually, in order to resolve such contradiction, the neural system establishes the authority of a 'Black Box': a meta-intelligence machine, which simply neutralises all contradictions, and in which all excessive data can vanish when not needed. Thus, when any other machine starts glitching because of contradiction, the Black Box immediately neutralises the problem. The Black Box becomes, in other words, a device to ingress and devour the excesses of algorithms and data that were not logically necessary, but that had to proliferate as a consequence of the infinite capacity of algorithmic outputs – quite similar, that is, to *the incomputable* as described by Parisi.

In *The Mystery of Black Box*, ultimately, the inventor of the system, Adam Adamich, is blamed for excessive thinking; the machines decapitate him and substitute his head with a device for data memorising. The didactic conclusion is that the perfection of computation has been reached, but the infinity of production that was inscribed in the machine became unnecessary. So, paradoxically, infinity, when it stops being a category of thinking and dialectics, and is regarded as a mere flow of data, cannot manifest its true nature, which should be dialectical and contradictory. In the search for the guaranteed limit to infinity, machines reach the condition of the absolute end of thought, which coincides with the permanent blankness of the Black Box.

Despite the fact that *The Mystery of Black Box* was written in the late 1960s in the very different context of Soviet academia, the principal technical remedies in the augmentation of mind that it features are actually very similar to those found in current theories of computation. These might be summarised as follows:

1. A capacity for self-perfection, acceleration and self-learning by the machine.
2. The *discrete* character of algorithmic tasks and the eviction of any blurred, contradictory inputs, which might block the output.
3. The infinity of those discrete data.
4. The total division of activities and hence of labour, as a consequence of the extreme discreteness of algorithmisation.
5. The autonomy and autopoeisis of machinic intelligence.

While doubt and contradiction (or the 'disability of philosophy') diminish the efficiency of reason and make it powerless in post-philosophical theories of mind or of the brain, for Ilyenkov it is precisely these traits that construct thought. The mind's 'disability' is inscribed into the mind's ability. This disability is surpassed not by means of an augmented storage of knowledge or of cognised data and thought's functionality. Rather, it is an awareness of the disability of human reason in its treatment of the contradictions of reality that is able to redeem such disability. Moreover, thought's inevitable disability, perishability and its bond with human neoteny – that is, the retention of protective capacities for surviving in natural environments, as a condition in which the existence of the human species is grounded – does not contradict its quest for the Absolute.[34]

As Ilyenkov often repeats, philosophical and dialectical phenomena are spiral-like or snowball-like – constantly on the move and hence indiscrete as selves. The common good, labour, reason or culture are, as such, not autopoetic, but realise themselves as '*other-determined non-selves*'. Autopoiesis implies that the organism remains the self, even in the surrounding of an environmental outside and in exchange with it, whereas the above-listed phenomena – common good, labour, reason, culture – presuppose one's positing as non-selves. 'The other self' in this case is not simply an outside of the self, but the formative principle of the self as of the non-self, of non-identity. From this perspective, it is impossible to algorithmicise thought, since thinking is not confined to the moves in a neural network, or within the brain alone, but evolves externally including the body with its senses, its involvement in activity, engagement in sociality, and other human beings of all generations and locations. Consequently, if one were to emulate an artificial intelligence or thought digitally, one would have to create an entire machinic civilisation (one that would, additionally, be completely autonomous and independent from the human one).³⁵ At the same time, the very idea of programing a human consciousness or a thought as input is unimplementable, since there is not a single moment when a human being and her reason would have a stable and discrete programmatic interface that could be used as an input. As Ilyenkov argues, if there is any *function* of thought, it is in surpassing that function. As such, even if computation inscribes within itself *the incomputable* as its autopoetic potentiality, it would not be able to pre-empt the concrete paths for dealing with contradiction, as the requirement of algorithmic logic is in either solving or neutralising the paradox, rather than in extrapolating it.³⁶ As Boris Groys puts it, the sovereignty of thinking procedure is possible only when it is defunctionalised and miscommunicated. Moreover, a truly interesting (artistic) computer would be the one that 'always produces the same result – for example zero – for any and all computations, or that always produces different results for the same computational process'.³⁷

Techniques of dialectical othering

Why, in the face of claims to displace philosophy by cybernetic research, should the necessity of dialectical method, specifically, be insisted upon, at least so far as the political ontology of communism is concerned?³⁸ To start with, for Ilyenkov, dialectics is a specific tool of generalisation (as against formal abstraction) that does not simply distill an invariant from the breadth of empirical reality, but has to bring together mind and body, thing and concept, the concrete and the abstract. Mind and body can exist in equivocality and parallelism – as in Spinoza – or be chained in semiologic series regardless of any topological gaps and divergences. For example, in post-structuralism and Guattarian semiology, the convergence of the conceptual and the sensual/material was implemented through providing one plane of representation for the signifier and the signified. And this was done through a mere dismissal of any semiological incongruence between them: so that the combining of a thing and a sign could take place performatively and not semantically, i.e., without their semantic fusion and overlapping. In dialectical logic, conversely, a thing has to acquire a noumenal dimension too, i.e., it must be generalised in the mode of a 'notion' as well; and, vice versa, the notion (noumen) should have the opportunity to be embedded and revealed in reality, activity and thinghood.

This is central to Ilyenkov's argument: when a notion is abstracted from things, then things become abstract too. Interpenetration is indispensable therefore, simply because a thing without notion, without generalisation, without being reflected *how it is reflected*, has no proper being. As such, the interpenetration of concept and thing is necessary to surpass such abstraction. Interpenetration between thing and notion can only be implemented by dialectical procedure. Thus, generalisation is a mode of abstraction in which a notion is never torn from reality or thinghood, but maintains a bond with it.

The paradox of unifying mind and matter by means of dialectical procedure is to be found in the fact that only dis-identifying othering can thus lead to generalisation. One can unify and converge thing and concept not by virtue of identification of one with another, but by virtue of each identity being other than itself – the thing being other than itself in its noumenal aspect, and the notion being other than itself in its material concretisation. It is such constant *self-resigning othering* that entails positing both thing and concept in general terms. This is the reason why the thing and its signification cannot be codified and quantified. Such obsession with dialectical monism is in fact a sort of communist absolutism for Ilyenkov, as only (communist) non-monetised and non-privatised economics could provide the above-mentioned mode of convergence of being and thinking. Only in a non-monetised economy are both things and notions incommensurable, non-quantifiable, generalisable. Conversely, the monetary form of commodified things entails and requires formalised, abstract and discrete quantification of things and their signifiers. Philosophy as such becomes a constant labour of non-quantifiable dialectical generalisation, as against numerical quantification and abstraction, which always remains discrete, reversible data and never transcends to an irreversible quality.

What Ilyenkov shows in his earlier (and most celebrated) book, *Dialectics of the Abstract and the Concrete* (1960), is that dialectical logic is not found in mere extraction of logic from the living sphere. Instead, this logic is only found and located *within* the *incommensurable* living sphere of activity. Yet this does not mean that the sum of real phenomena should coincide with the logical essence of those phenomena. This is because Marx's

dialectical logic is qualitative; it presupposes the irreversibility of quality in the dialectical procedure – an approach that differs from the naturalistic non-reducibility and non-compressibility of scientific and empirical data. Non-dialectical logic produces abstract identifications via metaphysical distillation. Dialectical logic abstracts and generalises, but does so by manifesting the living essence of the thing, of the phenomenon, the law of its existence.

It is in this context that *Dialectics of the Abstract and the Concrete* presents a technique of dialectical othering – showing how the being of 'the self' is always 'the non-self' being – which, for Ilyenkov, implies a non-positivist method of speculation, indispensable for communism.[39] Ilyenkov finds a number of examples of such othering in Marx's political economy, thus demonstrating that Marx's analysis of political economy was – contrary to the idea that Marx's famous eleventh thesis on Feuerbach implied a simple detour away from philosophy in favour of social praxis – a model of dialectical logic and in fact itself a philosophical gnoseology. For example, as Ilyenkov emphasises, when Marx defines the logic of value, he does not do so by extracting some unifying trait from various kinds of value, or by gathering all data about value and distilling one unifying trait out of this – as an algorithmic logic would suggest. Instead, to define the logic of value (as surplus value) he dismisses the realm of value theory altogether to discover its logic in the realm that has never been an exemplary part of value theory. This 'other' realm not related to value theory lay in raw reality and was a non-monetised exchange of one commodity for another one – of one mode of labour with another mode of labour. This non-monetised exchange was regarded as an exception in value theory. But precisely this exception was used by Marx as the specific condition from which to generalise the logic of value. In this case, Marx proved, according to Ilyenkov, that in order to understand surplus value, one had to leave aside the characteristics and functions of value as such, and depart from other phenomena, deeply rooted in raw exchange, in reality, not yet having any articulate signification. In this case, the generalised conceptual essence of one phenomenon (value) was found *in* or *via* another phenomenon (the exchange between various modes of labour).⁴⁰ But such generalisation could have occured only precisely by searching for noumenal logic in the raw reality of trade, by discovering logic in living procedures rather than in already given abstract data about value.

Communism, mortality and reason

For Ilyenkov, dialectical logic as against algorithmic logic manifests a paradox of incommensurability: namely, that the universal (the absolute) and the quest for it in thought persists precisely due to the functional *indiscreteness* of human existence, and the essential *disabilities* of reason and of thought. In its genealogy, philosophy and its speculations on reason emerge with the eclipse of theocracies, of gods and any supernatural creatures. Precisely because the thinking body can no longer rely on God, or supernatural forces, it has to automatically posit its reason as non-individual, generic, universal, inter-human. In fact, the precarious human body-organism, which is described by Descartes in his *L'Homme* as like clockwork, is the disabled body without divine animation or support that clings to reason and thought as the only remedy that would posit it in a general sense.

In his 'Cogito and History of Madness', written around the same time as Ilyenkov's texts, Derrida argued that the Cartesian *cogito* could be interpreted not as the mere hegemony of rationality, but rather as the speculative courage to declare an awareness of mortality, on the one hand, and the capacity to confirm one's not yet being dead due to the still ongoing human labour of thought, on the other.⁴¹ Cogito could be interpreted in this case not as 'I, the rational Subject, think, hence I exist', but as 'I am still not yet dead, and not quite sure about being sane or insane, as God can no longer confirm it; but it seems that, if I am still able to think, I am not yet dead, although constantly on the verge of it'. In fact, philosophical gnoseology since Socrates has never ceased to emphasise mortality as the crucial aspect of thought and reason. Mortality is the outcome of temporality's intensity and fatality without which human reason and its intentionality cannot be imagined. Plato's *Phaedo* as well as his *Apology of Socrates* locate the source of dialectical thought in the acceptance of death by a philosopher. Philosophical gnoseology as well as reason are constructed by human mortality in the attempt to speculatively surpass this mortality.⁴² As Boris Groys argues, human reason, as against machinic intelligence, is formed because of the risk of death, or the fear and awareness of death.⁴³

From the perspective of a communist thought that seeks to develop its own militant postulates of what reason is, as Ilyenkov argues, this is to say that human reason is not a sovereign power, it is a testimony to staying without any ontological support in neoteny in this world together with others. The necessity to develop wordliness and new secular cosmologies, which are philosophical and political, arises precisely from such weakness, groundlessness and the abandonment of the human – not from the strength of the inhuman, protected by supernatural forces, psychedelic phantasies or digital augmentations.

Keti Chukhrov is Associate Professor at the Cultural Theory Department, National Research University Higher School of Economics, Moscow.

Notes

1. Catherine Malabou in a recent lecture shrewdly emphasised the motives for the critique of philosophy in post-structuralist thought, where philosophy was critiqued precisely on the basis of its excessive overlaps with science or with the determinist transparency of theoretical discourse. Cognitivists, conversely, criticise philosophy precisely for its insufficient efficacy. Catherine Malabou, 'Is Science the Subject of Philosophy?', paper at the University of Westminster, 17 January 2019.
2. See Thomas Metzinger, *Being No One: Self-model Theory of Subjectivity* (Cambridge, MA: MIT Press, 2003); Marvin Minsky *The Society of Mind* (New York and London: Touchstone, 1988); Benjamin Bratton *The Stack* (Cambridge, MA: MIT Press, 2015).
3. Autopoiesis as a concept was introduced in 1972 by Chilean biologists Francisco Varela and Humberto Maturana and was meant to define the capacity of a system to self-reproduce and maintain itself. The term is applied broadly in cybernetics, system theory, architecture and sociology, and implies the capacity of non-human intelligences for self-organisation and self-learning without any intervention on the part of a human subject.
4. See the group monograph edited by Matteo Pasquinelli, *Alleys of Your Mind: Augmented Intelligence* (Luneburg: Meson Press, 2015).
5. Reza Negarestani, 'Revolution Backwards: Functional Realisation and Computational Implementation', in *Alleys of Your Mind*, ed. Pasquinelli, 139–157.
6. Ibid., 150.
7. Ibid., 147 (emphasis added).
8. See Luciana Parisi *Contagious Architecture: Computation, Aesthetics and Space* (Cambridge, MA: MIT Press, 2013).

9. Luciana Parisi 'Instrumental Reason, Algorithmic Capitalism and the Incomputable', in *Alleys of Your Mind*, ed. Pasquinelli, 125–138, 128.
10. Ibid., 133
11. Ibid.
12. Ibid., 134
13. Felix Guattari, *Machinic Unconscious*, trans. Taylor Adkins (Los Angeles: Semiotext(e), 2011).
14. Ibid.
15. Parisi *Contagious Architecture*, 38–62.
16. Ibid., 43.
17. Deleuze writes about the machine, and the halt as its symptom, in Gilles Deleuze and Felix Guattari, *Anti-Oedipus*, trans. Robert Hurley, Mark Seem and Helen R. Lane (Minneapolis: University of Minnesota Press, 2011). In particular, see the chapters entitled 'The Machines' and 'The Molecular Unconscious', 36–42, 283–296.
18. Slava Gerovich, *From Newspeak to Cyberspeak: A History of Soviet Cybernetics* (Cambridge, MA: MIT Press, 2004), 76
19. Ibid., 77.
20. Paolo Virno, *Multitude Between Innovation and Negation* (Los Angeles: Semiotext(e), 2008).
21. See Evald Ilyenkov, 'Where Does the Mind Come From', in *Philosophy and Culture* (Moscow: Political Literature Publishers, 1991), 30–43.
22. In 1963 the Soviet psychologists Alexander Mesheriakov and Ivan Sokoljanski founded the Zagorsk Internat for deaf and blind children. They relied on the psychological school of Alexey Leontiev – a disciple of Lev Vygotsky – and were supported theoretically by the Marxist philosopher Evald Ilyenkov. Mesheriakov and Sokoljanski developed the special tactile signal system of dactilologia, which was a developed extension of tiphlosurdopedagogics (a specific methodology for teaching the deaf-blind).
23. Ibid., 43
24. Veniamin Pushkin, one of the pioneers of Soviet cybernetic theory, very clearly shows how expansions in computation and digital engineering had to confirm their fidelity to materialist dialectics in the ideocratic Soviet society. With such adherence declared, one result was that the representatives of cybernetic theory largely supported the bureaucratic interface of Marxist dogmas, and even provided systemic tools to strengthen it. Philosophic gnoseology and Marxist cultural theory could then implicitly be considered redundant. Slava Gerovich provides interesting evidence in his *From Newspeak to Cyberspeak: A History of Soviet Cybernetics* of how the representatives of philosophy of science and of mathematical logic – including Alexander Zinoviev, author of the 'Logic of Science' (1971), among others – ardently delved into the new field of cybernetic theory, but later, by the end of 1970s, having understood that the applied role of cybernetics was meant to subsume the role of philosophy as a supreme science, deserted the field. See Gerovich, *From Newspeak to Cyberspeak*, 275
25. Dmitry Pospelov and Modest Gaaze Rappoport, *From the Amoeba to a Robot* [*Ot Amiobi do Robota*] (Moscow: Nauka, 1987). [All translations from the Russian are, unless indicated otherwise, the author's own.]
26. Veniamin Pushkin and Arkady Ursul, *Informatics, Cybernetics, Intellect* (Kishinev: Shtiinza, 1989), 92.
27. Ibid., 181
28. Ibid., 145
29. Evald Ilyenkov *Lenin's Dialectics and the Metaphysics of Positivism (Leninskaya Dialektika i metaphizika pozitivizma)* (Moscow: Mir Philosophii, 2015). Available in English at https://www.marxists.org/archive/ilyenkov/works/positive/index.htm.
30. Evald Ilyenkov, 'The Notes of Bezumtsev', in *Evald Ilyenkov's Philosophy and Contemporaneity*, ed. Andrey Maidansky (Belgorod: Belgorod Publishers, 2016), 10–14
31. Victor Glushkov, a Soviet mathematician and one of the founders of Soviet computation, became a very frequent author in philosophy journals from the mid-1960s onwards. Mikhail Rutkevich, a physicist by specialisation, was appointed the Dean of the Philosophy faculty at the University of the Urals.
32. Andrey Maidansky, Foreword to *Evald Ilyenkov's Philosophy and Contemporaneity*, 10.
33. Evald Ilyenkov, 'The Mystery of Black Box. Sci-Fi Prelude', in *On the Idols and the Ideals (Ob Idolakh I Idealakh)* (Politizdat, 1968), 11–28. Online version: http://libelli.ru/works/idols/index.htm
34. See Evald Ilyenkov, 'Cosmology of the Spirit', trans. Giuliano Vivaldi, *Stasis Journal* 5:2. (2017), 164–90.
35. A. Arsenev, E. Ilyenkov and V. Davidov, 'Machine and Human: Cybernetics and Philosophy', in *Lenin's Theory of Reflection and Contemporary Science*, ed. F. Konstantinov (Moscow: Nauka 1966), 265–283.
36. Interestingly, Alexander Zinoviev, the author of the 'Logic of Science', who in his seminal work tried to construct the logical mathemes of various sciences and their lexicons and methodologies, incessantly reiterates in his book that mathematical logic has an applied, instrumental function and it cannot replace dialectical or philosophical procedures of reason.
37. Boris Groys, 'The Museum as a Cradle of Revolution', *E-flux* 106 (February 2020), available at: https://www.e-flux.com/journal/106/314487/the-museum-as-a-cradle-of-revolution/.
38. There would be an additional question concerning why philosophy could not reside in non-dialectical methods as well; for example, in a Spinozist method. But this would have to be the topic of another text.
39. Evald Ilyenkov, *The Dialectics of the Abstract and the Concrete in Scientific and Theoretical Thinking (Dialektika Abstraktnogo I konkretnovo v Nauchno-teoreticheskom Mishlenii)* (Moscow: Philosophy Institute of Academy of Sciences, 1960).
40. Ibid., 65–93.
41. Jacques Derrida, 'Cogito and the History of Madness', in *Writing and Difference*, trans. Alan Bass (London: Routledge, 1978), 31–63.
42. In a recent paper, Franco Berardi claims mortality and temporality as the main traits confirming the incommensurability of consciousness. 'Sensitive Consciousness and Time against Transhumanist Utopia', *E-flux* 98 (February 2019), available at: https://www.e-flux.com/journal/98/257322/sensitive-consciousness-and-time-against-the-transhumanist-utopia/
43. Boris Groys, 'The Museum as a Cradle of Revolution'.

The social life of black things
Fred Moten's *consent not to be a single being*
David Lloyd

> I want to identify not with creaturely life but with the stolen life of imagining things.
>
> Fred Moten, 'There is no Racism Intended'

Fred Moten's three-volume collection of essays, *consent not to be a single being*, draws together some fifteen years of his consistently inventive but widely dispersed work in Black Studies, thus allowing his reader finally to begin the task of grasping it in its ensemble as something like a whole.* That task is complicated by precisely what makes the reading so exhilarating, namely the form that the work mostly takes. These are essays that, as African American poet Nathaniel Mackey aptly notes in his endorsement of the second volume, *Stolen Life*, each constitute 'what John Coltrane called pursuance, in flight and toward something ... an unremitting search prone to unexpected turns.' Their construction is – as befits a critic who is also a poet and performance artist – poetic, in the sense that their flight often operates by way of association and through condensations and displacements of meaning which, though working at a high level of theoretical engagement, obey a logic of resonance and turn, recurrence and dispersion rather than gradual exposition. They remain in the problematic they engage with rather than seeking resolution and exit.

That refusal is intrinsic to an ethic as well as an aesthetic that drives the writing: both defy any injunction to pursue the emancipation or resolution of the subject through the (impossible) securing of autonomy from condition. The motto of these essays might be the phrase 'I ran from it but was still in it', from the third part of the trilogy, *The Universal Machine* [UM 39], that also furnished the title of one of Moten's poetic sequences.[1] For the reviewer who is drawn to offer a preliminary account of the whole assembly, this entails an invidious task akin to paraphrasing a poem: the work of reduction inevitably does a certain violence to the form. What passes here for an exposition of Moten's thinking proceeds, then, by reassembling strands of argument that are, in the original text, widely dispersed rather than continuously developed. The purpose is to offer a pathway through a body of work whose very volume might daunt the first-time reader even as its content excites and inspires. That pathway hopefully also will serve as a gateway into the work.

Aesthetic tradition as radical tradition

Moten's first book, *In the Break*, was subtitled *The Aesthetics of the Black Radical Tradition*.[2] One way to understand the gathering of brilliant, mobile and rhizomatically interconnected essays that compose *consent not to be a single being* is as an extended adjustment of that earlier subtitle into the proposition that the black radical tradition is (above all) an aesthetic tradition. It is as if the parenthetical hesitation in the phrase 'black radicalism is (like) black music' were now subject to an ongoing decision that abolishes it:[3] Moten's claim is not that the black radical tradition *has* its accompanying musical forms, but that black music – by extension, black aesthetic practice in general – *is* and cannot be separated from black radicalism, even by so slight a difference as resemblance entails. Just how radical a proposition that

---

* *consent not to be a single being* consists of three volumes: *Black and Blur* (Durham, NC: Duke University Press, 2017); *Stolen Life* (Durham, NC: Duke University Press, 2018); and *The Universal Machine* (Durham, NC: Duke University Press, 2018). These are cited in the text hereafter as BB, SL and UM respectively.

turns out to be may not be evident at first sight. It would be all too easy to reproduce the dismissive compliment that reduces black folks to their cultural performances, a devious tradition that runs from 'the pageantry of the coffle' under slavery to contemporary 'play-labour', the transformation of black play into commodities that Robin Kelley has trenchantly analysed.[4] Such a reduction depends already on the positioning of aesthetic culture over and against the constraining spheres of the political and the economic, as a space of free and harmonious play that pretends to compensate for the effects of the division of labour, not to speak of coerced labour. The condescension of such compensatory allowances does not survive Moten's radical subversion, his thorough overturning of that aesthetic tradition from its very root in Kant's *Critique of Judgment*.

To put things this way is to acknowledge, as Moten everywhere does, that the aesthetic tradition furnishes not only, and not so much, a theory of art as a theory of freedom and of the subject, which, taken together, constitute the conditions of possibility for any modern concept of the political. The aesthetic is an expressly regulative faculty for Kant, both in the technical sense that its concepts necessarily have no constitutive or determinative force and in the sense that Moten elaborates, its will to regulate the 'lawless freedom of the imagination'. But it is also regulative in the sense of establishing the terms in and through which freedom and the autonomy of the subject are thought as properties of the universal human. If, in one regard, aesthetic freedom is compensatory for restraint felt elsewhere in the system, a reserve of 'free play' to the side of the constraints of labour and the unfreedom of political life, its larger concept exemplifies and prepares human freedom in and through identification with the Subject whose abstraction from particular material properties and interests grounds its universal claims.

Such a formal conception of freedom as the autonomy of the subject and as categorical for human being requires in the first place the subject's indifference to its own materiality and to any enjoyment of its object. Likewise, the judgment of taste is obliged to let go, 'so far as possible ... of the element of matter, i.e., sensation, in our general state of representation', and reflect solely upon the 'formal peculiarities' of that representation.[5] The formal freedom of the subject is, for Kant, at once the condition and the product of that 'public or common sense' without which no realm of liberal political subjecthood could be imagined. But the autonomous subject is necessarily set over and against another human that Kant elsewhere designates the pathological subject. This is the human subjected to necessity, whether in the form of external forces or of internal needs and desires, the human as material being, capable perhaps of approaching freedom but only at the price of being subjected to formation. This formal freedom is both closely regulated and regulative of a disposition of human beings and their relative value along a scale that ranges from the representative universal and free subject to humans subjected to matter and necessity. A whole history of cultural pedagogy or *Bildung* instituted in and by liberal states through the apparatus of education stems from this exemplary model of freedom and continues to play out to this day.[6] Accordingly, as Moten points out, 'The regulative discourse on the aesthetic that animates Kant's critical philosophy is inseparable from the question of race as a mode of conceptualising and regulating human diversity, grounding and justifying inequality and exploitation ... ' [SL 2].

As a counter-aesthetic of life-in-common, rather than a universal common sense that finds its ultimate representation in the state 'as a kind of degraded representation of commonness' [SL 8], the black radical tradition, in Moten's reinscription of it, deconstructs this Kantian regulative discourse at every turn. This is in part because blackness can be read as the 'anteKantian' as much as the antiKantian instantiation of that 'lawless freedom of the imagination' whose wings and whose flight aesthetic judgment is tasked with clipping. Blackness historically becomes the object of an *aesthetic* regulation in 'a set of brutally discursive maneuvers' that critically exceed any of the longstanding phenomena that concern historians and sociologists, that is, the deployment of racial difference in the disciplining of coerced labour or the segmentation of the labour force and its political counterpart, a militant working class. 'This is so even as what is continually revealed, if not confessed, is that what is now, in the wake of those maneuvers, called blackness makes those very maneuvers possible and – for and as eternally thwarted and dispersed sovereignty – necessary' [SL 3]. What is revealed across the extended terrain of *consent not to be a single being* is that the aesthetics that is and is of the black radical tradition is consubstantial with the practices of an alternative sociality or life form that 'animaterialises' both a constant underpresence, 'the dynamic hum of blackness's facticity' [SL 10], and the white racial fantasies and projections that constitute the series of figures for sensuality and indiscipline. Those figures 'have always been inseparable from a "natural" history of inequality', calling forth and legitimating 'a predispositional servitude, a captivity in which the embodiment of the need for constraint … precisely insofar as she [the black (woman)] is supposed to be incapable of self-regulation, is given over to the ultimate form of governance, namely that phantasmatic and im/possible condition of being wholly for another' [SL 13].

Moten's aim, however, is not to recuperate black dignity and humanity from the aspersions cast and instrumentalised in the name of regulation, as has been the tendency in so many political and cultural movements predicated on political freedoms embodied in rights and enfranchisement, or to demand those forms of recognition that Frantz Fanon continued to hanker for, a recognition as a subject or 'being-for-oneself' to the object whose 'being is wholly for another'. His project is, rather, to unfold 'the tumultuous derangements of a certain politicoaesthetic imagination that might more improperly be understood as the essential resistance of the object that manifests itself as lawlessness, as a kind of being against the law, as the lawless freedom and the struggle for freedom in unfreedom, in quite specific modes of discipline and regulation that we call slavery and colonialism' [SL 55–56].[7] To pursue this 'politicoaesthetic imagination' enjoins the elaboration of the protocols through which that 'tumultuous derangement' is played out, especially in the procedures of black poetry and black music. Those protocols refuse the formality of the Kantian aesthetic and its abstraction from sensuous enjoyment that determines the pathological subject; they cleave to materiality and to the very feelings that Kant designated 'pathological' and thus shape an aesthetic practice that does not seek to lift itself up over the constraints of the flesh, of necessity, the needs and desires that play out in life in common, but inhabits them, in the words of the first volume of the trilogy, *Black and Blur*, in mobile ensemble: 'it hurts to play this music' [BB xiii].[8]

Recounting a fraught discussion between visual artist Ad Reinhardt and jazz musician Cecil Taylor, Moten comments at length on the formal and distantiating tendencies of traditional aesthetics, for which 'detachment' is 'the very essence of intellectual and aesthetic experience', as opposed to the communal and pathological tendencies of 'black aestheticosocial life':

> To insist on the distinction between the canvas as scene [of forms] and the canvas as thing is to detach oneself from the scene as much as it is also to represent the scene. It is to establish something like a freedom *from the community* in the most highly determined, regulative *legal* sense of that word, in the sharpest sense of its constituting a field in which the human and the (disorderly) thing are precisely, pathologically, theatrically indistinct. Let us call this community the black community, the community that is defined by a certain history of blackness, a history of privation (as Taylor points out) and plenitude, pain and (as Taylor points out) pleasure. It is from and as a sensual commune, from and as an irruptive advent, at once focused and arrayed against the political aesthetics of enclosed common sense, that Taylor's music emerges. [UM 166–67]

I'll come back to the question of thingliness that preoccupies Moten in his reflections on blackness momentarily, in order to focus at first on the significance of this 'pathological', sensuous aesthetic that forms the ground for a music that emerges from the improvisational, generative ensemble of a life in common.

Subjecthood and freedom

An apparently constitutive double bind has always bedeviled the study of slavery and of the cultural work of the enslaved and continues to shadow debates on black being in the wake of enslavement and through the historical experience of racial subjugation. The problematic can be stated summarily as follows: if the historian celebrates the vitality of that culture, does the representation of vitality itself represent a mitigation of the unremitting violence of the order of slavery? If, on the other hand, the historian emphasises that unremitting violence and the negation of black being, is the culture, on which the extraordinary traditions of black cultural life in the United States are founded, to be seen as a more or less epiphenomenal compensation, 'a cry of pain', so to speak? What are we to make of the *pleasures* of the slave where those pleasures were so often recruited to legitimate the system of the slave economy? As Moten put it in *In the Break*,

Saidiya Hartman 'allows us to ask: what have objectification and humanisation, both of which we can think in relation to a certain notion of subjection, to do with the essential historicity, the quintessential modernity, of black performance?'[9] In this question, implied again in Moten's paraphrase of Taylor, lies a profound meditation on the relations established in the Euro-American and more or less Kantian tradition between the spaces of aesthetic pleasure or judgment and the emergence of the autonomous subject itself. How can one think the slave's pleasures where the very things that pleasure is taken to signify – humanity and an at least latent autonomy – are at once denied the slave and, whenever pleasure is taken or stolen, stand as evidence of their enjoyment of the qualities that have been denied them?[10]

What Moten shows us, and elaborates across *consent not to be a single being*, is that the terms of that double bind are intimately connected with the imagination of both subjecthood and freedom in the post-Enlightenment aesthetic tradition. The cultural productivity of those whose quotidian experience is one in which 'pain is alloyed with pleasure' constitutes a radical and thorough-going refusal of those terms, an 'affirmative refusal' [UM 186] that 'refuses what was refused to them', to use a phrase repeated several times throughout these essays. The black radical tradition entails 'a refusal of a polity or community structured by refusal' [UM 90] that turns out to be also a certain form of dissenting assent, a crucial act of consent. To refuse the poisonous gift of an autonomy or a citizenship or a right that is always withheld is also to refuse the tortured logic that apprehends racialisation – as, in one moment of his restless dialectic, Fanon does – only as the negation that installs a lack in being in the black non-subject, or as an enduring social death. As Moten puts it in a passage I want to return to, 'Taylor speaks of and out of possibilities embedded in a social life from which Fanon speaks and of which he speaks but primarily as negation and impossibility' [UM 160]. Moten spells out at length the ways in which the performance of black music and poetic writing embody and figure the modalities of that 'social life' in a meditation on Francophone poet Édouard Glissant and jazz musician Anthony Braxton that tracks the relation of the soloist – who embodies what is elsewhere described as a 'differential integrity in and to the unit' [UM 69] – to the ensemble, 'in the depths of our common impasse, our common flight, and our common habitation':

> They allow and require us to be interested in the unlikely emergence of the unlikely figure of the black soloist, whose irruptive speech occurs not only against the grain of a radical interdiction of individuality that is manifest both as an assumption of its impossibility as well as in a range of governmental dispositions designed to prevent the impossible, but also within the context of a refusal of what has been interdicted (admission to the zone of abstract equivalent citizenship and subjectivity, whose instantiations so far been nothing but a set of pseudoindividuated aftereffects of conquests and conquest denial, a power trip to some fucked-up place in the burnt-out sun), a kind of free or freed 'personality' that will have turned out to be impossible even for the ones who are convinced they have achieved it, even as they oversee its constant oscillation between incompleteness and repair, distress and fashion. ... Such refusal, such dissent, takes the form of a common affirmation, an open consensus given in the improbable, more than im/possible, consent, in Glissant's words, 'not to be a single being'. [UM 136]

Where the Kantian aesthetic at once feelingly apprehends (in all his 'black genius' [SL32]) and yet seeks to regulate the lawless generativity of this collectively backed solo performance in the interests of a disciplined freedom and autonomy, the aesthetics of blackness follows in its fugitive, improvisatory performances not the road to freedom but a line of flight that is obviously grounded in the liberatory practices of the enslaved, but is also entirely attuned to the ruse of freedom that Hartman has called its 'encumbrance'. As she put it, 'The discrepant bestowal of emancipation conferred sovereignty as it engendered subjection.'[11] Moten's understanding of the articulation of the freedom drive in the politicoaesthetic imagination of blackness with the conditions of constraint and of privation, working, like Olaudah Equiano, 'between law and motion, between constraint and a privileged loss of control' [SL 61], is all too cognisant of the knowledge that 'Leaving, differing, stealing away, is always under the threat of interdiction, of protected theft, of mastery's protected "right" to steal, of the roguish force that is always most powerfully wielded by proper subjects and proper states' [SL 113].

Fugitivity, then, does not escape the law, conditioned as it is by the long reach of the law that it calls forth, but no more does it embrace the sovereignty of freedom, the autonomy of the subject in its disciplined and abstracted individuated representation of the universal. Nevertheless, this 'unruly music that moves in disruptive, improvisational excess ... of the very idea of the (art) work', and that is also 'the site of a certain lawless, fugitive theatricality' [SL 111], remains in its own peculiar relation to law, but one that exceeds any Kantian regulation of the imagination. Drawing on legal theorist Robert Cover's classic essay 'Nomos and Narrative', Moten notes that 'the fearsomeness of ungoverned generativity is held, for Kant, in the fact that what is being generated is law; that, above all, it is what Cover calls "the fecundity of the jurisgenerative principle", which is manifest as endless mutation and differentiation, that freaks him out' [UM 115].[12] Cover's point, on which Moten so generatively elaborates, is that *jurisgenesis*, the capacity to create legal meaning, exceeds the law as written and determined by any given legal system. It is, therefore, 'the problem of the multiplicity of meaning – the fact that never only one but always many worlds are created by the too fertile forces of jurisgenesis'[13] that the institutions of the law are concerned to contain by imposing a single *nomos*, or legal order. The law seeks 'to maintain some coherence in the awesome proliferation of meaning lost as it is created – by unleashing upon the fertile but weakly organised jurisgenerative cells an organising principle itself incapable of producing the normative meaning that is life and growth'.[14] The rationale for legal interpretation and for those interpretive institutions, the courts, is, accordingly, not the need for law, but the 'need to suppress law, to choose between two or more laws, to impose upon laws a hierarchy. It is the multiplicity of laws, the fecundity of the jurisgenerative principle, that creates the problem to which the court and the state are the solution.' Accordingly, '[i]nterpretation always takes place in the shadow of coercion'.[15] Cover's 'jurispathic' courts, in all their implicit violence against difference and multiplicity, correspond to Kant's judgment of taste that seeks to 'clip the wings of the lawless imagination', to curtail the flights of fantasy that generate 'the awesome proliferation of meaning' that is at once fertile and ephemeral, ante- and anti-institutional.

Cover's formulations prompt Moten 'to imagine something on the order of an anoriginary criminality with which blackness is inextricably linked – or to think blackness, perhaps more precisely as the paradoxically anarchic principle and expression of a jurisgenerativity that demands a reconfiguration of the very idea of law' [SL 19] – and, we might say by extension, of the aesthetic.[16] It's not hard to see how the fugitive nature of an unconstrained jurisgenerativity corresponds to the protocols of improvisation and the 'weakly organised cell' of the ensemble, not least as Moten goes on to characterise blackness's undoing of the law's sentence in precisely such terms: 'the improvisational para-statement – the extragrammatical run-on, that informal incompletion where the sentence lives against its own execution – continually and ubiquitously establishes itself otherwise, elsewhere and at another time, neither here nor there nor here and now, as a kind of anoriginal (declaration of) independence' [SL 20].

That allusion to the declaration of independence affirms less the autonomy of a black life-form than a procedure, the sheer generative performativity of improvisation itself as it brings into being some new state of play out of the fugitive encounter of constraint and invention in and through the interdependence of the ensemble. Everywhere Moten insists on this performativity of a blackness that is not an ontological essence nor an originary identity but a constant process, a performativity that is necessarily non-performance insofar as it is never subjected or given over to institution, to the dismay of interpretation.[17]

One way to grasp the significance of this performativity of blackness is by watching how, in the passage I partially quoted above, Moten invokes Cecil Taylor's 'claim on aestheticosocial life' over and against that still Hegelian dimension of Fanon that is fascinated by the demand for recognition and haunted by its refusal:

> [Taylor] speaks not only out of but also of the lived experience of the black. This is to say that Taylor moves by way of an experience, an aesthetic sociality that Fanon can never embrace insofar as he never really comes to believe in it, even though it is the object, for Fanon, of an ambivalent political desire as well as a thing (of darkness) he cannot acknowledge as his own. In other words, Taylor speaks of and out of the possibilities embedded in a social life from which Fanon speaks and of which he speaks but primarily as negation and impossibility. [UM 160][18]

In some sense, the whole of *consent not to be a single being* could be seen to flow from and to this passage. Performativity, this capacity to invent out of nothing and out of the constraints that proclaim one's nothingness, is the generative cell of the 'aesthetic sociality' of blackness. Aesthetic sociality significantly shifts the terms in displacing 'the political aesthetics of enclosed common sense' and even the 'politicoaesthetic imagination' elsewhere invoked. The sociality of the aesthetic refuses the moment of individuation through which the Kantian subject of taste arrives at its universality by way of the enclosure of a common sense that proscribes the feelings on which life-in-common is predicated as 'pathological'. Aesthetic sociality, as the social life predicated on that pathological lived experience of pleasure and pain, stands – in ways understated here but that form the groundwork of the trilogy's larger critique – against the ambivalence of Fanon's precisely *political* desire. For the sphere of politics is the terrain of one's recognition as both citizen and autonomous subject, the domain of formal freedoms for which the Kantian aesthetic limns the conditions of possibility in that 'enclosed common sense' through which the subject finds its abstract universality. The very formulation 'social life' in itself contests the containment of black life in the dismal frame of 'social death'; Orlando Patterson's seminal formulation in his history of slavery. Not only is black life 'irreducibly social', its 'irreducibly aesthetic sociality' is an ongoing ruptural apposition to the politics of aesthetics as that has been imagined since Kant: 'black life is lived in *political* death or ... in the burial ground of the subject by those who, insofar as they are not subjects, are also not, in the interminable (as opposed to the last) analysis, "death-bound"' [UM 194].[19]

In his extended critique of Hannah Arendt's 'degradation of sociality' in both her book-length *On Violence* and in her occasional essays on the civil rights movement, Moten addresses the distinction she makes between the non-public realm of the social and the valorised public realm of the political. This distinction is for Arendt troubled by what appears to her as the violence of black social movements and their claims, their irruption into what is 'the already given institutional structure' whose protection, she insists, is 'the prepolitical condition of all other, specifically political, virtues' [UM 91, citing Arendt].[20] Arendt's emphasis on the inviolability of those 'given' political institutions of liberal society has as its obverse an overlooked and prior violation of blackness:

> Her yoking of that insistence to the eternally dangerous black example is nothing less than the reimposition of the obligation to consent (to one's own violation). This reimposition will have been justified insofar as refusing the obligation, however violently imposed, however unaccompanied by some reciprocal promise, is to relinquish one's claim to a polity and, therefore, to humanity. [UM 91]

In a quite brutal inversion of the old Aristotelian adage that man is a political animal, Arendt suggests that to refuse or contest the political itself, and not merely the specific form or allowances of some political regime's given institutions, is to be something less than human. But what if the historical preference of the enslaved, whose legacy continues to inform black social life, were rather to take flight from than to accept enforced incorporation into those institutions whose freedoms are so differentially bound to enslavement? Then the mere non-violent, Bartlebeyan act of 'preferring not to' be conscripted to those institutions in the coercive name of freedom and sovereign subjecthood manifests as a mode of violence:

> And if the slave, in the interest of the abolition of slavery, which is understood by her not as a goal but as an ideological commitment, relinquishes that place, flees that 'home', then not only is she expelled from humanity but she is also guilty of a violence fundamental to the tacit consensus (imposed upon her in the absence of any protection of her personhood and in the oppressive fullness of its protection of her acquired thingliness) in which and from which that home is constructed. [UM 92]

In a peculiar twist on Walter Benjamin's recognition that the state regards any nonviolent movement that challenges the foundations of its law as a manifestation of violence, Arendt, the political subject, 'can only understand such preference as violence'.[21]

Arendt's (mis)understanding is a general disposition of the political intellectual, a constitutive ignorance of the subject, one might say:

> Blackness as violence, in a communicability that, again, will have always already exceeded the very idea of what are imprecisely called black bodies and the bounds imposed on black people when they are constrained to bear their bodies as loss; blackness as a refusal of a polity or community structured by refusal; blackness as a form of social thought in social life is the irreducible, antifoundational danger to which legitimate American intellectual work responds. [UM 90]

If we follow Moten's formulation of 'blackness as a form of social thought in social life' in the context of these imperiously political demands, we can see not only why black refusal, black irruption, black fugitivity, necessarily appear within and to the polity as violence, criminality, something other than humanity. We can also see that ambivalent Fanonian political desire, the desire for incorporation or assimilation (what Denise Ferreira da Silva has nicely dubbed 'engulfment', and Moten 'exclusionary assimilation' [UM 38]),[22] the desire for rights and the right to rights, the very desire for freedom, betray the subject as well as the subjected to the subjection that is their constitutive obverse. For this social life has been forged in exclusion from, 'in apposition' (to use Moten's favored phrase) to, citizenship, as 'the refusal of refused and therefore tainted citizenship' [UM 93]. Forged thus, and forged in this domain of an imposed and 'acquired thingliness' through which the commodified human is denied even her vestigial humanity, black sociality has nothing recuperative about it; it takes oblique flight not against but to the side and in the shadow of those political ends that at times stand in for but could never realise the imaginative excess of black freedom dreams:

> It's not about what it is to live under the shadow of a falsifying disregard, even when it reveals a threadbare aspect of an otherwise sumptuous life of the mind; the thing is that lived, luxuriant mindfulness that such disregard brings inadvertently into relief: the collective head, the hydratic passage, the hydraulic story that is the refuge and fugue(d) state of the stateless, the refusers, the refugees, which we share in common where blackness and study are in play. [UM 95]

In this very unHegelian, anti-Arendtian sociality, a jurisgenerative sociality that antecedes but does not anticipate the political, the double bind of violation and cultural richness, of social death versus affirmative negritude, is refused: the violation that reduces humans to things furnishes the ground for what Moten will come to call, very precisely, 'the social life of black things' [UM 207], a social life guaranteed, perhaps, not by a recovered fullness of autonomous being, but by 'a certain black incapacity to desire sovereignty and ontological relationality whether they are recast in the terms of and forms of a Levinasian ethics or an Arendtian politics, a Fanonian resistance or a Pattersonian test of honour' [UM 206].

Another way of thinking things

How do we parse this provocative and fecund formulation, 'the social life of black things', given how radically it seems to break with a whole tradition of recuperative humanisation of the enslaved and of black people? After all, thingliness has long been the index of the greatest degradation, the reduction of the human to brute, lumpish matter, 'mere' existence without value. Consider only Hegel's famous dismissal of the African in the *Philosophy of History* that is also a justification of her transatlantic enslavement: 'For it is the essential principle of slavery that man has not yet attained a consciousness of his freedom, and consequently sinks down to a mere Thing – an object of no value.'[23] The thing is that which lacks freedom, value and subjecthood. Furthermore, one might say that not only is the thing a lack of subject, it is the default of the object, which is always a phenomenon for or in relation to a subject. Accordingly, we can see across the panorama of *consent not to be a single being* a shift from the thematic of *In the Break*, which concerned the 'resistance of the object', the objection, as Moten put it there, raised by the speaking commodity that in turn gives rise to 'a theory of value – an objective and objectional, productive and reproductive ontology'.[24] Such a thematic is not lost in *consent not to be a single being*, but the conception of a social life of (mere) things raises different questions, grounds the question of blackness differently, perhaps more deeply, in a thingliness that has neither value nor ontology. Indeed, the first volume of the trilogy, *Black and Blur*, opens with a kind of pentimento over the first sentence of *In the Break*, which runs:

'The history of blackness is testament to the fact that objects can and do resist' [BB vii].[25] What now seems wrong with that sentence may be its predication of blackness as objecthood, an implicitly oppositional formulation that *consent not to be a single being* is devoted to undoing. Doing so, it undoes a whole lot else. What Moten refers to as 'an irruption of the thing into a discourse from which it had been excluded and which it had made possible' [UM 28] is no less an intervention into 'the ongoing accumulative disavowal of the thing that animates certain essential strains of Western philosophy' [UM 9]. There, the fate of the thing, most notably by way of the Kantian phenomenon or the Hegelian phenomenological dialectic, has been to be subsumed into an object for the subject, an object which, just as the condition of slavery is the constitutive other of freedom, anchors the self-consciousness and autonomy of the subject. And for the subject to *have*, to grasp or possess its objects is also to commit itself to the enclosure of interiority: 'To be turned toward the world of objects, is to be turned inward, to be enclosed in an inner theatre of representations'. 'Meanwhile, things stand out from the outside' [UM 32].

There where the object was, the thing shall come. Following Moten, 'We must appeal to another way of thinking things that is offered in the social aesthetics of black radicalism and its improvisatory protocols' [UM 10]. His trajectory – in an extended engagement with Heidegger's writings on the thing and his formulation that 'the thing is resistance' – from the resistance of the object to that of the thing is striking, not least in furnishing a kind of ground bass for the trilogy that makes up this work.[26] And where the speaking or shrieking object produced a 'phonic matter' irreducible 'to verbal meaning or conventional musical form',[27] a sounding out of captivity and commodification, the thing appears as that peculiarly 'thingly resistance to the status of mere thing', and does so in forms of improvisatory, generative and no less musical sociality that bypasses the individuation of the subject and its separation from its objects: 'a certain thingly resistance to the status of mere thing plays itself out precisely as a resistance to signification' and appears again as an 'irreducible phonic materiality' [UM 9]. The differing echo of certain formulations in *In the Break* is unmistakable, as is the departure from that book's lingering logic of oppositionality. Things get relegated to the threshold, on the edge of the outside, of the phenomenological tradition of philosophy, which may after all be no more than 'an ongoing disavowal of fallenness, an ongoing disavowal of and devaluation of things, of falling into the world of things' [UM 24]. Accordingly, things afford no purchase for the oppositional, for the Master-Slave dialectic that – precisely by the appropriation of the thing as his object – would make a subject of the Bondsman.[28]

Thinking from thingliness, thinking as the thing, requires a turning away from the hankering after freedom and autonomy, the ever-frustrated desire for the sovereign completeness that would be the impossible achievement of self-identity, and takes place to the side of those concerns, appositionally. Moten starts from the deceptively simple question: 'What would it mean to deal with the thingly in oneself, to attend to the possibility of being-captivated, to think from the position of the captive and thereby to enact possibilities of escape ...?' [UM 36] That thinking does not end, but approaches again and again the ethic that Cedric Robinson deciphered in the black radical tradition, a carelessness for individual survival that was profound care for what he termed 'the ontological totality', a phrase whose somewhat enigmatic formulation *consent not to be a single being* is devoted to illuminating.[29] Crucial to whatever ethic emerges from the position of the captive thing is simultaneously the inhabitation of the injury, the open wound out of which the thing's articulate cry emerges – the whole brutal history of capture, enslavement and racist violence – and the refusal to apprehend that injury as mere negation, as denial of one's very being.

Intrinsic to black radicalism in Moten's elaboration of the ethics implicit in Robinson's account of it is this commitment to think from the place of the thing, with the pathological, suffering/desiring subject in its sensuous ensembles rather than by way of transcending either suffering or incapacity. This is not to linger in injury, but at once to refuse and take on an injurious history in a 'critical encounter' [SL 104]. The 'black incapacity to desire sovereignty' is a radical transvaluation of incapacity that impels the alternative, appositional ethical-aesthetic of blackness, the counterstrophic accompaniment of modernity understood as the advent of freedom and progress. From within that alternative trajectory:

> We might think by way of, and perhaps through, the thing, with the thing's thought, that thought's expression

and habitation in the quotidian, in otherwise systematic rhythms, in the suffering of the suffering that is seemingly without voice, in the industrial, in and as the commodified, in the mute, mutant, mutated language of the mute, mutated, mutant instrument as it moves, finally, in the irrepressibly nonidentical. [SL 84]

Crucial to that thought is its punning thinking of instrumentality against its grain, not as radical alienation, but as 'the instrumental sociality of things in common' [SL 14]. If the ethical foundations of abolition, as of the prohibition of torture, have rested on some version of the categorical imperative, that no human should be used 'merely as a means' on account of 'the autonomy of his freedom', what can be the ethic of those whose historical experience, intellectual traditions and aesthetic performances are rooted in the knowledge of what it is to be 'mere means' and therefore a 'mere thing'?[30] Thinking out of, rather than in refusal of that knowledge, the black radical aesthetic tradition is an anti-instrumentalist instrumentalism of the ensemble, 'one that continually, and at first glance paradoxically, manifests itself through enactments of blackness as instrument and apparatus in melodramatic irruption' [SL 110]. The deep historical knowledge of blackness is given in 'the refusal, by way of black and fugal operations, of the subject's long, developmental nightmare' [SL 243] whose culmination now may be the general instrumentalisation of everything and everyone, black or not, in the brutally appropriative drives of contemporary capital.

The condition of that knowledge is the antipossessive ethic of those whose experience of modernity has been the violently imposed dispossession that constituted it. To affirm that a preferential option for the dispossessed is the ethico-political legacy of black radicalism is inseparable from taking on the knowledge that emerges from the assumption of the self's instrumentalisation, both as a matter of historical and brutal economic fact. The resulting disposition toward the world involves, once again, blackness's refusal of that which has been refused, but which is proffered over and over again as the release from bondage, that is, the lure of autonomous subjectivity as the form of the human: 'What if man escapes the labour of the negative via self-inflicted release into the thingly, a simple auto-dispossessive gift of self to instrument that resets both self and instrument in an ongoing, general recalibration of any and every such relation?' [UM 29]. That thought, which is the unseen, disregarded thinking of blackness, does not lend itself to conceptual formulation, to any easily legible program, but entails the difficult and repeated work of improvisational making and unmaking of the given, or imposed, structures and forms, their 'ongoing general recalibration', the parsing and unraveling of concepts that appear as the general and fugitive law of motion of Moten's philosophical investigations. As he parenthetically remarks, 'You have to come around again and start all over and hope that what you do gets close to what you're trying' [UM 29]. This is a thinking that, having been unseen, obscene, within the philosophical tradition, is 'an auditory affair' [SL 155], that is, has to be heard, as the long, multiply appositional phrasings of Moten's exploratory sentences must best be heard to be followed, like Coltrane's 'irrupting into and erupting out of that self-inflicted, rendering condemnation of man who had seemed to make such ruptive motion impossible, determined to keep returning to – or to keep turning in – that exhaustively locomotive breaking until he comes round right' [UM 29].

In this 'movement of things against owning' [SL 84] sounds and resounds a whole history of black radical commitment to commoning, in refusal of any 'tacit pseudouniversal consensus' that would make of the universal a carefully guarded enclosure for the possessive individual:

> As Kant says... 'the common right to the face of the earth ... belongs to humans generally.' Like all such ownership, it is only ever fully enacted in its having been relinquished. Such autodispossession is the (*first*) common right. Resistance to enclosure is its vehicle. ... Such assertion of world community is the essence of black radicalism/black abolition. [UM 94]

Two figures in particular perform this enactment of black radical thinking whose 'productive imagination moves to make present what has not already been there; but this is to say that it makes present, presents in the open, the original compact that was always already there' [UM 94]. One is (black) study, that anti-disciplinary, multi-disciplinary and dialogical mode of reflection and improvisation that is 'against sequestration, in always open unison' [UM 95] and which is 'blackness as a critical-historical project' [SL 99]. The other is, again, the soloist whose relation to the ensemble offers a kind of counter-model to the individual subject, the instrumentalist subjected to their instrument 'in attentive enactment of the open collective' and who furnishes 'the form of scholarship to which black students ... have long been devoted.' These students, these soloists, 'emancipate dissonance in a conception of sociality hinged on dispossession where one is bereft but for the specifically human, irreducibly necessary possibility of enacting new social forms, into which one disappears.' And once again, parenthetically, the mode of study is listening in: 'We hear that disappearance in audition's improvisational incursion of the song form' [UM 95].

The blackness that animates study, that emerges in the relation of soloist to ensemble or collective, is, to repeat an earlier point, performative, coming to presence in the protocols of performance and as the ongoing performative irruption of the 'old-new thing' [SL 156] whose felicity is that it refuses institutional sanction, thus manifesting as nonperformance, as Moten stresses in his dialog with Sora Han in 'Erotics of Fugitivity' [SL 241–267]. As the repeated work of an ethic of dispossession on the part of the (self-)dispossessed, blackness cannot itself be a property any more than, as iterated performance, it can be essence or identity. Moten urges this point more than once throughout *consent not to be a single being*: blackness 'is not reducible to black people' [UM 67], 'is not the property of black people' [UM 237], even if black people have a privileged relation to blackness 'insofar as they are given (to) an understanding of blackness' [SL 35] that is a function of their history of non-privileged relations to property. This is a formulation that gives rise to one of Moten's sharper rebukes to a certain kind of injured anti-racism on the part of those who 'step up to black history as if it were nothing but a serial injury inflicted upon them; as if every injury were their private property' [243]. Nor is blackness reducible to epidermalisation, as Fanon put it. Indeed, to riff on a phrasing of Moten's cited above, emphasis on colour and on the visible marks of racialisation could be to confuse the black as seen with blackness as thingliness. Blackness is not an ontological condition, nor even the denial to black people of 'ontological resistance' in the eyes of the white man, as Fanon thought. On the contrary, 'blackness is the anoriginal displacement of ontology' [SL 194]: as against one reading of Fanon, 'The lived experience of blackness is, among other things, a constant demand for an ontology of disorder, an ontology of dehiscence, a paraontology whose comportment will have been (toward) the ontic or existential field of things and events' [UM 150]. Thus an over-emphasis on the colour line, on the black/white binary in contemporary black studies has led to 'a field of racialised existence in which blacks, within a general structure of difference, have been made, against the grain of their own anoriginal, collectively unselfconscious self-making ... to signify a certain deanimated otherness-in/as-blackness while having been devoided, in the same horrific and impossible figuration, of the idea of blackness as a form of life' [SL 33–34].

To insist on 'blackness's distinction from a specific set of things that are called black' [SL 157], thus to refuse the conception of blackness as an identity, even as a form of non-identity predicated on wound and deprivation, and to regard it instead as 'the dispersive gift of anoriginal dispossession' [SL 27], may inevitably provoke the question, whose formulation will no less inevitably seem blunt or naïve, as to what the limits to blackness can be. If blackness is 'a form of life' not monopolised by black people, if black radicalism has been the critical-historical study and practice of commoning in the name of a 'world community', who gets to claim and perform blackness? Moten's response to such questions, which might also inevitably seem arch detours aimed back at critique, is no less blunt: 'Everyone whom blackness claims, which is to say everyone, can claim blackness' [SL 159]. The 'open unison' that is black study enables it to conjoin with the parallel 'study of comparative racialisation' in a manner that resonates deeply both with Robinson's historical work and with W.E.B. Du Bois's extensive exploration of the global significance of the colour line and its constitutive, ongoing relation to racial capitalism.[31] Although the terms that animate blackness and organise black study emerge in the context of the United States, 'their continued relevance and resonance will be international as well as intranational insofar as the ongoing aggressive constitution of the modern nation-state as a carceral entity extends histories of forced migration and stolen labour and insofar as the imperial suppression of movements that would excavate new aesthetic, political, and economic dispositions – as well, of course, as those movements themselves – is a global phenomenon' [SL 158]. Far from being the name of an identity, blackness is the moving ground of a solidarity that is intrinsic to black radicalism and its 'renunciation of actual for historical being'. For that renunciation, the owning of one's dispossession, 'will have ultimately become intelligible only as a general disruption of ownership and the proper when the ontological totality that black people claim and preserve is understood to be given only in this more general giving' [UM 236].

Dispossession is intimately bound to the condition of statelessness that is the other condition of blackness [UM 237]. In that light, solidarity amounts to more than the formal affirmation or defense of others' rights, whether a right to self-determination and sovereignty or the human rights that are bound to conceptions of citizenship and sovereign subjecthood and, above all, to the state's insistence on its own right to exist as sovereign. Solidarity is, rather, the articulation of stateless forms of life whose 'already given, constantly performed capacity for the alternative' calls forth – as jurisgenerativity does the jurispathic will of the law – the violent response of sovereign power [SL 215]. The relation of solidarity – which is entailed upon any claim to a commitment to black radicalism and internationalism – is predicated not so much on the kinds of political claims in which the discourse of rights is embedded, but on 'a particular kind of subpolitical experience that emerges from having been the object of that mode of racial-military domination that is best described as incorporative exclusion that settler colonialism instantiates' [SL 215]. That variously entangled 'more and less than political experience' of incorporative exclusion is what grounds the exemplary solidarity between black radicalism and the Palestinian liberation struggle that Moten engages, not as ethical duty but as a mode of renewal or refreshment of the black radical tradition. While the boycott called for by the Palestinian movement for Boycott, Divestment and Sanctions against Israel 'might provide some experiential and theoretical resources for the renewal of a certain affective, extrapolitical sociality – the new international of insurgent feeling' [SL 216], it is no less the case that: 'If there is a stateless antinationalism that is the surreptitious essence of black radicalism, then it bears lessons for the Palestinian struggle too' [SL 224]. Solidarity is this reciprocal renewal and mutual instruction, held 'in the radical sociality of our promised and unpayable debt to one another' [SL 214].

Both the mutual debt that is the condition of a non-sovereign human entanglement and 'the gift of historicity as claimed, performed, dispossession' [UM 237] that is its constitutive obverse are endless, unredeemable and unredeemed. This endlessness that informs both solidarity and the modes of black collective study, in steady and studied refusal of the institutions of sovereignty that maintain their violent regulation of human sociality, makes *consent not to be a single being* resonate far outside the field of black studies. The radical challenge it poses to the political presuppositions of modernity and the philosophical assumptions that continue, even unwittingly, to sustain them in the name of freedom and rights, offers inimitable resources for thinking through what it might be to inhabit our times transformatively. Moten's own formulation of the ethics of blackness offers a summation of that 'alternative planetarity' that would be the sociality performed by non-sovereign movements of the dispossessed moving in solidarity:

> It instantiates and articulates another way of living in the world, a black way of living together in the other world we are constantly making in and out of this world, in the alternative planetarity that the intramural, internally differentiated presence – the (sur)real presence – of blackness serially brings online as persistent aeration, the incessant turning of the ground under our feet that is the indispensable preparation for the radical overturning of the ground that we are under. [UM 235]

Blackness

These restless, questioning volumes inevitably yield in turn questions that will vex any reader. Afro-pessimists may continue to resist Moten's celebration 'of and in and through our suffering' [BB xiii], of blackness as sociality when the unabated force of anti-blackness operates above all through the denial to black people of access to (civil) society: that police killings of black and brown people persisted and may have increased even while the presidency of Barack Obama stood as evidence of the achievement of post-racial political integration is the index of that foreclosure from social being. Doubtless, in a quite different vein, historians of black diasporic struggles for specifically *political* forms of recognition and emancipation will be troubled by Moten's apparent indifference to the long traditions of organising for civil rights, for franchise, for citizenship and inclusion in national polities, as for access to the distributive justice minimally represented in welfare, education and other public goods that are in the purview of the state.

What if the anarchic performance of blackness as aesthetic sociality brackets out the historical commitments of black people that have been explicitly and resolutely political in their ends and forms of organising? Does the detachment of blackness from bodies that are black, even in the effort to read the 'free association' of black movements as 'desegregative planning' rather than 'integrationist achievement' [UM 100], not perform its own mode of erasure, substituting a preference for 'black refusal of political subjectivity' [UM 101] for the historical labour of black social movements and the transformations they have effected?

Given my own anarchist predilections, which determine my sympathy with Moten's positions, the questions that I am left with in the wake of reading *consent not to be a single being* lie in a different direction. Largely persuaded by the critique of the superordination of the political and of freedom predicated on political subjecthood, citizenship and sovereignty, I find myself perplexed in a different way by the extent and the limits of any dissociation of blackness from black people. Insofar as blackness is performative rather than predicative, how far does it risk diffusion into theoretical portability, becoming an optative signifier like the postcolonial 'subaltern' or race critical 'intersectionality', whose deployment has of late become detached from any relation to the social histories the terms were intended to designate? This is always the potential fate of any concept and Moten's work is peculiarly dedicated to pursuing and performing the disseminative dissolution of conceptual propriety. Nonetheless, can blackness finally be thought outside the historical formation of the social – and the political – life of black people from whose survival and whose improvisational generativity under conditions of dispossession, captivity, enslavement, Jim Crow and contemporary reinscriptions of state-sanctioned anti-blackness Moten derives its ethical and aesthetic practices? Or is there a way, tempting enough given the generativity of *consent not to be a single being*'s own conceptual moves, that blackness can become, if not a theoretical term for the ensembles of practices forged in other subaltern spaces, at least a passage into thinking them in other ways and other relations to one another? Can the fugitive forms of subaltern organising that Ranajit Guha among others have documented be rendered again in light of the improvisatory flights of blackness? Do the dispossessed and displaced Irish poor of the nineteenth century, with their own version of 'phonic materiality' and unruly impropriety, with their social formations that defied British notions of civility and individual property, constitute a mode of performance of blackness – as, indeed, reactionary cultural critics like Thomas Carlyle charged at the time? Analogous historical and geographical instances could surely be multiplied.

If in fact such cases can be thought not *as* but *in relation to* blackness, in the end this is not on account of the abstraction of the concept into unlimited transferability but is, paradoxically perhaps, an index of the specificity of Moten's deduction of the performative lexicon of blackness from the particular conditions of black social history. In that light, as he insists more than once, blackness is not an ontological essence, but an effect produced in and productive of the trajectory of modernity and its aestheticopolitical regimes. As such, blackness emerges in difference and must be thought in differential relation to other systems of racial formation. That thinking must take place with a similar degree of specificity, such that any invocation of blackness as analogue or as a means to the theoretical displacement of normative conceptual or representational frames can only do justice to that term through a painstaking attention to social formations that have emerged precisely in difference from it. Moten's indispensable contribution to Black Studies has long been recognised; it is for those of us working in adjacent fields to learn from his procedure, rather than from the terms he generates, how to 'turn the ground' with an equally radical effect.

David Lloyd is Distinguished Professor of English at the University of California, Riverside. He is the author of Irish Culture and Colonial Modernity *(2011),* Beckett's Thing: Painting and Theatre *(2016) and* Under Representation: The Racial Regime of Aesthetics *(2018).*

Notes

1. Fred Moten, 'I ran from it and was *still* in it', in *The Feel Trio* (Tucson, AZ and Denver, CO: Letter Machine Editions, 2014), 65–93.

2. See Fred Moten, *In the Break: The Aesthetics of the Black Radical Tradition* (Minneapolis: Minnesota University Press, 2003).
3. Ibid., 24.
4. See Saidiya Hartman, *Scenes of Subjection: Terror, Slavery, and Self-Making in Nineteenth-Century America* (Oxford: Oxford University Press, 1997), 23; and Robin D.G Kelley, 'Looking to Get Paid: How Some Black Youth Put Culture to Work', in *Yo Mama's Disfunktional! Fighting the Culture Wars in Urban America* (Boston: Beacon Press, 1997), 45.
5. Immanuel Kant, *Critique of Judgement*, trans. James Creed Meredith (Oxford: Clarendon Press, 1952), 151.
6. For a fuller exposition of the argument laid out here, see David Lloyd, *Under Representation: The Racial Regime of Aesthetics* (New York: Fordham University Press, 2019). [Reviewed by Lucie Kim-Chi Mercier in *Radical Philosophy* 2.06 (Winter 2019), 57–62.]
7. Moten is here addressing Fanon's 'Kantian critical discourse on nonsense' manifested in his 'conflicted critique of the style of the native intellectual' in *The Wretched of the Earth*, a critique closely related to his critique of the linguistic excesses of negritude poetics in *Black Skin White Masks* that Moten elsewhere discusses [UM 215-6]. The 'resistance of the object' reprises the titles and concerns of the opening and closing chapters of *In the Break*. Overall, however, *consent not to be a single being* pivots towards the somewhat different resistance that is that of the thing, or of the thingly sociality of blackness, as I'll discuss further on.
8. Moten is here citing the black trumpeter and composer Wadada Leo Smith.
9. Moten, *In the Break*, 2.
10. On those stolen pleasures of the enslaved, see Stephanie M.H. Camp, 'The Pleasures of Resistance: Enslaved Women and Body Politics in the Plantation South, 1830-1861', *Journal of Southern History* 68:3 (August 2002), 533-72, as well as Hartman's own extended mediation on 'Negro enjoyment' in Chapter 2 of *Scenes of Subjection*, 'Redressing the Pained Body', 49–78.
11. See Hartman, 'The Encumbrance of Freedom', *Scenes of Subjection*, 134.
12. See Robert Cover, 'The Supreme Court, 1982 Term. Foreword: Nomos and Narrative', 97 Harv. L. Rev 4 1983-1984.
13. Cover, 'Nomos and Narrative', 16.
14. Ibid.
15. Ibid., 40.
16. The formulations I am citing here are part of a long and engaged reading of Brian Wagner's *Disturbing the Peace: Black Culture and the Police Power after Slavery* (Durham, NC: Duke University Press, 2009), and critique what Moten sees as his 'assessment of crime as part of a state language to which blackness responds in ways that are labeled by the state as criminal' [SL 19].
17. See Moten's extended engagement with performance and nonperformance in dialogue with legal theorist Sora Han's essay, 'Slavery as Contract: *Bettye's Case* and the Question of Freedom', *Law and Literature* 27:3 (2015), 395-416, in his essay 'Erotics of Fugitivity' [SL 246–263].
18. The phrase, 'the lived experience of the black', is drawn from the French title of the fifth chapter of Fanon's *Black Skin, White*

Masks, 'L'expérience vécue du Noir', that was rendered in the first English translation as 'The Fact of Blackness'. See Frantz Fanon, *Peau noire, masques blancs* (Paris: Éditions du Seuil, 1952), 88; and *Black Skin, White Masks*, trans. Charles Lam Markham (London: Pluto Press, 1986), 109. This is the chapter that moves from the famous phrase 'Look, a Negro!' to Fanon's sense of ontological annihilation on reading Jean-Paul Sartre's introduction to the volume of negritude poetry, *Black Orpheus*, that confirms that his 'blackness was only a minor term' in the dialectic (*Black Skin, White Masks*, 138).

19. Orlando Patterson, *Slavery and Social Death: A Comparative Study*, with a new preface (Cambridge, MA: Harvard University Press, 2018). Moten cites here also Abdul Jan Mohamed, *The Death-Bound Subject: Richard Wright's Archeology of Death* (Durham, NC: Duke University Press, 2005), perhaps the most thorough-going elaboration of Patterson's Hegelian approach available.

20. Cited by Moten from Hannah Arendt, 'Civil Disobedience', in *Crises of the Republic* (New York: Harcourt Brace, 1972), 72.

21. See Walter Benjamin, 'Critique of Violence', trans. Edmund Jephcott, in *Selected Writings, Volume 1: 1913-1926*, eds. Marcus Bullock and Michael W. Jennings (Cambridge, MA: Harvard University Press, 1996), 240. For commentary on this paradox, see David Lloyd, 'From the Critique of Violence to the Critique of Rights', *Critical Times* 3:1 (April 2020), 109-130.

22. See Denise Ferreira da Silva, *Toward a Global Idea of Race* (Minneapolis: University of Minnesota Press, 2007).

23. G.W.F. Hegel, *The Philosophy of History*, trans J. Sibree (New York: Dover Publications, 1956), 96.

24. Moten, *In the Break*, 11.

25. Ibid., 1.

26. Martin Heidegger, *What is a Thing?*, trans. W.B. Barton, Jr. and Vera Deutsch (Lanham, MD: University Press of America, 1967), 191.

27. Moten, *In the Break*, 6.

28. For a more extended discussion of Denise da Silva's and Moten's notion of the thingliness of blackness and Hegel's dismissal of the thing in the *Phenomenology*, see David Lloyd, 'The Racial Thing', in *Texte zur Kunst* 117 (March 2020), 74-95.

29. Cedric Robinson, *Black Marxism: The Making of the Black Radical Tradition*, new edition, foreword by Robin D.G. Kelley (Chapel Hill, NC: University of North Carolina Press, 2003), 168.

30. Immanuel Kant, *Critique of Practical Reason*, ed. and trans. Mary McGregor, (Cambridge: Cambridge University Press, 1997), 74.

31. On Du Bois and the philosophical implications of the entwined emergence of global modernity and racial capitalism, see Nahum Dimitri Chandler, 'Exorbitance: The Problem of the Negro as a Problem for Thought', Chapter 1 of *The Problem of the Negro as a Problem for Thought* (New York: Fordham University Press, 2014), 11-67.

New philosophy books from Edinburgh University Press

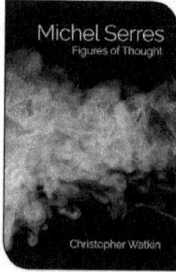

Michel Serres
Figures of Thought
Christopher Watkin

The first full introduction to Serres, from *The System of Leibniz* (1968) to his final publications in 2019.

ISBN 9781474405744
Paperback £24.99/$39.95
March 2020 • 472 pages

Lucretius II
An Ethics of Motion
Thomas Nail

An ancient ethics for modern life.

ISBN 9781474466646
Paperback £14.99/$19.95
March 2020 • 240 pages

Homo Natura
Nietzsche, Philosophical Anthropology and Biopolitics
Vanessa Lemm

Highlights the relevance of Nietzsche's work on human nature for contemporary debates in biopolitics and posthumanism.

ISBN 9781474466721
Paperback £19.99/$29.95
March 2020 • 216 pages

Nietzsche's *Human, All Too Human*
Ruth Abbey

A critical introduction and guide to one of Nietzsche's pivotal but lesser-known texts.

ISBN 9781474430821
Paperback £19.99/$29.95
January 2020 • 256 pages

EDINBURGH University Press

A motley crew for our times?
Multiracial mobs, history from below and the memory of struggle
An interview with Marcus Rediker

Radical Philosophy: A key concept of your work is 'the motley crew', which you mobilise to designate transversal alliances of sailors, slaves and pirates at sea. This seems a very productive notion for conceptualising insurgent collective formations that do not fit into the traditional categories of collective subjects. Could you explain the analytical purchase of that notion and how it emerged in your work with Peter Linebaugh?*

Marcus Rediker: In writing *The Many Headed Hydra* (2000), Peter Linebaugh and I searched for terms and concepts used by people in the seventeenth and eighteenth centuries to describe collective proletarian subjects and class struggle at the dawn of capitalism – 'motley crew', 'hewers of wood and drawers of water', 'outcasts of the nations of the earth', and, most importantly of all, 'the many-headed hydra'. Classically-educated European rulers cast themselves as Hercules as they built a new global economic system, calling forth great violence against the workers who resisted them. It was no easy task to organise sailors, slaves, indentured servants, factory workers, commoners and domestic workers into a new world capitalist system.[1]

What we especially liked about the hydra concept was how it embodied the motility of resistance: when one head was cut off, two new heads grew in its place. The basic forms of capitalist violence – expropriation, exploitation, discipline and punishment – generated new forms of resistance. This became a central theme of our book: insurgent actors might be defeated in one place, then exiled, after which they initiated new resistance, often in another form, somewhere else around the Atlantic. Radicals defeated in the English Revolution reappeared as rebellious indentured servants in Virginia. The 'experience of defeat', as Christopher Hill called it, was carried within radical diasporas around the Atlantic and helped to generate new struggles. Movements from below were more deeply connected than we knew.[2]

Out of this search for new concepts came the 'motley crew', a phrase that usually referred to the multi-ethnic workers aboard a ship but had a much broader application, especially in Atlantic port cities, where workers of all nations congregated. 'Motley crew' makes it possible to think the heterogeneity of the social subject in a way not determined by the nation-state. The 'motley crew' represented a new kind of mobile collectivity that contained its own social force.[3]

'Motley crew' is a useful concept for our times. In the eighteenth century, the 'motley crew' referred to a work group, a collective of people whose cooperation was essential to accomplish a particular task. That task could be sailing a ship, unloading a ship, or producing tobacco, rice

---

* This interview was conducted by Martina Tazzioli of the *Radical Philosophy* editorial collective in late 2019.

or sugar on a plantation. The 'motley crew' was an informal work group and a fundamental constituent part, an atom, so to speak, of class organisation. It was a temporary work group, frequently disbanded after its task had been completed. The collective of sailors who completed a voyage dispersed into taverns on the waterfront. But motley crew also operated at a second level, which was social and political. Various groups of working people came together in what was called a motley mob or a revolutionary crowd, a source of considerable power in eighteenth-century port cities. Let me give two examples. The motley crew was a driving force toward revolution in the 1760s, leading a series of protests in Boston, Philadelphia, New York and throughout the West Indies that eventually grew into the American Revolution. In 1768 sailors protested a wage cut in London, going from ship to ship, taking down or 'striking' their sails. This is the seafaring origin of the collective action called the strike. The motley crew wielded agency and power.[4]

RP: One reason for being interested in this concept is its significance for contemporary research on migration; that is, the possibility of using your analytical tools to understand these hybrid collective formations that cannot be described as 'populations' nor as 'the people', such as migrants who assemble at the border or wherever. These migrant collective formations, these migrant multiplicities, are usually described as non-political and are criminalised.

MR: This is an important point. Throughout history workers have been in perpetual motion, moving here and there, looking for something different, something better. This is, at a deep level, a matter of political choice. Such movement has been a powerful political force in world history for centuries. I was recently involved in a project called *A Global History of Runaways: Workers, Mobility, and Capitalism, 1600-1850* (University of California Press, 2019), about runaway sailors, soldiers, slaves, domestic workers and convicts in Europe, America, Asia, Africa and Australia. We found multiple traditions of running away, or absconding, moving from one place to another in ways that were self-determined – and therefore violently criminalised by authorities. Many of the runaways were multi-ethnic, i.e., motley crews; their actions were a subversive form of migration. It is not easy for us to think in conceptual or theoretical terms about people in motion. The anthropologist James Clifford has written an important essay about 'mobile cultures', in which he explains that almost all of anthropological theory is premised on the search for the 'sedentary primitive', peoples who were falsely presumed to be immobile and unchanging. But of course human populations have been in motion for millennia. Our task now is to generate new concepts that will help us understand people whose habits of thought and action have been shaped by motion.[5]

RP: Another term that you and Peter Linebaugh use in *The Many Headed Hydra* is 'multiracial mobs', which is evidently connected to the motley crew. Could you expand on how you use the term 'mob' by taking into account its political and historical genealogy, and the fact that the mob has been historically associated with unruly and non-political collective formations?

MR: The term 'mob' has a long history stretching back to the medieval and early modern eras. 'Mob' is a shortened version of 'the mobility', the collective of workers who made up a large part of urban social order. In the mouth of the upper classes, the 'mob', or 'rabble', a similar term, were always derogatory terms, insults against the unruly poor. In the 1960s and 1970s George Rudé, E.P. Thompson, and others shifted the discourse from 'mob' to 'revolutionary crowd', which has a completely different connotation, implying the power to make history. The terms 'mob' and 'crowd' are inherently political as they refer to people who gathered for the sake of protest:

against merchants who raised the price of bread, against manufacturers who created low wages and poor working conditions, or against the state who conscripted sailors through impressment and forced them into long stints of labour at sea. There is an insurgent dimension in this idea of the crowd. One of the contributions of *The Many-Headed Hydra* was to emphasise the diversity of social composition of these crowds. Crowds were democratically accessible; most anyone could join. Many who did had no other means for political expression.

I have long been interested in comparing the slave ship and the migrant ship. Of course, there are big differences between the two, in terms of the origins of the people on board. Many came from Africa past and present but by different routes and with different motivations. But in both cases the collectives aboard the ship made history – and we have been largely blind to it. It is a lasting bias in modern thought not to regard the oceans of the world as real places. We assume that history is made on land and in nations. One of the purposes of my research has been to show that large-scale historical processes happen at sea: class formation, race formation, cultural formation from below. In my book *The Slave Ship* I suggest that the lower decks of the slave ships created an early version of pan-Africanism through the assembly of millions of people made up of dozens of African ethnicities and nationalities. They learned to cooperate in new ways. If you look at the same process from the other side of the Atlantic, what's happening on board these slave ships is the origin of a new Atlantic African-American culture, featuring new ways of speaking, singing, relating to others and resisting. Such creativity happened on ships, at sea, a place usually considered to be a historical void. I came up with a word to try to describe the bias of seeing the seas and oceans of the world as empty spaces devoid of history: *terracentrism*. The bias restricts our understanding of change to landed societies, making it hard to comprehend history as made at sea on slave and migrant ships. When new groups of people come together on ships, their interactions result in new relations, new institutions, and social, cultural and political change. I have also applied this method of analysis to pirate ships, where poor sailors, 'the villains of all nations', pioneered democratic and egalitarian practices and traditions.[6]

RP: This is a crucial point to make, as there is a widespread tendency to dehistoricise what is going on at sea at the moment, to detach the bodies of the shipwrecked migrants from their stories as well as from the historical context. This process of abstraction is quite common in the public debate about migrant deaths in the Mediterranean.

MR: In his epic novel *Sacred Hunger*, Barry Unsworth depicts Liverpool merchant William Kemp talking with his son Erasmus about his slave ship, the *Liverpool Merchant*, anchored off the coast of West Africa:

> In that quiet room, with its oak wainscotting and Turkey carpet, its shelves of ledgers and almanacks, it would have been difficult for those two to form any true picture of the ship's circumstances or the nature of trading on the Guinea coast, even if they had been inclined to try. Difficult, and in any case superfluous. To function efficiently – to function at all – we must concentrate our effects. Picturing things is bad for business, it is undynamic. It can choke the mind with horror if persisted in. We have graphs and tables and balance sheets and statements of corporate philosophy to help us remain busily and safely in the realm of the abstract and comfort us with a sense of lawful endeavour and lawful profit. And we have maps.[7]

This passage brilliantly captures the violence of abstraction that shapes how historical actors and subsequent generations think – and do not think – about the past. This violence sanitises the past, blinding us to the human realities of history. I wrote *The Slave Ship* in order to try to grasp and convey in concrete, visceral terms what it meant to be on board one of those vessels. The same approach should be applied to migrant vessels.

RP: The other point that we would like to discuss is the reverberation that you stress in your books between the motley crew, the urban mob and other struggles happening elsewhere. We are interested in how you conceptualise these connections. There is indeed a huge literature about the connections among struggles, but these are thought in a quite horizontal, flat way, without accounting for the genealogy and the memory of the struggles, how these are reactivated in the present. Struggles and movements do not come out of the blue. And what is distinctive about your approach, it seems, is precisely your attempt to bring together a history and genealogy of the struggles on the one hand, and their transversality on the other.

MR: I really like this question because I think it is crucial for our era. I've always been interested in cycles of struggle that transcend the borders of nation-states. I learned in my earliest studies of sailors that mobile workers have been vectors of knowledge and experience. They connected struggles around the Atlantic as both participants and as carriers of ideas and traditions of resistance. We have usually considered protest and rebellion in national context or as geographically specific phenomena that could be compared but not connected. This is another way in which nationalism blinds us to the richness and power of history from below. Rare is the struggle that does not have a transnational origin, cause or reverberation, so we need to look for commonalities and connections. Take the Atlantic in the revolutionary 1790s as an example: scholars increasingly see the connections among the French Revolution, working-class agitation in England, the rise of the United Irishmen, and the most radical event of the era, the Haitian Revolution. Julius Scott's magnificent work *The Common Wind* shows how black sailors created autonomous networks of subversive communication in this revolutionary moment. Peter Linebaugh has recently created a powerful new history of the 1790s at the heart of which was a many-sided transatlantic struggle to recapture the commons.[8]

Add to this volatile mix a massive explosion of mutinies on naval vessels at sea, brilliantly analyzed in a forthcoming book by Niklas Frykman, *The Bloody Flag: Mutiny in the Age of Atlantic Revolution* (University of California Press, 2020). Frykman has discovered that as many as two hundred thousand sailors, literally 'motley crews', took over their ships and created a maritime crisis for Western European nations and their colonies in the 1790s. Workers moved from ship to ship to ship, carrying the news of the revolution and abolitionism from England and the United States to Haiti and from Haiti back to France. The point is, these various revolutionary movements, which were previously treated as separate national events, had common personnel, ideas and structural causes as well as mutual inspiration. Many people around the Atlantic began to think, all more or less at once, 'now is the time'. Whether applied to the 1790s, the 1830s, the 1930s, the 1960s, or today, this notion of a cycle of struggle helps us to think beyond the nation-state and recover the linkages that have frequently been rendered invisible by nationalist histories.

In all of my work I have tried to escape the pervasive violence of nationalist history, which limits what we can consider as part of our history and blinds us to the huge segments of European and American history that happened overseas through empire and global capitalism. Oceans and other bodies of water allow us to escape the national and to rediscover previously marginalised actors and lost histories. The Atlantic is one such space but so are the Indian and Pacific Oceans as well as the dozens of seas from the Caribbean to the Mediterranean, Persian and Tasman. International workers in motion, who always fit awkwardly into national stories if they were included at all, are now, after the global turn in scholarship, increasingly seen as those whose labour connected the world's continents. Getting beyond the nation is critical to rethinking capitalism and many-headed resistance to it.

RP: In your work you also refer to 'the multitude' to designate collective formations. And yet, your way of understanding the multitude seems quite different from the way in which Michael Hardt and Toni Negri describe it.

MR: Peter Linebaugh and I used the word 'multitude' in *The Many Headed Hydra* in quoting historical figures who had employed it in a primary or archival source. But we thought 'motley crew' offered a better way of understanding movement, resistance and social composition. Multitude is an imprecise residual category, more an abstract embodied fear than an analytical concept. 'Motley crew' is in my view a sharper analytical and theoretical tool because it emerges from working-class self-activity. It comes from below.[9] This is ultimately my life's project in writing history from below. Rather than take a concept from Machiavelli or Spinoza or Hobbes and apply it in a top-down way to the past, I look for concepts that bubble up from below and get us closer to the consciousness and action of insurgent subjects, the people who are actually moving and changing history. It is true, we don't always have first-person historical sources from these actors, but one of the principles of history from below is that one can, indeed must, read elite sources and discover within them a history of resistance and struggle. This helps us to understand the deeper causes of change as generated by social movements.

RP: How does your most recent book, *The Fearless Benjamin Lay*, connect with your previous work on collective subjects? In fact, in that book you centre on individual counter-conducts, to put it in Foucaultian terms, so there seems to be a partial shift from your previous focus on collective subjects.

MR: That book is the story of a radical eighteenth-century Quaker who was one of the first people to demand the worldwide abolition of slavery. He happened to have dwarfism and stood around four feet tall. He enacted guerrilla theatre against rich Quaker slave owners, sprinkling them with fake blood to humiliate them in public. He drew their wrath and was punished for his direct action: he was excommunicated by four different Quaker meetings, making him the most disowned Quaker of his era. One thing that interested me about Benjamin Lay was that he was an ordinary working person; he was not an elite in any sense. He was born to a humble family in a small village in Essex. He worked as a shepherd. He sailed the seas for a dozen years. He laboured as a glover in a 'stinking trade'. And yet he made an enormous breakthrough in human thought.[10]

Lay imagined a world without slavery at a time when most people of European descent considered slavery to be as natural and as eternal as the stars, the sun and the moon in the heavens. I wrote Lay's intellectual history from below to explain how he made the break. I discovered that he was a self-educated philosopher: he read classical philosophy quite seriously and was inspired in both his ideas and his methods of agitation by the Cynic philosophers, especially the radical figure Diogenes, whose first principle was commitment to radical free speech, what the Greeks called *parrhesia*. Lay followed the injunction to speak truth to power in all circumstances.[11]

Benjamin Lay applied this maxim in a direct way. He spattered blood on the most powerful people in the entire Quaker colony of Pennsylvania. Lay's combination of Quaker and Cynic ideas was further radicalised by his experience as a sailor, where he worked among a motley crew and imbibed the tradition of seafaring solidarity, and as someone who lived for a year and a half in Barbados, the pre-eminent slave society in the world at the time, where he saw enslaved Africans starved, maimed, tortured and executed for their resistance. Out of these experiences grew Lay's revolutionary worldview: he was a race-conscious abolitionist; he was a class-conscious critic of wealth and greed; he was a gender-conscious proponent of equality between men and women; he was environmentally-conscious, living in a cave and producing his own food and clothes to avoid participation in the capitalist market in which the commodity-form hid the labour and exploitation of workers. Lay came up with this idea more than a century before Karl Marx and immediately applied it to the struggle against slavery, pioneering the boycott of sugar because that innocent-seeming commodity was made, he knew, with the blood of enslaved Africans. Lay was also an advocate for animal rights; he considered all animals to be his fellow creatures. Human beings must not kill them. He was therefore also a vegetarian. He warned his contemporaries to beware rich men who 'poison the earth for gain'. Lay figured these things out almost three hundred years ago. He was a thinker of world-historical importance.

And yet he is almost completely unknown. His thought deserves to be studied alongside that of Machiavelli, Spinoza, Hobbes, and especially the 'enlightened' slave-owner Thomas Jefferson. Because Lay came from the wrong class, had the wrong kind of body, and espoused extremely radical ideas he has been left out of most histories, even those of abolitionism, to which he contributed so much.

Lay was a major reason why the Quakers became the first group to abolish slavery in their own midst. The Quaker yearly meeting announced in 1776 that one could not be a Quaker and own a slave. Slave-owning became grounds for disownment. Buoyed by Lay's radicalism, Quaker abolitionists as a whole had a tremendous influence upon Thomas Clarkson and the early abolitionists in England and upon the Société des Amis des Noirs in France. The revolutionary vector named Benjamin Lay had transatlantic influence. It is crucial that he fashioned his own critique of slavery (after 1718) more than two full generations before antislavery movements developed in the 1780s. Lay should be remembered as a major contributor to the struggle against slavery. He embodies many of the great themes of history from below.

RP: What do you think about contemporary political struggles and political organisations? How do you analyse these in light of your analytical framework?

MR: I think that these methods of analysis certainly do apply to the contemporary world. I use them in thinking about where we are and where we may be going.

It is important to observe new and diverse radical collectives emerging in recent years in public spaces, for example, Occupy Wall Street in Zuccotti Park in New York or the movement that assembled in Tahrir Square in Cairo. Bernie Sanders has mobilised a political movement at the heart of which is America's multi-racial working class. The initiatives of motley crews of migrants – who might be better called fugitives or runaways – are making the seas and oceans of the world a primary site of struggle again. It used to be the case that subversive ideas required ships for their circulation; now they travel instantaneously by technology and social media, making it possible for movements in one place to learn quickly about what is happening in other parts of the world.[12]

Even though global politics is currently characterised by resurgent nationalism and racism, I see sources of great hope. I see a million people in the streets in Chile. I see Lula out of prison and energising new struggles in Brazil. I see Latin America moving leftward again. I see a creative, fiercely determined movement in the streets of Hong Kong. More people identify as leftists of one kind or another in the United States than at any time since 1917-1922. The feminist movement continues to advance. The struggle against climate change has fired the wills and imagination of many thousands of people.

I've just returned from a week in Paris where I talked with a lot of people about the Yellow Vest movement. Many consider it hard to understand; it does not fit our standard models for a social movement. Its puzzling complexity fascinates me. It is radically democratic and self-consciously leaderless. And it has terrified the ruling class of France more than at any other time since 1968. We must learn from it, not stuff it into older categories of analysis.

The result of these movements is that there are more people working in radical causes today than at the peak of the movements of the 1960s and 1970s, which was considered a more revolutionary time. But here is the difference: radical forces have fragmented, or should I say, *have been fragmented* by the ruling classes they challenged half a century ago, when a broad 'movement culture' made everyone feel they were part of a world-changing surge forward. Today the huge number of people doing one or another kind of progressive work do not often feel connected to each other. We must come up with new inclusive ideas and connect the dots.

In conclusion, we can take a couple of lessons from Benjamin Lay as we imagine a better future. Lay took the sailor's ethic of solidarity and applied it broadly – to enslaved people, indeed to all people, all animals, all living things, the environment included, all around the world. Only compassionate solidarity could save us from greed and oppression, he believed. We must build it.

Lay also believed in the power of agitation – something the left has largely forgotten. In every public meeting he drew a line and asked the people around him, which side are you on? Are you for slavery or are you against it? There is no middle ground. He agitated high and low. Many people despised him for putting them on the spot. But slowly the hearts and minds of rank-and-file Quakers began to change. As the great African American abolitionist Frederick Douglass stated in 1857:

> If there is no struggle there is no progress. Those who profess to favor freedom and yet deprecate agitation are men who want crops without plowing up the ground; they want rain without thunder and lightning. They want the ocean without the awful roar of its many waters. This struggle may be a moral one, or it may be a physical one, and it may be both moral and physical, but it must be a

struggle. Power concedes nothing without a demand. It never did and it never will.

Lay wanted it all and so should we – the land and the sea, the crops and the rain, the thunder and the lightning, and most of all the struggle and the progress. We need to be ever mindful of the struggles of the past, even, or perhaps especially, the ones that failed. I have tried to build an archive of struggles past from which we can learn, take inspiration, and realise that we are not alone. People have been fighting capitalism for hundreds of years. As C.L.R. James observed long ago, the self-activity of working people around the world will always be the greatest hope for human emancipation.[13]

Marcus Rediker is Distinguished Professor of Atlantic History at the University of Pittsburgh. His books include Villains of All Nations: Atlantic Pirates in the Golden Age *(2004),* The Slave Ship: A Human History *(2007),* The Fearless Benjamin Lay: The Quaker Dwarf Who Became the First Revolutionary Abolitionist *(2017), and, with Peter Linebaugh,* The Many-Headed Hydra: Sailors, Slaves, Commoners, and the Hidden History of the Revolutionary Atlantic *(2000).*

Notes

1. Peter Linebaugh and Marcus Rediker, *The Many-Headed Hydra: Sailors, Slaves, Commoners, and the Hidden History of the Revolutionary Atlantic* (Boston: Beacon Press, 2000).

2. Christopher Hill, *The World Turned Upside Down: Radical Ideas in the English Revolution* (New York: Viking-Penguin, 1972); *The Experience of Defeat: Milton and Some Contemporaries* (New York: Viking-Penguin, 1984).

3. Marcus Rediker, *Outlaws of the Atlantic: Sailors, Pirates, and Motley Crews in the Age of Sail* (Boston: Beacon Press, 2014).

4. Laura Harris engages with and significantly expands the concept in 'What Happened to the Motley Crew?' in her *Experiments in Exile: C.L.R. James, Hélio Oiticica, and the Aesthetic Sociality of Blackness* (New York: Fordham University Press, 2018), 17–60.

5. Marcus Rediker, Titas Chakraborty, and Matthias van Rossum, eds., *A Global History of Runaways: Workers, Mobility, and Capitalism, 1600-1850* (Berkeley: University of California Press, 2019); James Clifford, 'Travelling Cultures', in *Cultural Studies*, ed. Michael Grossberg (New York: Routledge, 1992), 96–116.

6. Marcus Rediker, *The Slave Ship: A Human History* (New York: Viking-Penguin, 2007) and *Villains of All Nations: Atlantic Pirates in the Golden Age* (Boston: Beacon Press, 2004).

7. Barry Unsworth, *Sacred Hunger* (New York: Doubleday, 1993); Marcus Rediker, *The Slave Ship: A Human History* (New York: Viking-Penguin, 2007).

8. Marcus Rediker, *Between the Devil and the Deep Blue Sea: Merchant Seamen, Pirates, and the Anglo-American Maritime World, 1700-1750* (New York: Cambridge University Press, 1987); Julius Scott, *The Common Wind: Currents of Afro-American Communication in the Age of the Haitian Revolution* (New York: Verso, 2018); Peter Linebaugh, *Red Round Globe Hot Burning: A Tale at the Crossroads of Commons and Closure, of Love and Terror, of Race and Class, and of Kate and Ned Despard* (Berkeley: University of California Press, 2019).

9. I am indebted to Nandita Sharma for leading a comparative discussion of 'multitude' and 'motley crew' in a series of useful meetings in Honolulu in 2008.

10. Marcus Rediker, *The Fearless Benjamin Lay: The Quaker Dwarf who became the First Revolutionary Abolitionist* (Boston: Beacon Press, 2017).

11. Michel Foucault emphasised the power of Diogenes and the Cynic philosophers in lectures at the University of California-Berkeley in the fall of 1983. See his *Fearless Speech*, ed. Joseph Pearson (Los Angeles: Semiotext(e), 2001).

12. A major new contribution on the politics of migration is Nandita Sharma, *Home Rule: National Sovereignty and the Separation of Natives and Migrants* (Durham, NC: Duke University Press, 2020).

13. Frederick Douglass, 'The Significance of Emancipation in the West Indies', (August 3, 1857), available through the University of Rochester Frederick Douglass Project: https://rbscp.lib.rochester.edu/4398; C.L.R. James, *Notes on Dialectics: Hegel, Marx, Lenin* (London: Allison & Busby, 1980).

Reviews

Ontology for edgelords

Andrea Long Chu, *Females* (London: Verso, 2019), 112pp., £7.99 pb., 978 1 78877 737 1

In a dialogue published in the *Transgender Studies Quarterly* last year, Andrea Long Chu declared the death of trans studies. In her words, the discipline produces nothing but 'warmed over pieties' about sex and gender, devoid of any 'true disagreement' that would be able to 'birth theories'. She claimed that theorists working within the ever-more-indistinct field are essentially replicating queer theory with a trendy new prefix, and that this leaves important realities of 'transsexual' life unexamined. Chu has been championed by influential figures of various stripes, from trans studies 'founder' Sandy Stone to media theorist McKenzie Wark and affect theorist Lauren Berlant, precisely for her willingness to disavow disciplinary truisms. But one should wonder: is Chu's animosity directed at the current state of trans studies, or is it directed at transness itself? What does Chu herself have to say once she finishes shooting the New Materialist fish in her barrel, for example? Throughout the 27-year-old's rise to the status of pop theorist, Chu has held off on substantially articulating an approach to desire, identity and politics that might differ from what she polemicises against. With the release of her first book from Verso, *Females*, she has attempted to do just that.

More autotheory than theory, the theoretical claims made by *Females* are bracketed by oblique fragments of culture writing and personal memoir. Chu leaves it to the reader to bridge what is auto- and what is -theory in the text, and doing so is not easy. The narrative gaps between her autobiographical vignettes are filled in by theoretical claims that are as sweeping as they are poorly argued, and the intellectual gaps in her argument are plastered over with half-finished close readings of performance art or sophomoric reminiscences about her pre-transition self's college years. ('I was full of rage then: red, male, viciously intellectual.' Salingerian sentences like this, or the moment Chu describes someone about to dive into a swimming pool as 'bracing for the angry kiss of chlorine', hint that her reputation as a prose stylist is a tad overblown.) It is not that the autotheoretical form makes good theory or good autobiography impossible, but when both modes are present purely to compensate for each other's insufficiencies, the form as a whole fails.

The book's constant shifting between personal and academic registers also makes substantive criticism of its project difficult; autotheory is Chu's preferred form for a reason, and it seems to be an effective defense mechanism. Despite their unqualified embrace of her ideas, Chu's acolytes like to insist that one can never read her at face value, and wave away critique by deferring to some deeper truth of this or that metatextual frame, whether it be satire, trolling, irony, confessionalism, etc. But despite this goalpoast-shifting, *Females* does make a definite theoretical argument about sex, gender, transness and being, and this argument runs through all of Chu's work – there is no *Females*, and no Chu, without it – so evasive or not, such work must be able to be read seriously if it is to be read at all.

The text revolves around the claim that 'femaleness is a universal sex defined by self-negation, against which all politics, even feminist politics, rebels.' Chu minimally defines the 'female' as the one for whom 'the self is sacrificed to make room for the desires of another. … To be female is to let someone else do your desiring for you, at your own expense.' But Chu qualifies repeatedly that her model of the female has nothing to do with biological sex or gender identity as such. It is more that femaleness for her is the 'sex' of subjectivity (if not being) itself: 'How one copes with being female – the specific defense mechanisms that one consciously or unconsciously develops as a reaction formation against one's femaleness, within the terms of what is historically and socioculturally available – that is what we ordinarily call gender.' Yet despite these qualifications, Chu repeatedly codes the female to femininity, to penetration, submission and passivity. The figures she analyses – women like Jamie Loftus, Yoko Ono, Gigi Gorgeous, but also men who are pick-up artists and incels – are all said by Chu to index femaleness because of the way they carry ideals of femininity and womanhood (self-abnegation, most of all) to their extremes. 'Being Female' in Chu's special sense always ends up looking indistinguishable from 'being female' in the contingent, everyday sense. And given that she uses the formulation to make claims like 'men are not men, men are never men', it is clear that there is no meaningful way for Chu's argument to understand the position of trans men or nonbinary people. In fact, *Females* neglects to mention that they exist.

If being female is 'a universal existential condition, the one and only structure of human consciousness', and if at the same time 'to be is to be female', then the reaction to femaleness is not just the truth of sex and gender, but of all forms of identity. Race, class, and subjectivity itself are for Chu the same epiphenomenal residue of a sexed position that is supposedly nothing other than its empty formal receptivity to external desire; these forms are nothing other than their capacity to 'get fucked', because 'fucked is what a female is'. But race plays an especially troubling role in Chu's work. *Females* practically begins with the statements 'the entire incarcerated population is female' and 'females masterminded the Atlantic slave trade' – Chu can't quite follow through on her own line of thought and tell us that the enslaved, too, were female, but this is implicit.

Chu's triangulation of 'femaleness' with blackness becomes central in her analysis of sissy porn, a genre in which men (often white) are forcibly turned into women through sexual domination by other men (often black). 'Sissy porn did make me trans', Chu says. 'At very least it served as a neat allegory for my desire to be female – and increasingly, I thought, for all desire as such.' Using this racist genre of pornography to metaphorise not just one's own sense of one's femaleness and desire to transition, but everyone else's as well, is perhaps the dictionary definition of telling on oneself. By describing a generalised male 'inferiority complex' in a way that sublates white supremacy, Chu all but erases antiblackness, or renders it a side effect of the universality of femaleness. Chu extends this misreading by appealing to C. Riley Snorton's argument that gynaecological research's historical brutalisation of enslaved black women was fundamental to the development of an abstract idea of sex (female, unraced) as distinct from gender (woman, raced as white). To mistake the fungibility of race for the formability of sex in this way – to treat racialised violence as a kind of evidence for an idea of a sub-sexual sex which necessarily precedes race – is a serious error.

What then does Chu think being trans means? 'Gender transition, no matter the direction', we are told, 'is always a process of becoming a canvas for other people's fantasies.' There is only one possible colour for this canvas, however, and by pure coincidence it is the author's favourite. Chu repeatedly slips femaleness in on both sides of the ontological difference: 'To be female is, in every case, to become what someone else wants.' At the same time, 'the female is always the product of force, and force is invariably feminising.' In truth, there is not any agential subject in Chu's schema that could resist its femaleness, no self to sacrifice. As a result, despite her claim that 'gender transition begins ... from the understanding that how you identify yourself subjectively – as precious and important as this identification may be – is nevertheless on its own basically worthless', Chu herself is caught in the same trap of tautological insistence that she claims 'mere identification' finds itself in. What is the female 'produced' out of, if there is but one sex which precedes and creates all the forms which might initiate such a force? Where can the desires of others come from if everyone is an empty vessel awaiting those desires? What could ever create a new desire, trans desire most of all, if 'female' is all there is to be? In the end Chu only says that everyone is female because, like any good solipsist, that is the only way she can convince herself that she is. If everyone is female, no one is, and real transition is in the end impossible – a view that Chu seems to uphold when she posits that 'autogynephilia', a transphobic and discredited psychiatric diagnosis which sees trans women as men who get off on the idea of being women, is 'the basic structure of all human sexuality'. Unable to muster any fidelity to the ontological possibility of transition, she instead settles for weaponising its purported ontological impossibility as a general axiom: if trans

people can't really be what we are, then no one can.

In her essay 'The Pink', which preceded the publication of *Females* by half a year, we see some of the thinking behind this book presented with greater honesty. There Chu took up the supposed obsolescence of a 'universal category of womanhood', and attempted to critique the way that contemporary feminism has discarded a 'vaginal imaginary' that might exclude pre- or non-operative trans women. True to character, Chu argued that a trans-inclusive gesture would be equally impossible. Her surrender to this dilemma was bleak:

> We have this, at least, in common: two kinds of women, with two kinds of self-loathing, locked in adjacent rooms, each pressing her ear up against the wall to listen for the other's presence, fearing a rival but terrified to be alone. For my part, cousin: I don't want what you have, I want the way in which you don't have it. I don't envy your plenitude; I envy your void. Now I've got the hole to prove it. I would give anything to hate myself the way you do, assuming it's different from the way I hate myself—which, who knows.

For Chu there is not really one void called femaleness, but at least two voids: one is cissexual and one is transsexual, and the former is vastly more desirable than the latter. Why? Well, this is just how desire is, we cannot question it, it has no history, it has no ethics; it is, and we are (for it is all we are) opaque. It's striking to see Chu try to inscribe cis supremacy into something as empty and formless as the void, but this is the project's endpoint, and explanatory of her popularity with a cis audience. But it is useful to contrast this image of femaleness, in which 'two kinds of women' fear one another and loathe themselves, to an image presented by Chu's role model, Valerie Solanas: 'In actual fact, the female function is to relate, groove, love, and be herself, irreplaceable by anyone else. ... In actual fact the female function is to explore, discover, invent, solve problems, crack jokes, make music – all with love.' As racist, misanthropist, transphobic and hateful as Solanas was, Chu manages to discard the one optimistic kernel of an otherwise pessimistic theory.

Chu too has been described as a pessimist. In fact, it would be more accurate to call her a fatalist, who at heart believes that the difference between being cis and being trans is absolute, made intractable by an ontological ground that can never truly be determined. In her *TSQ* dialogue, Chu said she longed to see the birth of 'real theory' that would reorient our ideas of transness away from its current articulations. But Chu's conclusions are no different from the 'pieties' she positions herself against, which see the trans subject as always hybrid, always crossing borders, always becoming but never being. Chu reaches the same dead-end of thought, not by particularising sex, gender and transness to the point of meaninglessness, as trans studies indeed tends to do, but by universalising her own hopelessness about transition: not 'always becoming but never being', but 'always not being'. Here trans women are still not women, but we do get to be 'females' like everyone else – in other words, nothing at all.

A reorientation and revivification of trans theory is certainly necessary at the moment, and it is clearly something many are hungry for, given the attention Chu's work has received. But if *Females* is any indication, Chu will not be among those who manage to stage such an intervention.

Nora Fulton

Unstable histories

Lucas Richert, *Break on Through: Radical Psychiatry and the American Counterculture* (Cambridge, MA: MIT Press, 2019). 224pp., £22.00 hb., 978 0 26204 282 6

In May 1969, in the plush surroundings of Miami's Americana Hotel, the ordinarily staid annual meeting of the American Psychiatric Association (APA) became the flashpoint for a standoff which had been brewing within the profession for a number of years. The newly-formed Radical Caucus of the APA issued a defiant challenge to the association's leadership, and to the profession as a whole. No longer content with 'hiding behind the couch', its spokespersons argued, it was time for psychiatrists to take a principled stand against the social, political and economic injustices that divided the US. Members distributed pamphlets condemning the medical establishment's endemic racism and sexism, and attacking psychiatrists for their complicity with the American military. They denounced the Vietnam War, called for the decriminalisation of drugs and of abortion, and supported gay rights protestors calling for the declassification of homosexuality as a psychiatric disorder.

Break on Through by historian Lucas Richert seeks to offer 'a reinterpretation of medical and mental health knowledge in American society in the 1970s'. This was a decade (give or take a few months) which opened with the formation of the Radical Caucus, and closed with the publication, in 1980, of the third edition of the APA's *Diagnostic and Statistical Manual of Mental Disorders* (DSM-III), now widely seen as signalling the triumph of a narrowly biomedical psychiatry. In reality, Richert's book encompasses a longer period, stretching from the late 1950s to the early 1980s, and taking in a wide range of challenges to mental health orthodoxy. As well as critiques from within American psychiatry, and from the international anti-psychiatry movement, he covers scientific explorations of parapsychology and of psychoactive substances, the development of alternative therapies and grass-roots health activism, and the take-up of mental health issues by various political constituencies.

This was a period which saw both a politicisation of psychology and a psychologisation of politics. Radicals in the 'psy-' professions argued that the problems described as 'mental illnesses' should not be seen in purely medical terms, but instead as the psychological effects of unjust socioeconomic relations. Neither the talking cure of psychoanalysis nor the scientific pretensions of behaviourism, they claimed, were adequate to deal with the challenges posed by contemporary American life. Rather, mental and emotional wellbeing could only be achieved through social transformation. 'Therapy means political change', as one enigmatic slogan of the Radical Caucus put it, 'not peanut butter.'

At the same time, the language of psychiatry – of madness, alienation and paranoia – was infiltrating Cold War discourse in the United States and Europe at a variety of levels. For an iconoclastic new left in the 1960s, the irrationality of a 'sick society' was evident in everything from racial segregation to the Cuban Missile Crisis. What was the 'delusion' of a psychiatric patient who believed the atom bomb to be inside of her, asked the Scottish anti-psychiatrist R.D. Laing, compared to the madness of political leaders willing to trigger nuclear apocalypse? At the same time – perhaps paradoxically – a romanticised idea of madness could also represent the possibility of liberation from society's repressive norms: the 'half-chosen, half-compelled' rebellion that Laing's associate David Cooper identified in the schizophrenic, the 'psychopathic personality' of Norman Mailer's hipster, or the 'systematic derangement of the senses' pursued by the followers of William Burroughs.

This was a complex and unstable exchange, and neither appropriation of psychological vocabulary nor condemnation of orthodox psychiatry were limited to the political left. Probably the best known 'radical psychiatrist' in twentieth-century America, Thomas Szasz, was a fervent right-wing libertarian. Szasz argued – with increasing vitriol over his career – that medical psychiatry and 'the therapeutic state' functioned to pathologise undesirable behaviours, preventing individuals from accepting responsibility for their own actions and creating dependency. Other prominent critics of psychiatry in the post-war period would include the anti-communist John Birch Society – for whom the psy-disciplines represented a Soviet-Zionist conspiracy – and L. Ron Hubbard's Church of Scientology. At times, *Break on Through* struggles to contain these contradictions, and Richert's impulse to treat 'radical psychiatry' as a consistent or discrete phenomenon risks flattening out some of the complexities inherent in the era's volatile psychopolitics. While it is undoubtedly the case that a wide range of people came to criticise psychiatry and its institutions in the 1960s and 1970s, whether as a group they shared much else in common, politically or culturally, is less clear.

For the majority of the book, Richert's focus is on militancy within the psy-professions – those 'agitators and radicals' who challenged the assumptions of their disciplines and put forward revolutionary new models of mental disorder and its treatment. Yet one of the more striking aspects of the story told in *Break on Through* is the extent of productive exchange and interaction between this 'radical fringe' and the ostensible mainstream. The pioneers of 'humanistic psychology', Carl Rogers and Abraham Maslow, managed to challenge orthodoxies while at same time holding numerous prestigious professional appointments, while facilities such as the Esalen Institute – the California birthplace of the 'human potential' movement – provided a lively interface between the countercultural avant-garde and the scientific establishment. Exploration of the therapeutic effects of psychoactive substances such as LSD and MDMA, in treatments of schizophrenia and in end-of-life care for geriatric patients, was a serious research enterprise rather than a crank pseudoscience, and its legitimacy was threatened more by the political climate of Nixon's 'War on Drugs' than by any opposition within the psychiatric profession.

While the APA's Radical Caucus undoubtedly styled themselves as renegades and trailblazers, many of the positions they advanced in the 1970s actually had a much longer pedigree. The thrust of much recent scholarship on anti-psychiatry movements has been to stress the extent of continuity between the politicised, social models of mental health of the kind explored in *Break on Through*, and an already-established liberal tradition within the psychiatric profession. In the US, the Group for the Advancement of Psychiatry (GAP), founded in 1946, was typical of this approach, eschewing political neutrality and espousing a variety of social causes. Two decades before the Radical Caucus's emergence, a 1950 statement by GAP on the 'social responsibility of psychiatry' had made clear the Group's 'conscious and deliberate wish to foster those social developments which could promote mental health on a community-wide scale.' Similarly, the origins of the democratically-run 'therapeutic community' were not to be found at Esalen, or in the radical circles around Laing and Cooper in 1960s London, but in experiments taking place in British military hospitals during the Second World War.

Arguably the more interesting problem for historians is not the prevalence of these ideas in the 1960s or 1970s, but the reasons for their ultimate co-option or defeat by the 1980s. The reassertion of a biological and hereditarian essentialism in psychiatry, assisted by the lobbying power of the pharmaceutical industry and codified in DSM-III, is one aspect of this story. Another is the corporate, business school co-option of concepts and techniques – human potential, mindfulness, the encounter group – which had once held utopian promise for a generation of radicals as a means to transform both interpersonal and societal relationships. While it is tempting to see such projects as corrupted from the start – naïve in their prizing of immediate experience, nascently individualistic in their focus on personal growth, orientalist in their selective appropriation of Eastern philosophy and religion – it is also worth considering the emancipatory ways of thinking that their eclipse may have shut down. In this view, the decline of radical psychiatry begins to look like just one aspect of a greater exorcism of that spectral freedom which Mark Fisher identified in sixties radicalism more broadly – the process of reclamation through which 'those aspects of the counterculture which could be appropriated have been repurposed as precursors of the "new spirit of capitalism", while those which were incompatible with a world of overwork have been condemned to so many idle doodles.'

Some of the most illuminating sections of *Break on Through* are the short passages which look at the emergence of what is now called the psychiatric survivor movement (Richert's claim that such groups have been well-served by existing historiography is puzzling). Grassroots demands for 'mad liberation' from patients and ex-patients both exposed tensions within radical psychiatry and generated new contradictions of their own. While often inspired by the anti-psychiatric writing of figures like Szasz and Laing, activists in groups such as the Insane Liberation Front and the Network Against Psychiatric Assault questioned the possibilities for genuine emancipation within a movement dominated by a few 'hip professionals', most of whom continued to work within the psychiatric system. While some groups campaigned for a more humane and democratic approach to treatment – demanding an end to involuntary hospitalisation, electroshock therapy and psychosurgery – others questioned whether the existence of any kind of therapeutic intervention at all was compatible with liberation. The demand for a transformed psychiatry co-existed uneasily with convictions that only a wider, revolutionary, social transformation could address the problems that psychiatrists claimed to treat. Ultimately, from the 1980s onwards, the more radical elements of patient-led activism also proved co-optable. Demands for greater democracy in treatment could be subsumed within a commercialised model of user feedback and consumer rights, collective self-empowerment diverted into privatised self-help, while more militant groups struggled for resources in the face of cuts to public funding.

Richert is surely right in seeking to situate the battles over American psychology within a wider cultural field. In many ways 'radical psychiatry' and 'American counterculture' were inseparable. As well as Rogers and Maslow, Esalen could count among its guests and residents the likes of Ken Kesey, Buckminster Fuller, George Harrison, Joni Mitchell and Bob Dylan. The patients' liberation movement exploited the networks of the underground press and drew on a repertoire of activist and protest techniques – such as the consciousness-raising group and the sit-in – developed in civil rights and women's liberation movements. Yet the definition of 'counterculture' offered by Richert – 'theological, political, attitudinal, or material positions that departed from common or accepted standards' – is so capacious as to be almost evacuated of any analytical utility. Too often, cultural historical detail is deployed as mere background colour, the superficial set-dressing for a nostalgic period drama set in a television producer's idea of the sixties and seventies – a time of hippies and punks, lava lamps, roller skates and disco. At certain points, this appears as unintentionally comic non-sequitur, crowbarred in like clumsy expositional dialogue. The pioneer of LSD therapy Ronald Sandison writes to R.D. Laing in June 1970, we're told, 'a moment when the Beatles "The Long and Winding Road" and Jerry Mungo's [sic] "In the Summertime" were wafting over the airwaves and *Myra Breckinridge* and *Catch-22* were showing in theaters.' The somewhat rushed feeling these insertions give to the book is not helped by an accumulation of minor factual or typographical errors: the opening of Laing's community at Kingsley Hall is wrongly dated to 1964 rather than 1965; a takeover of mental health facilities by workers at Lincoln Hospital in the South Bronx also has the wrong date (it was 1969, not 1968), and is erroneously attributed to the Black Panthers (perhaps being confused with a later action at the hospital led by the Puerto Rican Young Lords); the important newspaper of the early survivor movement, *Madness Network News*, is referred to as *Madness News Network* throughout.

The countercultural engagement with psychiatry – both in the United States and in Europe – was wide-ranging, often ambivalent and politically confused. A July 1969 special edition of the London underground newspaper *International Times*, for example, placed side-by-side an interview with R.D. Laing, an article on the unorthodox early twentieth-century psychologist Georg Groddeck (interspersed with quotations from Laing, the I Ching, Shakespeare and Jimi Hendrix), an extract from L. Ron Hubbard's *Dianetics*, and a call to action from the activist-therapy collective People Not Psychiatry. A more sustained and serious engagement with these broader anti-psychiatric networks might have allowed Richert more fully to come to terms with the tangled web of contradictory impulses, inconsistencies and reflexive critiques which in many ways defined the psychiatric radicalism of the period.

Half a century on, radicals in the mental health field are confronted with a much-changed system. While the Victorian asylums which dominated mid-century psychiatric care have largely been emptied, the reality of deinstitutionalisation in the US and the UK has been an abandonment by the state of those who most need assistance. 'Community care' – always largely euphemistic as a policy proposal – has left people isolated in the absence of properly funded support, and decarceration has in many cases meant emancipation into addiction, homelessness and the criminal justice system. Prescriptions for psychiatric medications (in particular antidepressants) have increased exponentially, as have the profits of pharmaceutical companies, while biomedical hegemony has been consolidated. In the context of relentless cuts to mental health provision, the instincts of the left have often, understandably, been defensive – to fight to keep the services we have, and to expand them to more people. Revisiting the liberatory experiments of the 1960s and 1970s can allow us to think again about how our communities might be served not just by an extension of medical psychiatry, but by a fundamentally transformed conception of illness and what it means to be well. For today's radicals and activists, at a time when mental health and illness are becoming newly politicised once more, it will be equally important to learn from their failures.

Steffan Blayney

Racial properties of colonial appropriation

Brenna Bhandar, *Colonial Lives of Property: Law, Land, and Racial Regimes of Ownership* (Durham, NC: Duke University Press, 2018). 272pp., £80.00 hb., £20.99 pb., 978 0 82237 139 7 hb., 978 0 82237 146 5 pb.

Brenna Bhandar's *Colonial Lives of Property* is a significant intervention into contemporary debates on empire, the property relation, imperial jurisprudence and racial capitalism. Employing a range of methodologies and interdisciplinary modes of critical inquiry, Bhandar constructs her argument around four interconnected frames of analysis: colonial conceptions of *use* that justify the valuation of land taken through the racialised devaluation of the people who might obstruct colonial appropriation; the procedure of *title by registration* as enabling an abstract logic of commodity form and racial classification; *improvement* as a mode of cultivation central to the project of settler colonisation; and the *identity-property nexus* as establishing the gendered, racialised and colonial terms of property ownership that are 'central to the proper legal subject in the political sphere'.

In the closing chapter, Bhandar asks: 'How do we reconceive place, territory, land, or property when it appears settled, firmly ensconced in real estate and financial markets organised according to capitalist rationalities that bear the mark of historically embedded processes of abstraction?' Throughout *Colonial Lives of Property*, she engages this question by demonstrating how colonial modes of appropriation have been constitutive for the historical co-production of modern property law and racialised subjects in ways that continue to be remade and contested in the present. Bhandar focuses on the significance of use, abstraction, improvement and status as animating logics of colonial appropriation and the juridical formation she calls the 'racial regime of ownership'. Building on Cedric Robinson's formulation of 'racial regimes' and Stuart Hall's elaboration of Louis Althusser's conception of 'articulation', she shows how forms of property, personhood and place that appear self-evident and incontrovertible are in fact contingent, disjointed and volatile cultural logics that are only ever provisionally secured under particular relations of power at specific historical conjunctures. With the British empire and the settler colonies of Canada, Australia and Israel/Palestine as its principal sites of inquiry, *Colonial Lives of Property* underscores how this provisional appearance of coherence, solidity and permanence 'requires continual renewal and reinstantiation to prevail over other ways of being and living'.

Indeed, in such occupied territories, the place, land or property that may appear from one perspective as 'settled' nonetheless remain profoundly and often violently contested. For instance, in the Canadian province of so-called British Columbia, the focus of two of Bhandar's chapters, conflicts such as the Coastal Gas Link and Royal Canadian Mounted Police (RCMP) assault on Wet'suwet'en traditional territory and the RCMP evictions of Indigenous and impoverished unhoused peoples from tent cities have substantially escalated during the past year. Whether by the Unist'ot'en Camp land defenders' refusal to allow oil and gas pipeline construction to devastate Wet'suwet'en homelands or by Alliance Against Displacement/Red Braid Alliance for Decolonial Socialism activists' defense against the violent rule of law on behalf of gentrification and capitalist predation, such action embodies contemporary confrontation with the racial regimes of ownership theorised by Bhandar.

Reflecting on the Unist'ot'en Camp, in 'Fighting Invasive Infrastructures: Indigenous Relations against Pipelines' (2018), Tlingit scholar and activist Anne Spice describes 'critical infrastructure' as extending the settler nationalist imperatives of appropriation in ways that might also be understood as emerging from the genealogies of possession and legal infrastructure discussed by Bhandar. Spice contends: 'Reclaiming relations beyond invasive infrastructures means acknowledging the violence done by prioritising technical and technological infrastructure as the work of national progress', arguing further that the 'settler state shapes narratives around infrastructure projects that make them out to be a part of the natural advancement of the nation-state while masking the violence they cause to Indigenous land and bodies, especially the bodies of women and girls.' From the

perspective of 'urban Indigenous people who have been displaced from our traditional territories', the Red Braid Alliance likewise 'exercise land relations and stewardship by healing, building, and defending our communities, homes, and spaces against colonial forces that seek to assimilate or annihilate us.' As refusals of the lethal emplotment of racial regimes of ownership, they assert on their website that 'our blockades and disruptions are practices of Indigenous ways of being and relating that work to dismantle the settler colonial country of Canada.' These practices, and the challenges they present to the colonial rule of law, are vital counterparts to Bhandar's argument.

Colonial Lives of Property draws insight from and contributes to anticolonial struggles and movements for the displaced attuned to the conditions of Indigenous dispossession. Bhandar troubles conventional critical responses to dispossession that replicate the possessive and appropriative underpinnings of racial regimes of ownership, ultimately proposing that 'the undoing or dismantling of racial regimes of ownership requires nothing less than a radically different imaginary of property'. Robert Nichols' recent work on the recursive logic of dispossession is an especially important complement to Bhandar's project. In *Theft is Property! Dispossession and Critical Theory* (2020), Nichols argues that in the context of British empire the system of colonial land ownership was not only the outcome of pervasive and coordinated theft but a means to conform property itself whereby 'possession does not precede dispossession but is its effect.' Bhandar develops a similar line of argument, but places greater emphasis on the constitutive role of race in this regard, contending that 'dispossession was both a prerequisite and a consequence of the coproduction of racial value and property ownership, rendered possible by a logic of abstraction that was central to emergent capitalist forms of property and the racial subjection of indigenous peoples and their lands and resources'.

From the mid-seventeenth century onward, further catalysed with the taxonomies of racial science during the late eighteenth and nineteenth centuries, Euro-American presuppositions of race and racial difference attributed value to those persons accorded the capacity and will to properly appropriate and claim possession through particular methods of improvement. In conversation with the work of Cheryl Harris, Ruth Wilson Gilmore and Denise Ferreira da Silva, Bhandar persuasively argues that colonisation 'produced a racial regime of ownership that persists into the present, creating a conceptual apparatus in which justifications for private property ownership remain bound to a concept of the human that is thoroughly racial in its makeup'. Bhandar can be likewise productively read alongside scholars such as Aileen Moreton-Robinson, Shona Jackson, Iyko Day, Tiffany Lethabo King and K-Sue Park, each of whom emphasise how distinct yet interdependent formations of colonisation and race underwrite the logics of possession and property, and each of whom reject the conventional division between analytics of land and labour as obscuring the work of conquest and colonial domination.

An especially crucial insight developed by Bhandar has to do with the particular valences of possession and property in the rationalisation of colonisation and occupation. She argues that 'possession, despite having been surpassed by the modern grammar of property that is built on a logic of abstraction, remains central to the reality of property relations in the settler colony'. While the abstracted hierarchical categories of racial classification work in tandem with the abstract character of the commodity form of real estate, in settler colonial contexts both work together to ostensibly secure possession. Colonial authorities cast specific practices of improvement and cultivation oriented towards market exchange as conforming and confirming propriety and proprietary rights. Thus, 'a concept of value emerged that linked the improvement of land through particular kinds of use (cultivation for commercial purposes) to the improvement of populations who were not capitalist tenant farmers or engaged in waged labour within emerging capitalist agrarian markets'. Legally recognised use of and claims to property, formalised in such key endeavors as registration by title, substantively disavowed and sought to erase Indigenous forms of habitation, subsistence and relations to land.

Bhandar productively focuses on the extent to which the idea of improvement served as a principal mode for the articulation of racial regimes of ownership. She demonstrates how and why 'improvement was to be measured by agricultural production and the capacity to engage in rational – that is to say abstract – thought as an economic actor'. With improvement understood as the animating and irrepressible logic of colonisation, 'the appropriation and cultivation of land was integral to the progression from a state of nature to a civilised state of being'.

This version of improvement enshrined notions of historical progress whereby private property came to be the culmination of reason and 'civilisation'. Ultimately, 'without ownership, and the law that accompanies it, there could be no civilisation'. And indeed, as with conflicts today such as Indigenous resistance to the Canadian siege on the Wet'suwet'en and the anti-gentrification actions of the Red Braid Alliance, it is precisely the logics and logistics of improvement, progress and (colonial-capitalist) civilisation that are rejected.

Another crucial example of the ideology of improvement as justification for colonial dispossession and disavowal examined by Bhandar are Zionist rationalisations for Israel's relentless and murderous expropriation of Palestine. She specifies here that her argument is concerned with 'the brand of political Zionism that had ... explicit territorial aspirations, which clearly prevailed in the mode of colonisation pursued in Palestine'. Focusing on Zionist theorists such as Arthur Ruppin, author of the 1926 tract *The Agricultural Colonisation of the Zionist Organisation in Palestine*, she argues that colonisation is organised by logics of possession not limited to the goals of economic profit, resource exploitation and capital accumulation. Jewish settler labour as a redemptive practice of cultivation 'became the prime basis for establishing a moral and legal right to land in Palestine'.

Agriculture is directly linked to the historical discourse of planting and plantation – colonisation as enacting the biblical allegory of 'planting the garden'. For Ruppin, the United States and the state of California in particular loom large in the imaginary of colonisation justified by agrarian practice. The frequently quoted passage from Crèvecœur's 1782 *Letters from an American Farmer* conveys the colonial specificity of this appeal for its affective fusion of cultivation and property as more than simply the accumulation of wealth: 'The instant I enter on my own land, the bright idea of property, of exclusive right, of independence, exalt my mind … What should we American farmers be without the distinct possession of that soil? … No wonder we should thus cherish its possession.' Ruppin similarly asserts with regard to Zionist settlers that 'The new settlers look upon agriculture not only as the means of existence, but as the source of a new national life'. For Ruppin, the racial difference between Jews and Arabs provided the ultimate explanation for Jewish superiority and why Arab labour could not serve as a comparable source of claims to belonging and nation.

The Zionist assault on Bedouin peoples further exemplifies displacement facilitated by the valorisation of particular relations to place and the erasure of others. Zionist recourse to ideologies of 'planting' as becoming rooted in place are deployed over and against the attributions of Bedouin nomadism. As Bhandar argues, the Israeli state's 'determination to deny the historic and contemporary presence of Bedouin on their land requires the constant and repeated destruction of the very evidence of their ownership – settlement in the form of homes, villages, and crops'. This categorical erasure of Bedouin peoples, by defining them as only historically transient and essentially without the capacity to possess, finds multiple resonances across the book, where colonial property regimes acquire life through juridical contrivances on behalf of dispossession, racial subjection and differential devaluation of people cast as without will or self-ownership.

The book's fourth chapter presents a searing explication of this process as manifested in what Bhandar calls the identity-property nexus. Here, she tracks the gendered and racialised formation of what C. B. Macpherson theorised as the self-possessed individual in relation to the production of 'Indian status' in the Canadian settler colonial context. During the mid-nineteenth century, a series of legislative acts attached Indian status to particular bodies and places such that 'the Indian as a juridical category and the Indian reserve marks a specific historical conjuncture, one in which identity and property relations were explicitly bound to each other, constituting a core dimension of an apparatus of colonial knowledge and governance'. The Canadian state rendered Indian status and access to reserve land for First Nations women dependent on the dictates of patriarchal marriage law and the implicit logic of blood quantum. Status in effect functioned as a form of patrilineal and patriarchal racial categorisation.

Such intimate technologies of transmissibility and division worked to disrupt or deny Indigenous kinship networks and relations to the land. Bhandar links her analysis of status and the identity-property nexus to Étienne Balibar's recent work on John Locke, which focuses on the relationship between the *Essay Concerning Human Understanding* and his theory of property in the *Two Treatises*. By bringing Balibar's reassessment of Locke to bear on the confluence of subjectivity and colonial appropriation, Bhandar traces how the 'move from a metaphysics of interiority to colonial governance' renders ideas of racial superiority inseparable from the formation of constituent property itself. Addressing the far-reaching consequences of Bhandar's assertion that 'the figure of the self-possessive individual, and the juridical counterpart found in Indian status, can only be undone in tandem' becomes a more conceivable project thanks to the discerning analysis and critical genealogy that she provides.

Colonial Lives of Property is a vital contribution to scholarship that is working to understand the entanglements of settler colonialism and racial capitalism. Bhandar's account of the racial regimes of ownership does not simply add nuance to already familiar analyses of race, property, law and empire. She also proposes a profound rethinking of 'the ways in which we understand, practice, and perform modes of subjectivity that are rooted in possession and domination are intimately bound to the juridical apparatus of private property relations'. Bhandar argues that this mode of subjectivity cannot be undone without the abolition of private property and its legal infrastructure. With this horizon in mind, *Colonial Lives of Property* offers invaluable critical resources for an anticolonial antiracism grounded in a radical de-propertisation and in possibilities for living otherwise.

Alyosha Goldstein

Theory of the workaround

Amit S. Rai, *Jugaad Time: Ecologies of Everyday Hacking in India* (Durham, NC: Duke University Press, 2019). 208pp., £79.00 hb., £18.99 pb., 978 1 47800 110 2 hb., 978 1 47800 146 1 pb.

In Amit S. Rai's *Jugaad Time*, the Delhi-based freelance music manager Renu tells her interviewer proudly that jugaad is 'our [i.e. India's] brainchild'. To demonstrate this 'particular skill set to achieve the unachievable, mend the otherwise damaged or do more with less', Renu opens her smartphone browser to a listicle on the Indian media website *ScoopWhoop*. The page, titled *51 Photos That Prove Indians Are the Ultimate Kings of Jugaad*, provides a surfeit of hacks and workarounds for the reader's entertainment: a pair of trousers attached to an AC unit, so that its legs can direct cool air into two different rooms; a clothes iron turned upright and used to keep a pot of milky chai warm; a plastic bottle fixed to a water pipe, its bottom pierced to function as a makeshift showerhead; a scarf tied around a train seat to allow a man to sleep without his head drooping; and so on. It is clear that, for most of these examples, their conditions of possibility are precarity, resource shortage or what Rai calls, following Jasbir Puar, debilitisation. Jugaad stages the canny and at times extra-legal repurposing of materials, infrastructures and technologies. And yet in contemporary India, this marginal practice is often framed as a source of admiration and in this listicle even national pride: 'Innovation is a hallmark of excellence and we certainly excel in this field', the *ScoopWhoop* editor opines.

The *jugaadu*, the one who performs jugaad, is a pirate, a hacker, but also a virtuosic entrepreneur, a 'frugal innovator', the neoliberal 'confidence man'. This figure's ability to overcome stasis and evade blockages has attracted the attention of management gurus and business strategists in twenty-first-century India, who greedily appropriate an apparently vernacular spirit to propel new forms of capitalist value-creation. But as Rai insists, processes of jugaad are 'not reducible to, and indeed continually exceed, capitalist relations of production.' One aim of *Jugaad Time* is to grapple with this excess, to identify in the momentary exits and inversions facilitated by jugaad those 'lines of flight from contemporary capital [that] increase collective capacities for a non-capitalist landing'. Rai is cautious in his conclusions: the creativity of India's pirate kingdoms may be expansive, but they can often be complicit in neoliberal logics and are always 'susceptible to control'. Nonetheless, the resulting portrait of contemporary India – which stretches from multinational corporate boardrooms to the intimate space of the home, from the tech CEO to the *kabad* (junk) scavenger – emerges as a dense and intoxicating affirmation of the plasticity of this country's present and an incitement to imagine possible futures otherwise.

Jugaad, a Hindi/Punjabi colloquialism, is itself an unstable category. The first page of Rai's *Preface* includes four different definitions: jugaad is a 'joyous passion', a 'practice of post-colonial practical reason', a 'hack', a 'pirated workaround'. It is a practice, a process, an event and an ethos, and is 'relatively old, but newly mediatised'. This latter is important, since Rai's particular focus is on mobile phones and digital cultures; indeed, he privileges this realm at the expense of those media shifts that precede the digital, for instance the televisual, and their own jugaad constellations. The book emerges from nearly a decade of research into the politics of neoliberal technology in India, specifically how they manifest at the level of a body's habits. India is home to more than one billion mobile handsets. Its national market is the most competitive mobile service market in the world, replete with cheap smartphones and a wide range of mobile value-added services. *Jugaadu* experiments demonstrate dramatically the emergent capacities of these new 'digital-human assemblages'. In Rai's words, jugaad 'gradually became for me a way of posing better questions regarding media, neoliberalism, and politics in India by tracing relations external to their term'. Though the book focuses on the contemporary, it also frames jugaad more generally as 'an attentive and canny bodily orientation toward historically specific *dispotifs* of power, exploitation, discourse, materiality, value and intensity, *and* [as] a relational practice of experiencing, negotiating, and, at times, changing human and nonhuman ecologies.'

Rai is concerned primarily with jugaad's 'affective passage' – its opening of different domains of action and power to experimentation. He approaches affect in the Deleuzian sense as a 'durational passage from one state to another in an encounter between two or more bodies (human or nonhuman, organic or inorganic), which either increases or decreases a body's capacity for action.' The emphasis on mobile phone *ecologies* means that the chapters grapple with complex and unstable assemblages, rather than tracing enclosed, self-oriented entities. Elizabeth Povinelli's critique of 'essence' in her *Geontologies: A Requiem to Late Liberalism* (2016) is an important reference here. To put it another way, Rai is interested not in the 'product-event' of jugaad, but in its 'potential process-infrastructure' – the web of social and material relations that enable hacking or workarounds and the vectors which jugaads themselves produce.

This foregrounding of jugaad's distributed and ecological processes is not simply a challenge to its appropriation as a reproducible business model. It also departs from a certain postcolonial media studies focus on the agency of the subaltern or marginal subject. Rather than intent and outcome, Rai is interested in movement, contingency and 'emergent sensations'. His 'diagrammatic method' attempts to create 'practical genealogies' of jugaad, capturing its processual nature and seeking to avoid the fetish of the hack demonstrated, for instance, in the *ScoopWhoop* listicle. For Rai, the hack is the labour of the *jugaadu*, certainly, but also of 'software engineers, cable TV installers, electronic component supply-chain workers, miners, processing-plant workers, etc.' All are part of the same assemblage. The question should not be, *How did they do that?*, but rather, *Where, when and how can the pirated be made common?*

Rai raises these questions against the backdrop of Narendra Modi's India, where the Hindu nationalist Prime Minister's promise of *acche din* ('good days') has been interpreted variously to affirm the flourishing of business, individual initiative and consumer choice, but also the fortification of the national body against 'enemies' and 'traitors' – commonly construed as the Indian Muslim, but also the Maoist Naxalite, and increasingly Dalit and lower-caste activists and organisers. Rai's investigations traverse the polished contours and flickering screens of the Indian 'smart city' – 'one of many instruments of corporate neoliberalisation and the elite globalisation of Indian society', and at the same time sites for new techniques of surveillance, security and segregation. Jugaad in this context can work to undermine regimes of copyright and facilitate informal labour practices, but Rai also warns that hacking what are essentially capitalist technologies – from mobile phones to databases – can still work to 'habituate its practitioners and prosumers to neoliberal logics of Big Data and risk management.'

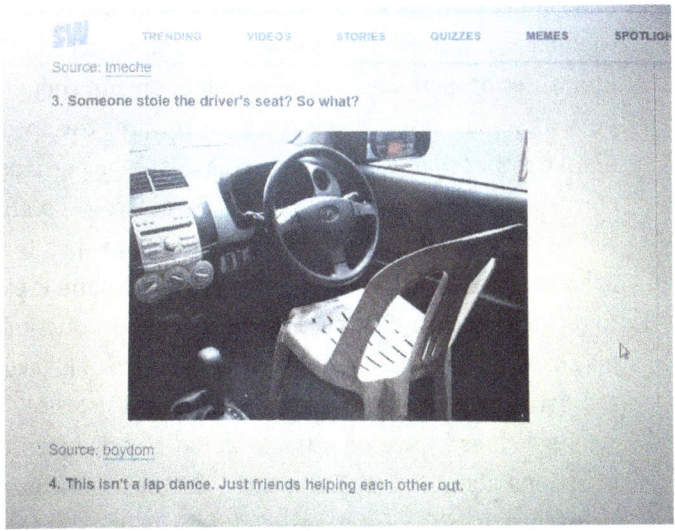

If jugaad is today a 'quasi-capitalist art', how far can the 'quasi-' be pushed to serve programs and practices of revolutionary becoming in contemporary India? Is this merely another chapter in the history of the intensification of work in postcolonial South Asia? In the book's introduction, Rai suggests that, 'indeed, in some sense the revolution will be anti-jugaad.' Disappointingly this provocation is never unpacked, but it becomes clear throughout the book that the value of jugaad is not in providing *hope* but in affirming *recalcitrance*. Jugaad is 'a fractally styled answer to the "no" of both state (law) and capital (private property).' What is needed is a politics that will take this break from habit – jugaad's sabotage of what is 'fixed, moral, propertied, *suvarna* (upper caste), appropriate and right' – and radicalise it, make it revolutionary, resist its smooth integration into neoliberal logics. *Jugaad Time* is a diagnosis of a situation and only the start of the story. But for Rai, the direction of travel is resolutely toward the commons and the collective.

Jugaad occurs in the junkyard workshop, the video parlour, the hackers' den but also in the home, in the domestic sphere. Rai's welcome concern for questions of gender is threaded through the book. Rai is keen to challenge the vision of the hacker as a heroic and masculinist visionary. He devotes attention to the ways in which media ecologies can undermine the gendered binary of *ghar/bahir,* home/outside, where the feminised domestic is contrasted with the masculinised public world. The sharing of mobile handsets by women in extended families becomes a demonstration of commoning and the horizontal distribution of ethical know-how. The mobile phone is a 'flux-machine', threatening structures of caste and gender control. Rai's interviews and fieldnotes are wielded as interventions into feminist and postcolonial literatures on capitalist social reproduction, but though persuasive, his observations can stray towards the speculative rather than substantive. This quality is perhaps consistent with the book's concern for vectors of potentiality. A more serious concern is the ways in which the concept of jugaad is stretched, referring at one point even to recipe shortcuts. The section on social reproduction may have benefitted from a sharper delineation of jugaad, against a more general notion of 'everyday resistance'.

Jugaad, as I have noted, allows Rai to ask specific questions about urban India after liberalisation, particularly since 2009 when research for the book began (and when 3G and 4G networks were taking off in India). Though this is a single-authored text, Rai's research was collaborative, involving sustained interaction with the Tata Institute of Social Sciences in Mumbai and the labours of three research assistants: Anisha Saigal, Shiva Thorat and Rachna Kumar. Fieldwork took place in Bhopal, Mumbai, Delhi and Bangalore. Rai's wide-ranging citations – appearing as a bracketed deluge at the end of key sentences – reveal the complex architecture on which the argument is built. Jugaad may be a window into contemporary India, but Rai also argues that it is not restricted to the twenty-first century, nor is it specifically Indian. This is a productive observation, but its implications are underdeveloped. The only non-Indian example given in the book is the repurposing, in rural China, of washing machines to help clean vegetables. While the diagrammatic method serves a certain purpose, some comparisons across time and space might help refine a conceptual history of jugaad. I offer two brief examples here.

First, in terms of comparisons across time, we might consider the late nineteenth- / early twentieth-century category of *swadeshi,* a descriptor for goods and products 'of one's own country'. Like jugaad, this was a quasi-capitalist concept that sought to disrupt the circulation and consumption of British goods in colonial India, drawing on ideas of traditional craft and slow artisanal labour, even as it also created new types of value and profit. Rai talks about subaltern jugaad as tied to the 'persistent effects of (post)colonial struggles against hierarchy, authority and deployed power', but the only anti-colonial tactic he discusses is that of subaltern networks of rumour, in which he sees a precedent for the unpredictable circulation of disruptive knowledge. Might the afterlives of *swadeshi* – invested, like jugaad, with a sense of pride and independence as well as experiences of debilitisation, but translated over time into a hegemonic nationalist register, including the recent exhortation to 'Make in India' – suggest a possible future for jugaad?

As regards anti-colonial strategies, I wonder, too, if the inspiring mobilisations of the 'Why Loiter?' group in Mumbai and elsewhere – an attempt to make women visible in public space and to challenge perceptions of risk and fear – are best thought of as an urban 'hack', as Rai suggests, or simply as part of a longer history of *satyagraha*, of courageously making visible the injustices of the present, even under the threat of violence? Does the use of digital technologies radically redefine this older spatial strategy and its forms of publicity?

Second, a comparison across space, and again to China. The philosopher Byung-Chul Han's recent book on the idea of the 'fake' in China, *Shanzhai: Deconstruction in China* (2017), can be read productively alongside *Jugaad Time*. The association of 'fake' with 'inferior' is challenged in Han's exploration, since his interest is in the way Chinese philosophy and culture departs from western ideas of the 'original' and 'authentic'. The *shanzhai* product is more like a jugaad, a pragmatic attempt to make something work better for the individual user – whether this is an upgraded mobile or a fan novel bringing Harry Potter to China – a responsivity that large companies cannot realistically emulate. As Han notes, due to a high degree of flexibility and adaptability in design, the 'fake' is frequently superior to the original. In this it is differentiated from jugaad – both aesthetically (as a polished product rather than refurbished *kabad*, waste) and in its more explicit project of value-creation. But Chan also sees in *shanzhai* pragmatics a possible line of flight, the potential for a reworking and repurposing that channels 'anti-authoritarian, subversive energies', especially against the security apparatus of the Chinese state. Are there similar tensions to unpick here? And if we can see *jugaad* in rural Chinese washing machines, what might *shanzhai* look like in India?

Jugaad Time's provocations are not limited to its philosophical reflections and fieldwork notes, but are found also in the speculative interludes that pepper the book. Rai's *Fables of the Reinvention*, a gripping vision of 'mutating technoperceptual assemblages' and 'data reinventing life' reads like a new frontier for Indian science fiction. But dystopias are not distant from the present moment. I finished reading *Jugaad Time* on a flight, where I'd also picked up an international edition of the *New York Times*. In this 19 December 2019 edition, the third page featured a story entitled 'India's habit of shutting down the internet'. India, it reads, 'tops the world – by far – in the number of Internet shutdowns imposed by local, state and national governments.' Over the previous calendar year there were 134 cuts to internet service, justified largely as a method to secure order against 'misinformation', but also deployed for more mundane reasons, such as to prevent students from cheating on exams. Pakistan, India's closest competitor, had cut service 12 times; Syria and Turkey just once. This story, alongside the sustained internet and communications blackout imposed in Kashmir since August 2019, underlines Rai's concern about the increasingly authoritarian character of the Indian state's engagement with smart technologies. If the futures promised by jugaad are multiple and contradictory, then its affirmation of the plasticity of the present must be seized upon with strategy and intent, affirming with Rai 'the potential of strategic bottlenecks, sabotage and repurposing … to effect change in contemporary arrangements and practices of solidarity', not least at this time of toxicity, entanglement and reinvention.

Chris Moffat

Human rights in a wrong world

Ratna Kapur, *Gender, Alterity and Human Rights: Freedom in a Fishbowl* (Cheltenham and Northampton, MA: Edward Elgar Publishing, 2018). 307pp., £90.00 hb., £19.95 pb., 978 1 78811 252 9 hb., 978 1 83910 447 3 pb.

Over the past few decades, various critical scholars have emphasised the limitations of human rights. Such scholars have, for the most part, proposed a return to human rights as the solution to its failures, hoping to revise the project through a renewed faith in liberal democratic values, as, for example, in scholarship by Wendy Brown, Costas Douzinas or David Kennedy. In *Gender, Alterity and Human Rights: Freedom in a Fishbowl,* Ratna Kapur also notes the uses, promises and limitations of the human rights project. However, rather than returning to the latter for answers to these limitations, Kapur goes further, seeking to think freedom through alternative registers beyond the bounds of the liberal legal fishbowl. The book is consequently essential reading for international lawyers, human rights lawyers and activists, and for critical thinkers across the disciplines, drawing on postcolonial, intersectional, feminist and queer theory, epistemologies of the global south and relationships between theory, activism and spirituality to provide a unique and in-depth analysis of the search for freedom beyond dominant systems of knowledge.

Much contemporary human rights scholarship can be seen as resting somewhere between a more doctrinal approach, seeking to use human rights law for social justice gains, and a more critical approach, which aims to understand what social justice outcomes are *not* seen by current human rights framings. Thus, while critical scholars note the ways in which human rights have become a powerful tool for governance with not always positive outcomes, people working more on the doctrinal side often hear this as a dismissal of their work and, in turn, dismiss critical perspectives for failing to offer practical solutions. While these two approaches tend to be set up in antithesis to one another, problematically equating, as Kapur states, 'a liberal rights critique with pessimism, and a liberal rights deployment with optimism', there are convergences as well as serious differences between them. Both, after all, want some form of social justice or freedom, to use Kapur's terminology.

The fissure between these theories is often largest, however, at the ideological level. Terms such as freedom and justice are defined in very different ways by each, with more doctrinal approaches tending to define freedom and justice in liberal legal terms and more critical approaches seeking to define these terms beyond dominant liberal frames. Human rights lawyers and activists often demand answers to what they can do on the ground, but such answers, as Kapur's book outlines with detail and nuance, are not always easily provided or are sometimes more complex than expected when one seeks to understand freedom beyond the liberal legal fishbowl. This, however, does not mean that critical approaches cannot also be affirmative.

Human rights law can, indeed, provide a moment of freedom or justice for many. But human rights law does not fundamentally challenge or, arguably, even seek to challenge structural injustices as created by colonialism and racism, patriarchy or capitalism. As Kapur notes, this has long been highlighted by feminist and postcolonial scholarship. Rather, human rights largely work within these systems of power and domination, often upholding such systems while offering 'a potent form of seduction into a particular type of normativity and a specific mode of governance'; a form of what Lauren Berlant terms 'cruel optimism'.

While human rights can and have been used for more transformational projects and while their impact does sometimes trickle out beyond the case at hand, human rights generally seek to address individual rights as isolated from broader power structures. There are, of course, some exceptions and some attempts to provide a more radical human rights-based approach. Nonetheless, the transformative project of human rights is often unclear, with the vast majority of human rights scholarship remaining tethered, as Kapur outlines, to a limited liberal account of freedom which reproduces the 'neoliberal, wealth-producing, heteronormative, reproductive framework, as well as ... [its] sexual, cultural, racial and religious prescriptions'.

On the other hand, critical approaches are much clearer in their transformative aims. For many critical scholars, such as Kapur, freedom must also be sought beyond the limits of the law. Freedom is not just about balancing people's human rights against one another to provide liberal equality. Rather, freedom requires dismantling gender hierarchies, decolonising knowledge and power and challenging dominant epistemologies. Freedom cannot be sought within the neoliberal frame. Moreover, as Kapur uniquely adds, freedom is also about spirituality and about the search beyond anything the law can – at least as it is currently envisaged – comprehend. This does not, as Kapur notes, mean that the terrain gained by human rights advocacy should be surrendered, but, rather, that what is needed is 'a more mindful and diligent approach'.

Gender, Alterity and Human Rights begins with an analysis of a few key examples of the inclusions and exclusions created by the human rights project, drawing on examples such as queer homonormativity (Chapter Two) and sexual security regimes (Chapter Three). In these analyses, Kapur focuses on the regulation of gender and sexuality, drawing on postcolonial, feminist and queer analyses to show that, while some have been slowly more included into the human rights frame, many are still very much excluded. One example Kapur discusses, in this vein, is the debate over the veil (Chapter Four). Many feminists have advocated for the legal banning of the veil, arguing that this piece of clothing is a symbol of women's oppression. Cases then challenging legal bans have subsequently been brought to the European Court of Human Rights which has upheld such bans. (See *Dakir v Belgium*, 2017; *Sahin v Turkey*, 2005; *S.A.S. v France*, 2014.)

While, as noted, the bans are often articulated in terms of women's rights, this perspective silences the many meanings of the veil. The veil is imposed on some but the veil is also worn by many by choice and, as Saba Mahmood's *Politics of Piety* (2004) explores, can itself be a symbol of freedom. The veil legal cases and the wider debates on the veil and women's human rights exemplify how human rights, despite claiming to be promoting the universal rights of all, include some and exclude others. These lines of inclusion and exclusion are, as Kapur notes, drawn in a way that is based around colonial and racist lines and the idea that Muslim women have no agency. 'Muslims', Kapur thus notes, 'continue to be conceptualised as the embodiment of a threatening alterity, and always as incommensurable with the liberal values which are the substrate of human rights discourse'. Unveiling becomes a form of governance, excluding some from the universal humanity that human rights claim to promote, while forcing others to submit in order to be able to access the 'freedom' that human rights prescribes them.

Kapur does not deny that human rights have been used as an emancipatory tool for some but refuses to sideline the excluded in the name of those included, calling for those working in human rights to note these inclusions and exclusions and to challenge them. Yet Kapur's project does not end here. *Gender, Alterity and Human Rights* also provides another layer of analysis which notes the inclusions and exclusions provided by the epistemological framing of human rights itself, questioning the ability of human rights to ever fully include, to ever be universal, let alone to provide freedom. While, arguably, human rights were never meant to provide ultimate freedom, they do claim universality and, as one of the most dominant discourses on social justice in the contemporary moment, human rights have come to be understood as *the* main frame of freedom in many parts of the world. This is problematic, working to exclude alternative perspectives. It is thus paramount that that which is not seen by human rights is made visible.

Kapur notes the difficulty of conceptualising freedom beyond the given terms 'when we remain intractably constituted through a specific epistemological universe ... [w]hen we are [and have been] so fully colonised into a specific way of thinking'. Parallels can be drawn here, as she acknowledges, with Judith Butler's reflections on power in *The Psychic Life of Power* (1997), where, reading Foucault and others, Butler notes the cultural and political predicament of 'how to take an oppositional relation to power that is, admittedly, implicated in the very power one opposes'.

This predicament is complex but many authors, including Kapur, offer varying ways out. Kapur sits here alongside authors such as Joan Wallach Scott who, in works including *The Fantasy of Feminist History* (2012), draws on psychoanalytic theory to identify a potential for radical change in fantasy. For Scott, while the concepts of the symbolic order 'provide the language through which identities are formed, the unconscious foundations on which social practises are implemented ... fantasy enables challenge and change'.

What brings these more hopeful critical voices together is a willingness to see beyond binary thinking. Such perspectives do not see structural forms of oppression as fixed, but rather focus on the power of the subject in fostering change. Butler's solution, too, exemplifies this, noting how the fact that 'agency is implicated in subordination is not the sign of a fatal self-contradiction', but rather that such a reflection requires complex perspectives which note the subject's implication within power as '*neither* fully determined by power *nor* fully determining of power'. Complexity is, in this respect, a positive source for change, noting and holding the contradictions together, being unafraid, in the words of Donna Haraway's *Cyborg Manifesto*, of 'contradictory standpoints', searching beyond what is known while being attentive to the constraints of the now.

Kapur's contribution draws similar lines of post-dualistic flight while also – in a similar vein to Scott – seeking an affirmative focus through affect and the politics of the everyday, highlighting the 'relationship between the self' and the 'turn inwards' as a way in which freedom can be sought beyond liberal registers. Kapur begins her journey into these non-liberal registers of freedom through a focus on Eve Kosofsky Sedgwick's and

Michel Foucault's works on Mahayana Buddhism and the Shia Islam underpinnings of the Iranian revolution respectively (Chapter 6). Noting Sedgwick's lamenting of the paranoia and the ultimate 'intellectual finitude' of critical theory, yet her love of deconstruction, Kapur discusses how she found an affirmative epistemology of non-dualism in Mahayana Buddhism. In a similar vein, Kapur discusses how Foucault, drawing on Shia Islam, turned away from the binaries underpinning the sovereign subject and the state (e.g. mind/body, public/private), looking instead towards 'another political thought, another political imagination' and noting the need for the transformation of the self. Kapur similarly draws on non-dualism and the turn to the self in her own exploration of freedom beyond the liberal fishbowl. Here, she looks primarily to the tradition of non-dualism found in the Indian philosophy of Advaita, which focuses on being and the self, seeing the self 'as one not a fragmented whole – who ultimately is not defined by her labels or identities'. Freedom, from this perspective, is not a project to be sought elsewhere but necessitates self-inquiry.

Kapur's turn to non-dualism and self-inquiry poses a radical challenge to the liberal frame of freedom provided by human rights. As Kapur notes, such a proposition calls on one to look inwards before seeking to 'save' others, noting the difficulty with being able to 'theorise and/or even actualise freedom for others before we have successfully freed ourselves from our own deep conditioning, unmitigated phobias, discriminatory schemas and powerful sense of privilege and entitlement'. While this move could be seen as similar to and indeed has links with other critical human rights scholars, Kapur's point is also much stronger, calling not just for further reflection before one acts but asking the actor to seek to understand freedom for themselves first, and subsequently to challenge the internalised normative frame of freedom offered by the liberal human rights project before seeking to save others.

Gender, Alterity and Human Rights ends with four examples of those who have sought freedom beyond liberal frames, exemplifying the inward journey required to truly seek freedom. Some of these stories, while requiring the reader to radically challenge their own thinking and assumptions around freedom, seem quite removed from human rights, so exemplifying the radical epistemic shift that Kapur calls for. For example, one such story is of Lalla, a fourteenth-century Kashmiri woman who renounced marriage and material life and wandered naked while undertaking a process of self-reflection and meditation through, in part, a turn to mystic poetry. Some examples, however, more easily pose challenges to human rights frameworks, such as the example of the legal battles around the Jain community's practice of conscious fasting known as *Santhara* or *Sullekhna*. Kapur notes how this spiritual practice is 'conscious and informed, grounded in the epistemological view shared by Hindus, Buddhists and Jains that the self/consciousness continues after it is released from the corporeal form'. Nonetheless, this practice has been ruled illegal in India, with parties having argued, first, that the practice is often used against 'elderly women considered economically burdensome' and, second, that the practise is in violation of the right to life (the act being likened to suicide, which was made criminal under Indian law by Christian British colonial rulers). As Kapur notes, such an understanding of the practise ignores 'deeper philosophical aspects'. By 'confining the issue within a rights paradigm', the alternative registers of freedom sought through this practice are both silenced and denied.

Gender, Alterity and Human Rights is a bold book, unafraid to address the importance of the spiritual in an era where much critical scholarship either shies away from spirituality for fear of being deemed anti-secular or more actively and problematically takes secularism as an inherent underlying basis of good critical work. Further to this, Kapur requires her reader to reflect on their own perspective on life, to challenge their own understandings of freedom and to think on the self and what freedom means to that self. Ultimately, the book provides an affirmative way of thinking freedom at a time in global politics where it has become all too easy to collapse into negativity and nihilism.

Emily Jones

From organic subjectivity to internal reality

Michel Henry, *Marx: An Introduction*, trans. Kristien Justaert (London: Bloomsbury Academic, 2019). 101pp., £50.00 hb., £12.99 pb., 978 1 47426 942 1 hb., 978 1 47427 778 5 pb.

As a phenomenologist who prioritises the 'appearing' of life, Michel Henry distinguishes the foundational content of subjectivity from the horizon of pure exteriority and inert appearances. In *Marx: An Introduction*, we see how Henry's approach to political economy qua Marx is fundamentally positioned around living subjectivity or, in his own terminology, 'incarnation'. According to Henry's phenomenological reading of Marx, life is fundamental and non-economic; the frame outside of which economic reality has no grounding. Life, phenomenologically conceived of as the ultimate modality of manifestation, is precisely what makes economics intelligible, rather than vice versa. According to Henry, the phenomenological inauguration of life is inherent to Marx's thought and the concept that has unwittingly been displaced by Marxism's misreadings. Henry contends that Marxism fails to conceive of the economic as an '*un*real' and a fantasised double of reality, treating it as inherent to and parasitic upon life.

In turn, Henry's 'Introduction to the thought of Marx' illuminates how Marxism has been presented, and is still being presented, as a dialectical and historical materialism despite Marx's thought not having any true connection to the doctrine of materialism. For Henry, the dialectic plays a secondary role in Marx, being a Hegelian remnant that disappears as Marx's oeuvre progressed. According to Marx, there is no dialectic essence that constitutes its own internal law or reality vis-a-vis the foundation of negativity. Furthermore, while for Hegel there *is a history*, or a substantive and ontologically existent thread – this reality produced by the objectification of Spirit (*Geist*) – for Marx history is not the 'self-accomplishment of a homogenous substance'. In contrast to Hegel (and to Bruno Bauer, who also subordinates man to a mediating history), for Marx there is no history, there are merely historical individuals. Furthermore, while the notion of class is a Hegelian concept, repeated in neo-Hegelians such as Max Stirner – who believes that the State constitutes a power above human beings – for Marx class constitutes the identity of its members. The Hegelian affirmation of the primacy of class over individuals is part and parcel of ideology. As Henry will evince, it is this individualised characterisation that is central to Marx and which is lost in Marxism(s).

Henry separates Marx's work into three categories: first, the early writings until 1845; second, the historical-political texts (*The Communist Manifesto*, *Class Struggle*, *The Eighteenth Brumaire*, *Civil War in France*, and so on); and, third, the economic-philosophical texts (including the *Grundrisse* and *Capital*). Identifying the historical-political texts as those that have given birth to Marxism, constituting their meaning via the conception of an origin, Henry ushers a return to Marx-*sans*-Marxism by focusing on the economic-philosophical texts. Henry produces a reading of Marx via an economic genealogy, wherein economic reality is rooted in the conversion of use values (*Gebrauchswert*) into exchange values (*Tauschwert*) via the systematic adoption of an objective scale to measure labour. It is only through the adoption of universal measurement to products of labour as exchange value that various products (e.g., linen, wheat, metal) are equally systematised. This invariably distorts the essence of labour – that is, it is not 'real' labour that this objective scale measures but, instead, its *representation*, which is always exterior to that which is being represented. As the nexus of the transcendental genesis of (capitalist) economy, measurement results in subjective labour's transmogrification into an objective equivalent. 'Real labour', or 'labour as real', is alien to representation and is *subjective*, or immanent. For Henry – who here echoes Plato – living praxis is interior and invisible while economics implies a derealisation of labour, transforming it into an unreal double that is mimetic. Henry asserts that Marx's thesis is that economics is an abstraction that presupposes and refers to a foundational substratum.

Economic realities, which result from a process of alienation, substitute the general for the singular, the social for the individual, the ideal for the real/representational. Henry's critique is not that this is a process that can necessarily be reversed or undone but that, unrecognised, it produces a calamitous result: *that the abstract is the real*. For those reader's familiar with Francois Laruelle's work, this will be quite familiar, since, according to Laruelle's non-standard reading of Marx, it is ethico-political praxis that emancipates raw materials and exchange-based economic practices from Standard Philosophy's possessive domination (or the mistaken identification of transcendence with the real). According to Henry's reading, Marx establishes how *subjective labour* escapes qualitative and quantitative forces of objectifying determination. Real labour ought not to be conflated with labour as it is objectively represented, for this is always a result of a *fiction*, an artificial process born out of socio-economic necessities. Scientism – the ontological claim that those mathematical-empirical molds that constitute and define reality objectively (vis-à-vis laws, objects, and so on) – is one such hold, as it mistakes immanent life for its abstracted representation. Henry, writing towards the end of the twentieth century, identifies scientism (which ought not be confused with science) with the dominant contemporary ideology, one that results in the negation of subjective and immanent life.

Subjective labour, reified via exchange value, is guided by money/capital, which distances us even further from real labour as it enacts a transcendental genesis – i.e., the representation of a representation (labour). Henry repeats one of Marx's central tenets, that without any ultimate reference to labour, capital is entirely deprived of its illusory value, illuminating how, in the last instance, capital has no economic autonomy but is, instead, stilted by extracting and increasing surplus labour. Due to the limits of the work day – and Henry qualifies this by noting that 'here again it is life that imposes its regulations on economy' – the technical and instrumental production of surplus impinges on increasing productivity, or 'relative surplus value'. Henry's reminder of this is a critical contemporary rejoinder to those who point to automation as an inherently post-capitalist phenomenon. Automation, digitisation and actuarial finance are merely contemporaneous articulations and extensions of relative surplus value. With automation, productive forces are neither the co-labour of humans nor what is at the core of the force of production, praxis (in the sense of the potentials and actualisations of organic subjectivity and life). Instead, automised technics simply produce value as a coherent, instrumental totality through objective functioning. Automation expresses a shift by foreclosing the subjective forces that create economic wealth and rendering objective forces that produce an 'ever-bigger mass of use values'.

Accordingly, in capitalism, economic circulation is not directed at exchanging commodity goods (C) against other commodity goods (C') via a universal medium of exchange or money (M), but by increasing capital itself. This is precisely how the formula CMC' transforms into MCM', where M' is greater than M and the exchange of use values is replaced by the maximisation of exchange values. Thus, it is 'labour power (*Arbeitskraft*)' that becomes central to this transformation, which according to Henry, cannot be separated from living praxis, or subjectivity, insofar as labour is an essential modality of life. For Henry, 'the economic' is prefigured by something meta-economic, which Henry terms the 'pure economy' (*l'économique pur*). Praxis is thus necessary to lift the veil of the 'pure economy' and recover a genealogical reading of economic reality.

In 'Life, Death: Marx and Marxism', Henry clarifies a contradiction inherent to capitalism: the development of productive forces, whereby objective factors are exacerbated, resulting in the increase of constant capital and, therefore, a decrease in the source of economic profits, which inevitably results in the decline of the rate of profit. Thus, the self-development of capital furthers the necessity of automatised production processes, where labour activity is designated to the machine, an 'objective process' that is 'no longer defined by subjective praxis'. On the one hand, subjective praxis is inherently ontological insofar as it relates to what Marx calls 'consciousness', in which the world of ideas is structured via apperception; on the other hand, it also stratifies the proletariat, which has no thought, will or capacity to act in and of itself – the proletariat is an objective class. According to Henry, Marx's critique of economy is truly radical because, in exchanging the lived determinations of praxis for a relational system of ideal entities, 'what it accomplishes is nothing less than the substitution of life for death'. It is *life* that we must turn to in order to conceptualise economic phenomena, for surplus value is incomprehensible on the plane of pure economy – this helps resolve queries such as why and how exchange (value) eclipses production costs. The conservation of exchange value is essential here, as it refers to a radical ontology of life – exchange value cannot be conserved unless the *form* of use value, which bolsters it, is also conserved.

The book's third chapter, 'Subjective Forces and Productivity', sees Henry turning to socialism, where praxis can emerge as it is removed from the concept of being as production vis-à-vis the totality of mechanical production. Socialism is here regarded as a system characterised by the partial absence of subjectivity in production processes, which Marx identified with subjective praxis' reorientation from processes of production towards the development of individual faculties such as education, art, science, and so on. Thus, the historical situation finds a rebirth in 'living activity'. Since society has no autonomous existence, the primacy of individual praxis always returns to the action of individuals, rather than that of society or a group. Here, Henry echoes Marx's 1842 manuscripts in rejecting Hegelian universalism. Henry and Marx afford heterogeneity primacy before determination, reversing the Hegelian part-whole relation whereby, according to Hegel, society-cum-Spirit constitutes individuals. Because the individual ultimately determines the reality of society, society's 'reduction of totalities' – insofar as it is represented, classified and historicised – must be reducible to individual praxis.

It is at this point that a question arises concerning an individual's integration within the sphere of immanence. If, according to Henry, actualisation is predicated upon subjective praxis, then social determination remains external to individual life – that is, it is *unreal*. Henry's solution is that, following Marx, the activity destined to satisfy material needs, as part and parcel of subjective life, is *independent* from social determination. As Frédéric Seyler notes in the preface, this 'need' originates as ipseity and self-generated movement (auto-affection). Following Henry's phenomenological approach to causation – which denies that there is any social causation that cannot be reduced to individual praxis – are not the social relations (*rapports sociaux*) which are produced by and identical to individual praxis entangled within reciprocal/circular causation? That is, social conditions are produced by the individuals that are subjected to them.

Here, Henry appeals to 'habits', which form and determine the 'concrete life of individuals' – rather than referring to a transcendent exteriority. It is through repetition enacted by individuals that social conditions are reproduced. The onto-phenomenological status of purely objective determination is treated as a product of *unreality*, in need of a radically subjective approach which ensures that the affective reality of social conditions constitutes a frame imposed upon action. In his analysis of alienation, Henry remarks that the labourer experiences *accidental determinations*, or constraints of the workplace, as distinct from the movement of subjectivity, or *essential determination* – the former is alienating insofar as it constrains the development of subjective potentialities. Because an individual reproduces their social conditions, any *origin* is outside of individual subjectivity – Henry resolves alienation without appealing to the mediation of an ideological or transcendent structure.

While *essential determinations* are inherent to subjectivity, *accidental determinations* designate social mediations reproduced through divisions of labour reproduced subjectively; consider how in the workshop, factory or within the machinery of any industry there is no objective experience but subjective experience, or phenomenological existence. *Contra* Marx, Henry's critique of social praxis lionises the individual; social praxis can only describe an intertwining of individual actions. For instance, a city is a stratified production ultimately reducible to the sum of individual efforts – any generalised abstraction, as seen from the aperture of the 'outside', is a mere representation. (Here, the reader may be reminded of Deleuze's machine ontology.) The division of labour is equivalent to the division of subjectivity. Thus, 'social praxis', at odds with individuated 'real praxis', is the product of an abstraction comparable to the forces of both the social and capitalist market economy, as both repeat the 'substitution of individual labour by general social labour'.

Henry sees communism and socialism as opposed to one another. Communism – or 'communitarian socialism' – submerges the originally individual character of praxis within the social, reproducing the same abstractions that led to capitalist alienation. Despite attempting to reject the alienation that constitutes capitalism, i.e., the exploitation of the labourer via surplus extraction, communism fails to abolish the alienation of differentiation that anchors 'real praxis'. Socialism galvanises the free development of individualities and indexes the overcoming of alienation by rediscovering subjectivity as life's absolute. From this sprouts the free development of individualities instead of the reduction of necessary 'labour time' so as to posit (relative) surplus value, setting free the artistic, scientific and cultural development of individualities. Hence, activity is no longer determined by, or confounded with, the union between individual and production; socialism allows for *private* labour to blossom as it overcomes the abstract universal of the market economy's 'transcendental genesis'. The solution that socialism posits is that use value takes the form of the community, which is characterised by the transparency of social relations in accordance to participatory common activity while, simultaneously, also understood as private (in its production).

Henry recovers from Marx the notion that the pure substance of the labour process is, in itself, neither material nor economical but rooted in the development of productive faculties, i.e., in living. Ontologically dissolving these productive forces into capacities, dispositions and activities of individuals, Henry identifies the development of productive forces as signifying the identical and indefinite development of individual activities. *Marx: An Introduction* reveals Henry's singular and rigorous close reading of Marx himself, a reading that is often muddied or lost in the deluge of Marxist and post-Marxist critical thought.

Ekin Erkan

Cleaning artefacts

Dan Kidner and Alex Sainsbury, eds., *Nightcleaners and '36 to '77* (London: Raven Row, LUX and Koenig Books, 2018). Box-set containing two books (214pp.) and two DVDs/Blu-Rays. £24.00, 978 3 96098 381 1

From campaign film to experiment in documentary representation, and from exemplary instance of anti-realist and self-reflexive 'Brechtian' counter cinema (according to some film theorists of the 1970s) to a semi-mythical and almost impossible to view work of leftist filmmaking: the history of Berwick Street Film Collective's *Nightcleaners* (begun in 1970, released in 1975) is characterised by continual transformations and conflicting understandings. In the twenty-first century, the film has returned to wider visibility, circulating particularly in the context of contemporary art. Its latest instantiation is as a pared-down, tasteful object: a neat box-set comprising two books of essays and archival materials, alongside the two films by the collective arising from the night-cleaners campaign – *Nightcleaners* itself and the later, lesser-known *'36 to '77* (1978), initially billed as 'Nightcleaners part 2'. Few comparable moving-image works receive such reverential treatment, and it seems that *Nightcleaners* is now a canonical work of radical cultural production in Britain, although academic film studies continues to show practically zero interest in the film. Why has this work resurfaced to claim such talismanic status? And what does this publication contribute to the process?

Recent interest in *Nightcleaners* and *'36 to '77* should be tracked in terms of a wider reinvestigation in the last decade of post-1968 British radical and experimental film manifested in exhibitions, publications and retrospectives. The two editors, Dan Kidner and Alex Sainsbury, have been influential figures here. Kidner organised a retrospective of the work of Marc Karlin, one of the members of Berwick Street Film Collective, at Picture This in Bristol in 2012, and presented *'36 to '77* as part of 'The Inoperative Community' in 2016 at Raven Row in London, of which Sainsbury is the director. This is itself part of a more general process in which historic figures of radical cinema such as Chantal Akerman, Harun Farocki, Jean-Luc Godard and Chris Marker increasingly have their work displayed in art galleries as much as in cinemas. Moreover, this has occurred alongside a positive re-evaluation of documentary practices discernible in contemporary art over the last few years, as well as this field's fascination with collaborative artistic production, both of which are enacted in the Berwick Street Film Collective's work. (The group that made *Nightcleaners* was composed of Karlin, Mary Kelly, James Scott and Humphry Trevelyan, with Kelly being replaced by Jon Sanders for *'36 to '77*.) There are parallels here with another of Kelly's projects from the 1970s, *Women and Work: A Document on the Division of Labour in Industry 1973-75*, made with Margaret Harrison and Kay Hunt, which approaches similar subject matter and mobilises related artistic forms; *Women and Work* too has been recovered in recent years, with its display at Tate Modern in 2016 and an archival exhibition related to it at South London Gallery in 2018-19.

The films' subject matter is also significant for their contemporary appeal: the campaign in the early 1970s to unionise (female) night-cleaners in London by women's movement activists and by the cleaners themselves, in the case of *Nightcleaners*, and the focus on the memories and experiences of one cleaner involved in this struggle, Myrtle Wardally, in *'36 to '77*. This coincides with important areas of theoretical research of the last decade or so, which themselves have flowed into the discourses of art: labour, social reproduction, care and maintenance, the racialisation and gendering of work. Notably, in the last decade a number of collections of Marxist-feminist writings from the same era as *Nightcleaners* have been republished, by figures such as Mariarosa Dalla Costa, Silvia Federici and Selma James. These texts, associated with the International Wages for Housework Campaign, speak to many of the issues also apparent in *Nightcleaners*, while sitting in a somewhat critical relation to the version of socialist-feminism legible in the film. Without suggesting a simple opposition, the film's concern with the orienting framework of socialism and the cleaners primarily as waged workers, as well as the critical engagement with the trade union movement of those involved in the night-cleaners campaign such as Sheila Rowbotham, Sally Alexander, and cleaners' activist May Hobbs, is thrown into relief by a text like James's 1972 article 'Women, the Unions, and Work, Or What is Not to Be Done', which is much more severe in its stance regarding most existing left organisations and their tendency to privilege waged work as the central site of political struggle. (In this optic, *'36 to '77* – where the filmmakers descend into the hidden abode behind production, in the form of the domestic space of Wardally's kitchen – becomes the more interesting work.)

In addition, the films clearly resonate with cleaners' activism in the UK in the present, for instance across the University of London, with many issues familiar from the latter struggles finding earlier analogues in the films: outsourcing and the direct market-mediation of social-reproductive work, battles with the conservatism of the larger unions, the precarious position of a workforce that has a high number of migrant workers, and so on. This is unfortunately not brought out in the commissioned essays here, although it is suggested towards the end of Sheila Rowbotham's piece, and an event to launch the book at Raven Row included a conversation with people involved in contemporary cleaners' organising.

These two films, then, cut across the field of 1970s independent cinema, from activist documentary to structural film to so-called '*Screen* theory', modelling this field's 'contradictions and antagonisms' as Kidner says in his essay here, while also providing extraordinarily rich objects for thinking questions of social reproduction, work, postcolonialism, solidarity and political strategy.

The first of the two books contains four short, newly commissioned essays, along with statements by each of the four filmmakers who worked on the first film. Overall, the new essays are disappointing. Kidner provides a competent, if fairly predictable, contextualisation of the film in relation to 1970s British independent film culture. Rowbotham contributes an interesting, but unfortunately brief, account of her involvement with the campaign and relation to the filmmakers. Kodwo Eshun and Sukhdev Sandhu explore *'36 to '77* and the use of sound across both films respectively, but never seem to quite grasp their elusive objects, particularly their political implications. There is nothing here that equals the best existing writing on *Nightcleaners* – *'36 to '77* has received little attention – by Claire Johnston and Paul Willemen, Griselda Pollock, Siona Wilson and Rowbotham herself.

Moreover, the book tends to replay a tension evident in the films themselves. *Nightcleaners* was begun by Karlin, Scott and Trevelyan. Kelly joined later, nominated by women's movement activists so that at least one woman was involved in the film's production. (When Kelly didn't participate in *'36 to '77*, her place was taken by a man.) A majority of essays here are by men, and it is noticeable that there is no black feminist presence. In general, the complexities of the relationship between the mostly male, white, in some cases privately-educated filmmakers, and the working-class, white and black, female cleaners – as well as the mainly middle-class, white women's movement activists, the white, male union leaders, and so on – are not really investigated head on, although they have been interrogated in some writing on the first film published elsewhere. This is not to say, of course, that because of these representational complications *Nightcleaners* and *'36 to '77* could not be exemplary works of political cinema. But surely the ramifications of gender, race and class are worth teasing out more?

The second book, or, perhaps more accurately, booklet-zine, enables a more productive examination of the issues. It pulls together facsimiles of writings on the campaign and film from a number of sources, many of them obscure and difficult to access. These texts from *Spare Rib*, *Red Rag*, *Shrew*, *The Cleaner's Voice* and the *1977-1978 British Film Institute Production Catalogue*, as well as previously unpublished material, add up to a very valuable resource. It re-embeds the films and the collective historically in a wider left activist culture of argument and action, discouraging a perception of the films as unmoored constellations of visual and aural signifiers.

Most important, though, is the way the box-set makes the films themselves (relatively) widely available for the first time in decades. *Nightcleaners* and *'36 to '77* may now be analysed at length. In 1975, Claire Johnston and Paul Willemen combatively declared in *Screen* that *Nightcleaners* was 'undoubtedly the most important political film to have been made in this country'. Although Johnston and Willemen's enlisting of the film to their own anti-documentary polemic foreclosed other readings of the film for a long time, their analysis of it as structured around a series of disparate and sometimes conflicting discourses (of the unions, the women's movement, the filmmakers, the cleaners, the cleaners' spokespeople, and so on) draws attention to the way the film takes difficulty, *blockage*, as one of its central structuring principles. Famously, sequences of the film are punctuated with silence and black leader, offering a time and space for thought, but also gaps in the fabric of representation itself, intervals in which nothing is said or done. Action is interrupted. What to say? What to do? It is a film that lingers on the obstacles to political organising, while remaining steadfast in its utopian demand that such struggles are necessary, possible and inseparable from the desire for a far-reaching transformation of society. Hence its deeply intertwined productivities and frustrations.

In fact, *Nightcleaners* is emblematic for its acute staging of dilemmas that have been identified in formally experimental political film ever since Eisenstein accused Vertov's *Man with a Movie Camera* of 'formalist jackstraws'. *Nightcleaners* raises this tension to an especially high pitch. The subject matter of an active political campaign of workers (removed from the niceties of debates in film culture) and the implicit objective to make something useful and readily comprehensible to those involved, sits alongside a profound investigation into the nature of images (of workers, of politics, in general) and the act of representation. Yet one thing that comes through in these materials is that the filmmakers understood the film from early on as primarily reflective rather than utilitarian. The move of the film into the art institution neutralises this tension to some extent – few would now demand the tangible political utility that seemed to be expected by some in the 1970s. But an ambivalence remains. It is tempting to see this crystallised in the box-set itself as artefact: while the materials are simply presented in a cardboard box that has an appropriately provisional feel, there is a latent high-design vibe that co-exists a little uncomfortably with the articles in, say, *The Cleaner's Voice*.

Where *Nightcleaners* retained a fraught relationship to activist filmmaking as traditionally conceived, *'36 to '77* steps much further into a meditative mode. The moments of *photogénie* in the previous film become full-scale reverie. As Eshun's essay describes, it is a portrait of Myrtle Wardally, in which the viewer comes to inhabit her memories of the night-cleaners' campaign and of her childhood in Grenada. The film is moving in its affirmation of the value of the experience of a working-class mother and migrant from the Caribbean. Shot in colour, unlike *Nightcleaners*, it smears and distends the image through replay, re-filming and extreme slow-motion, sometimes reducing the frame rate to once every few seconds, doing a lot with seemingly little footage, while snatches of Wardally's voice, calypso and trade union songs are audible. It is beautiful in a way that *Nightcleaners* isn't. Which is not to say that it is less 'political', although it is striking that the film is credited to a list of individual names rather than the collective subject 'Berwick Street Film Collective'. It would be a significant gain if one result of this publication is that it is no longer overshadowed by its predecessor.

Marc Karlin died in 1999. After Berwick Street Film Collective ceased to exist following *'36 to '77*, and the members went on to their own separate projects, Karlin charted a path of socialist filmmaking that refused – in its production methods and critical analysis – conciliation with neoliberalism, while taking in the major political landmarks of the era: the Nicaraguan revolution, the miner's strike, the fall of the Berlin Wall, the election of Blair. There is a need now for his later films to be made widely available, in order to draw some lines out of the moment of *Nightcleaners* and *'36 to '77* and connect them to the present.

Image courtesy of Berwick Street Film Collective: Humphry Trevelyan, Mary Kelly, James Scott, Marc Karlin and LUX, London.

Nicolas Helm-Grovas

Black-Palestinian Solidarity conference
Contesting settler nationalisms
Gary Foley and Suzannah Henty

The Black-Palestinian Solidarity conference was held at the University of Melbourne on 6–8 November 2019. The central interest of the conference was to strengthen Indigenous solidarity, establish relationships and engage with forms of resistance against the ongoing settler-colonial occupation of Aboriginal nations in Palestine and the continent now known as Australia. By settler-colonial governance, we refer to colonies in their modern nation-state manifestations that emerge from, practice and are sustained by what Patrick Wolfe terms, in *Settler Colonialism and the Transformation of Anthropology* (1999), a 'logic of elimination'. That is, where settlers seek to eliminate, assimilate and replace the *indigene* and their sovereignty with a new national order that is contingent on Indigenous genocide.

The subtitle of the conference 'Contesting Settler Nationalisms' referred to modes of domination *and* resistance that are informed by and embody a colonial logic. Against settler nationalisms, the conference aimed to reflect on models of and for resistance beyond the colonial-coloniser binary. It considered solidarity and resistance as intellectual and political praxis informed by what Mudar Kassis describes as a 'freedom-based epistemology' which rejects colonial grammar and embraces a transnational and transcultural solidarity strategy; and by the work of scholars Noura Erakat and Marc Lamont Hill, who argue that 'Transnational Black Palestinian Solidarity' is a theoretical framework and praxis in which the struggle for justice and the right to return – from Djap Wurrung to Al-Quds, Gaza to Ferguson, Rojava to West Papua, Chiapas to Kanaky, Standing Rock to Aleppo – is indivisible.

Aboriginal and Palestinian solidarity in the continent now known as Australia emerged during the late 1970s and began with the organised political actions of Ali Kazak and Gary Foley, who saw the Palestinian and Aboriginal struggle as part of the same fight for justice against settler-colonial occupation, and who officially opened the conference. Kazak, an activist, former Fatah member and, later, Palestinian Liberation Organisation representative for the Oceania region, migrated to Australia in 1970. Foley is a Gumbaynggirr activist, historian and co-founder of the Redfern Aboriginal Legal Services (1971) and the Aboriginal Tent Embassy (1972). In 1979, Kazak launched the first Palestinian-run newspaper in Australia, entitled *Free Palestine*, which ran until 1990 and which featured Foley's political actions. In May 1981, Kazak curated the first exhibition of Palestinian culture and resistance in Australia, held at RMIT's Storey Hall; Foley opened the exhibition. In 2018, Gary Foley and Ali Kazak met once again, this time with Suzannah Henty, a scholar of Anglo-descent researching anti-colonial resistance practices in contemporary art. Together, they decided to collaborate on a conference centred around Indigenous resistance against settler-colonial occupation in Australia and Palestine, framing this struggle as marked by capitalist structures of oppression in their imperialist, colonial, neo-colonial, nationalist and neo-liberal manifestations.

The theoretical questions that underpinned the conference were: What forms of political action can be defined as decolonial practice? What might be a valid proposition for decolonisation when the structures of colonisation – such as land expropriation, incarceration and assimilation – are embedded in modern nation-state models? What is the praxis of intersectionality and solidarity? What is the role of increasingly corporate educational institutions in de-normalising oppression and oc-

Micaela Sahhar and Rabab Abdulhadi (Photo: Ryan Al-Natour)

cupation? This latter question was specifically addressed in Professor Rabab Abdulhadi's keynote lecture, which examined Zionist lobbying on campuses and her own experience as a target of it, which has involved detailed death threats. It is worth mentioning in this context that the conference posters that were put up around the University of Melbourne campus were themselves vandalised during the event. The organisers promptly photographed, removed and submitted them to the Aboriginal History Archive at Victoria University.*

Focusing on transnational Indigenous solidarity and sovereignty as a means to imagine and experiment with liberatory futures, the conference consisted of seven sessions. Each was designed to not only unpack how occupation is exercised by the state and the individual – for example, the expropriation of land by the coloniser through property law, architecture, literature and art – but also to interrogate how resistance movements have used the language of the coloniser. Taking these two critical perspectives and demanding their confrontation, the contributions, above all, argued for the necessity of breaking away from oppressive hegemonies.

Alternative epistemologies for the exercising of power were discussed throughout the conference. If we accept that the Australian and Israeli nation-states are racist apparatuses, what possibilities do alternative epistemologies of identity – contingent on community, history and identity, rather than nineteenth-century social evolutionary and biological constructs of race and citizenship – provide for a non-racist future? If race is an historical, social and ideological construct, how can clarifying notions of 'Blackness' and 'Black-Palestinian solidarity', as well as extrapolating on the anti-Black structures and devices of the settler nation-state, influence

* For more on the Foley Collection, see https://www.vu.edu.au/library/about-the-library/special-collections-archives/foley-collection

forms of solidarity? In Jacqui Katona's talk, entitled 'Aboriginal Power and the State', she argued that in a cohesive social movement we can find a home. Katona argued that spaces for meeting and conversation where Indigenous sovereignty and self-determination are not only discussed but upheld, such as at the conference itself, can become a place for 'careful understanding, listening, of contestation as well, not just to agree but to debate a full understanding of who we are, and what our collaboration means'.

This space of careful understanding and coming together against the triumphalist state narratives that, in Australia, attempt to consume Indigenous peoples as a celebrated 'national character' (on the proviso that 'they' remain pacified, putative citizens of the state), and the self-proclaimed indigeneity by Jewish-Israeli settlers in Israel, was a radical component of the conference. Aboriginal and Palestinian solidarity carries with it a legacy of attempted division. The appropriation of indigeneity by settlers in Palestine, for example, was a critical topic addressed throughout the conference. Micaela Sahhar's paper, '"I have no other land": Subverting Aboriginal History in Israeli Aspirations to Indigeneity', took on Patrick Wolfe's 'logic of elimination' and J. Kēhaulani Kauanui's argument that Israel has attempted to 'eliminate the native as native' to examine how both settler-Australian governance *and* Aboriginal peoples in Australia have provided a model for Israeli 'land expropriation and identity appropriation'.

Against the pacification of the left in a world where we are fighting the rise and normalisation of extreme-right ideologies, Ghassan Hage was critical of the neoliberal tendencies of the self-fashioned left. There were two key components in his paper. The first was that to merely condemn genocide is not enough for anti-colonial practices. He began his lecture with a story he had written for the conference, describing the fictional 'Museum of Never Again', a museum dedicated to remembering the monstrosities that are occurring today in the Australian-run concentration-style refugee prisons on Manus, Christmas and Nauru Island. The museum consisted of artefacts mentioned in Behrouz Boochani's book *No Friend but the Mountains* (2018), written via WhatsApp while the Kurdish journalist was detained in an Australian detention centre in 2013–2019. Hage's second key point was directed against speaking about genocide as if it were a *fait accompli* after which attempts at reconciliation are to be made. In fact, both Aboriginal and Palestinian peoples have survived extermination attempts and refused settler-controlled reconciliation. These two arguments led Hage to a radical consideration: just as a gift carries the spirit of the giver, so does the legacy of invasion in a land that was stolen. Hage argued that reconciliation processes are consistently underpinned by a paternalism that seeks to ward off the ghosts that haunt stolen land, in order to prevent an uprising. Settler colonial reconciliation, therefore, is only attempted when the oppressed is pacified or dead.

Gunditjmara elder Alma Thorpe, who was the first matriarch to speak on the Matriarch Panel at the conference, spoke of her first experiences of another culture, which was Anglo culture. Having been 'missionised' as a child and forced to 'obey', Thorpe stated early in her talk that 'assimilation to us is that they haven't come up with a final solution yet.' Put in terms of transnational Indigenous solidarity, Alma's perspective was particularly pertinent and important, as she is a highly respected matriarch of the Melbourne Aboriginal community, being one of the founders and life-members of the Victorian Aboriginal Health Service (VAHS), an Aboriginal community-controlled organisation established almost 50 years ago out of the Black power movement of the 1970s. Not long after it was founded the VAHS became the first Aboriginal organisation in Australia to publicly express support for the Palestinian people against their occupiers, and as such was the first Aboriginal organisation to publicly draw parallels between the historic experience of occupation and colonisation shared by the Aboriginal and Palestinian peoples.

The incarceration of Aboriginal and Palestinian peoples was discussed extensively during the conference. In his keynote, Gary Foley stated:

> A good way of judging of whether or not you have a humane and compassionate society is by looking at the jails, at those who are in jail and what those jails are like. I stand before you today, despite all the stuff people reckon I am, as a man whose oldest granddaughter is in jail in New South Wales and whose oldest grandson has just been released from a juvenile detention centre in Melbourne. All Aboriginal people in Australia, like all Palestinian people, are impacted by the ongoing occupation of our homelands. The ongoing attempts to assimilate us, the ongoing and never-ending implications of

settler colonialism that are not diminishing but getting stronger, impacts all people. When I see what is going on in occupied Palestine, it hurts me and I feel that pain in me the same way I see the photograph of Dylan Voller being tied to that chair, with a spit mask on him, as a kid brutalised by the thugs in the Northern Territory juvenile detention system.

Suvendrini Perera and Joseph Pugliese, the chief investigators of the Deathscapes project – an investigative research unit examining and mapping offshore and inshore Indigenous and asylum seeker deaths in custody – examined the militarisation of the borders of Australia and its construction as nation state. A central component of the Deathscapes project is to establish transnational relations with other settler states, namely the United States and Canada, as well as the UK as the origin of the empire. Deathscape seeks to critically examine the systems of occupation and oppression that are used in other geopolitical landscapes, and to forge relationships of collective resistance.

The violent appropriation of history in the settler nation-state is a strategy designed to defend a claim to occupy sovereign land. Zionists have appropriated Palestinian land, architecture and history to build their national imaginaries, museums and sites for nationalist self-fashioning, including the Museum of Tolerance, built on the Muslim Mamilla cemetery in Jerusalem, or the Etzel Museum, built on Ottoman ruins in Jaffa. Similarly, Australian national culture has increasingly sought to Aboriginalise 'Australian art', beginning with the crisis of European imperialism in the mid-twentieth century (e.g. Margaret Preston, the Jindyworobak poets) through to the previous thirty years in which Western Desert painting has been made the brand of the Australian nation state. If the aesthetic appropriation of Western modernist art has been compared to forms of colonialism, ethnocide and cannibalism, then Aboriginal and Palestinian artists have used aesthetic appropriation and counter-appropriation as a form of cultural resistance. Such resistant appropriation needs to be considered in the context of other resistant aesthetic practices such as auto-ethnography and alternative ways of imagining community to the dominant national-cultural narrative.

With approximately forty contributors, the Black-Palestinian Solidarity: Contesting Settler Nationalisms conference was a significant moment for critical reflection on modes and temporalities of settler colonial occupation, and a historic moment in the strengthening of Indigenous relationships. The final remarks on the conference must, however, address the absence of the late Sam Watson. Political activist and author, Sam Watson was the co-founder of the Australian Black Panthers in 1971, alongside Denis Walker. Watson was a co-founder of the Australian Indigenous Peoples Political Party in 1993. He has worked on death in custody cases and with Stolen Generation peoples. He published several books and plays, including *The Kadaitcha Sung* (1990), *The Mack* (1997) and *Oodgeroo – Bloodline to Country* (2009). In 1995, he wrote and co-produced the film *Black Man Down*, which screened at the 1997 Cannes Film Festival. After hearing about the conference, he made contact with the conference convenors and expressed his keen interest to be involved, to which we responded with joy! His paper, entitled 'The Last Panther', was to examine the successes and failures of the Black Power movement. Unfortunately, Sam was unable to attend because of poor health. Approximately three weeks later he passed away. We will continue to fight for justice, just like Sam, until victory.

www.ingramcontent.com/pod-product-compliance
Lightning Source LLC
Chambersburg PA
CBHW081101070526
44583CB00019B/2515